CRABBE LIBRARY
EASTERN KENTUCKY
UNIVERSITY
RICHMOND, KENTUCKY

D1524821

FULL LENGTH ANIMATED FEATURE FILMS

THE LIBRARY
OF ANIMATION TECHNOLOGY

COMPUTER ANIMATION
Edited by John Halas

VISUAL SCRIPTING
Edited by John Halas

FULL LENGTH ANIMATED FEATURE FILMS
By Bruno Edera
Edited by John Halas

This book is sold subject to the Standard Conditions
of Sale of Net Books and may not be re-sold
in the UK below the net price.

FULL LENGTH ANIMATED FEATURE FILMS

by

BRUNO EDERA

Edited by

JOHN HALAS

Visual Communication Books
Hastings House, Publishers
10 East 40th Street, New York, N.Y. 10016

© 1977 Focal Press Limited
All rights reserved. No part of this publication may be
reproduced, stored in a retrieval system, or transmitted,
in any form or by any means, electronic, mechanical,
photocopying, recording or otherwise, without the
prior permission of the copyright owner.

ISBN 8038–2317–7

Library of Congress Catalog Card No. 76–45507

To Thérèse, Fréderic
and Daniel

NC1765
·E23

Printed and bound in Great Britain
by A. Wheaton & Co., Exeter

CONTENTS

410758

This is the first book ever written on the subject of animated feature films. For this reason it has not only an element of rarity but an aspect of pioneering which required a vast amount of fundamental research into the past through the film archives of many countries. It took Mr. Bruno Edera five years to collate the essential material, some of which has never before been published.

In spite of the basic technical differences, it is inevitable that the public should draw comparisons between live action and animated features and that these should reveal some interesting facts.

The first is the very low number of animated features which have so far been produced—some three hundred compared with hundreds of thousands of live action films.

Secondly, while live action productions have been developed to a truly international activity, especially since World War II, this only happened in animated feature films in the late sixties. Until then, production was mainly confined to the U.S.A., Japan and the U.S.S.R. It seems that animated features have flourished in direct ratio to labour availability in large countries with a strong and safe home market.

Following this, activity suddenly expanded and at present no fewer than twenty films are in production in countries as far apart culturally as England, Belgium, Korea, Sweden, Russia and Spain. Clearly, interest from the public, as well as animators themselves has gathered great momentum during the last few years.

There is another important factor which is a recent development. Hitherto, it has been maintained that apart from animated features made by the Walt Disney studio, any such film production carries a substantial financial risk, but this is no longer true. Fortunately films such as *Animal Farm* and *Yellow Submarine* (Britain), *Asterix* (France), *One Thousand and One Nights* (Japan), *Charlie Brown*, *Fritz the Cat* and *Heavy Traffic* (USA) have proved that other full length animated films can be financially successful and no greater financial hazard than most normal live action films. In fact, as a rule, an animated film has a longer money-earning life than a normal live action film, and can transcend international barriers.

The physical problem of production, however, is more serious from the animator's point of view. Basically, feature animation is a group activity requiring a number of artists' contributions from a number of artists over a very long period. Many films take three to four years to produce. Few animators are prepared to devote so much of their working lives just to do one film and many productions have been abandoned when patience as well as financial resources ran out. From the producers' point of view an animated feature is an enormous undertaking requiring elaborate planning, great skill and vast resources before even the most modest success can be hoped for.

There are, too, problems on the technical side. The anatomy of an animated feature is fundamentally different from a short cartoon or any other sort of film. The audience participation which is assumed with normal photographic identification in live films, cannot be so calculated in animation. The structural development of a storyline requires a rather different approach. The difficulties increase in proportion as the film is longer. The climaxing of situations must be carefully thought out to avoid a lapse in audience attention. Closer attention to sound track and sound effects is needed than with other films, and there is a need to vary visual style to maintain interest. Only a few artists throughout the world have the skill in collating these values—another reason why so few animated features have been produced.

There is also the problem of finance. A full animated production, especially in the USA, could be very costly. Today, however, with live action budgets reaching incredible proportions they no longer appear to be too expensive in spite of the very high labour expenditure. The Disney studio spends $3,000,000 to $4,000,000 on an animated feature. Other USA productions may cost less than $1,000,000. In Japan and Europe the cost may be half of those figures for a comparable film.

What does matter is the sort of market that a film will enjoy. Fortunately, the myths of animated features not having much box office potential have been exploded by the financial success of such films as *Jungle Book*, *Charlie Brown*, *Aristocats*, *Animal Farm* and the *Asterix* series, and there is no reason why the opposite should not apply considering the international appeal of the medium. It is of interest that *Aristocats* and *Lucky Luke* were leading the box office takings during the Christmas season in France a few years ago, and the former was the highest money earner during 1971 in Western Europe.

Robin Hood which opened simultaneously during Christmas 1973 in the USA and Britain also met with box office success. The success of feature length Cartoons will no doubt wet the appetite of the investors, who so far have shied away from uncertain investments.

Experimental films and those made by individual artists usually cost much less to produce, but the objectives of such films as well as their achievement, no matter how much sacrifice and devotion the work entails, are much narrower in scope. Such films end up in film festivals, unfortunately with no chance to reach a wider public. Finance causes fundamental problems in such circumstances and it is highly advisable for all producers to make sure that the resources are available before any work starts.

The prospect for the future of feature animation is very considerable. The vast potential of the medium has hardly been explored beyond the confines of the children's subjects and story films made until now. The flexibility of expression in the realms of fantasy and surrealism, poetry and drama is unique and remarkable, and with newly developing techniques such as machine tracing, computer generated animation and computerised rostrum cameras, one hopes that a substantial part of the mechanical labour will be saved, so that production can be made easier and faster and more encouraging to artistic creativity. Among all the media in film production here is one with an obviously healthy future.

ANIMATION TECHNIQUES

The animated film is a special branch of the cinema in which the cine-photography of live action is replaced by cine-photography either of drawings and paintings or of three-dimensional objects and puppets, basically by using the stop-motion or stop-frame process. This means that the illusion of movement can be introduced into the graphic image, as well as into puppetry.

There are other forms of approach, including experimental film production in which the stop-motion process is replaced to some extent by painting the images directly on to the surface of the film stock itself.

CELLULOID ANIMATION

Celluloid animation provides the smoothest and most flexible way of conveying complex movement, as well as systematising the production method through the various departments. Celluloid animation begins with the production of individual drawings on paper. Each drawing differs slightly from the next, following the content of the action. This is then traced with a fine ink line on to a thin, transparent sheet of celluloid, called the 'cel'.

These outline drawings on the cel are then painted in individually, using chosen colours which are carefully coded. So each animated drawing has become an opaque coloured shape on the transparent cel.

While this work is in progress, the backgrounds are designed and painted on plain paper. This artwork provides the scenery against which the character will move, and will eventually be placed under the camera as the first layer. The painted cels are then overlaid on the background in sequential order in accordance with the previously prepared camera chart.

The unpainted section of the cel allows the background to show through.

A further advantage in using cels is that the non-moving section of the character can remain static on one level, while the moving parts (arms, legs, head, mouth, etc.) can be replaced with other cels. It is normal to use from four to five levels.

Characters which do not need to move at all can also be left static in the scene.

Correct positioning is achieved by the use of peg bars throughout, which have matching holes in the paper and cels. These peg bars are also fitted on the camera table.

All the Disney features have been produced on the basis of cel technique. Only the manner of the camera work has differed. In *Fantasia* (1939/40), multiplane photography was introduced during the last section of the film to provide visual interest. The backgrounds were separated from the celluloids which were placed horizontally nearer to the lens. The panning background moved more slowly than the foreground, and those celluloids nearest to the camera were moved fastest. The correct relationship between the different levels was arrived at mathematically. This system, which imitated reality, was very expensive and has gradually been abandoned.

Most of the other feature cartoons produced around the world have used and are still using the cel method as the most practicable approach in cartoon production, especially in professionally organised high output studios.

COLLAGE AND DIRECT PAINTING ON TO FILM

The cel technique can be considered as the standard method for animated feature films, although there are other techniques in use, introduced since the mid-1960s. During that time a number of painters and graphic designers, such as Jan Lenica, Peter Foldes, Walerian Borowczyk and J. A. Sistiaga used an individual approach, introducing a variety of techniques into their productions which were previously tried out in shorter films.

For instance, Lenica, in his film *Adam 2*, used cut out shapes (collage) which were manipulated under the rostrum camera frame by frame. So did Borowszyk in *Monsieur et Madame Kabal*. Peter Foldes repeated the technique of drawing and painting figures in progressive motion under the camera and used camera cross-dissolves from one image to another extensively in order to advance an action. This technique, in *Je, Tu, Elles* (1971) was similar to that used in many of his shorts—*Short Vision*, *Animated Genesis* and *Visage du Femmes*. In Spain J. A. Sistiage simply recreated what he had painted on canvas, on the surface of the film celluloid—*Scope, Colour, Muda 75* (1970). He action-painted his feature film—nearly two hours' duration—by repeating the convention of abstract direct animation which, in fact, had been practised already for thirty years by Len Lye and Norman McLaren.

Such a brave attack direct on to the film stock may have horrified the purists, but the changing pattern of shapes on the film, and exciting colour

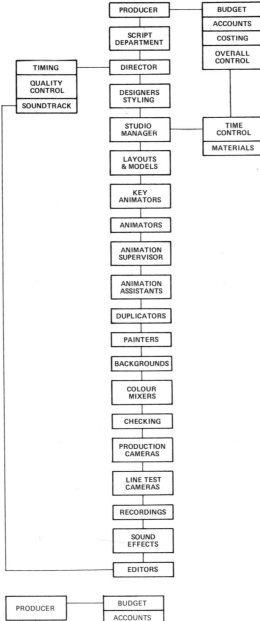

Structure of an Animated Film Studio of over 100 people engaged on the production of a Full Length Animated Film.

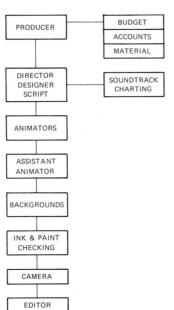

Structure of an average studio engaged on short films. It is customary that the director should write and design the script and draw the characters and backgrounds, but the latter may be the work of a specialist. The chart refers to a studio with a team of 12–20 people.

effects, even without a sound track, soon drew the audience into the spirit of the exercise. In the meantime, it destroyed several accepted concepts, such as that abstract cartooning cannot be maintained for longer than six minutes' running time, and that story development is essential in an animated feature film.

The basic disadvantage of painting directly on to film stock is that copies cannot be produced from the original without an extremely complex and costly laboratory operation.

SILHOUETTE ANIMATION

The technique Lotte Reiniger used in the silhouette feature length film *Prince Ahmed* (1926), can be compared with the Far Eastern hand-operated shadow puppet plays to which it bears a strong resemblance both in appearance and approach. The characters and the background were made with opaque black paper. The main features of the characters were joined with fine nylon thread which allowed the limbs free movement when manipulated frame by frame manually under the camera.

Today, instead of paper silhouettes, thin metal material is used which, because of its weight, lies flatter under the camera, and responds more readily to adjustments. The technique of silhouette animation is still mostly confined to Germany and China, but the fluidity of animation with this restrictive approach has greatly improved.

PUPPET ANIMATION

The difference between animated celluloid techniques and puppet animation is greater than is usually realised. Cartoon animation is basically two-dimensional, but can create an illusion of three dimensions when a figure is animated in the proper perspective. The individual celluloids are filmed by a stop-motion camera positioned horizontally, while in the case of puppetry it is vertical. A puppet set-up is usually made like a miniature live action set. The difference is that both the setting and figures are highly stylised, and the motion of the figures is advanced frame by frame.

While settings have not changed substantially, it is inevitable that the technique of puppet manipulation has been influenced by technology. Electronically operated puppets are now available and in fact were used for the first time as long ago as 1948 in *Alice in Wonderland*, made by the American producer Lou Bunin while he was in London. Ivo Caprino used a similar technique in Oslo, Norway during the early fifties, but only for the production of short films.

What is more significant is the development of the operation and control of the actual limbs and expression of the puppets. The early Russian puppet films, including the work of Starewitch, used

A puppet film production can be specified as a halfway operation between stop-motion animated film and live-action filming. The puppet animator takes the roll of the actors, and the camera operator the roll of the lighting camera man. The photography is normally carried out with three dimensional puppets and sets on a vertical angle instead of horizontal as in the case of flat cartoon animation.

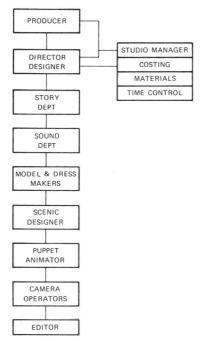

division of labour was adopted for puppet films as was used in cartoon animation. Sculptors made the figures, dressmakers made the clothes, scenic experts built the sets, and trained puppet animators manipulated the characters. As puppetry requires three dimensional light treatment, expert lighting cameramen also had to be employed. Until this period it seemed that the art of puppetry was mainly confined to Eastern Europe, although there was and still is a revival of object animation in Japan and China.

As the degree of labour and skill needed is even greater than that in the production of animated cartoons, this explains why there are so few animated puppet features. However the salacious appetite of television may change the situation and already there have been quite a number of nylon-thread operated puppet programmes which are photographed in live action. But these productions are not in the same category as full length animated puppet films because they are not conceived in the terms of stop-motion method.

It is highly probable that in future puppets will be electronically controlled and programmed by computer.

COMPUTER GENERATED FILM TECHNIQUE

This method will inevitably join the other accepted techniques in use within the next few years, and will have considerable influence on future film production.

Moving images can be generated through electrical impulses directly on the cathode ray tube which can then be photographed conventionally with a motion picture camera. Such images can be produced either through the digital system which instructs the computer in the many mathematical languages which are available today, or through the hybrid system. In the case of the latter the artist can manipulate the machine himself without necessarily knowing the mathematical language, and produce the images directly on to the cathode ray tube and from there either onto magnetic tape or film in colour or black and white. In both systems the advantage is that the images can be erased and mistakes rectified quite easily, and the correct information stored for future use.

A few years ago only linear and geometric shapes were possible on the computer but today figure animation can also be created as well as textured forms and shapes. As the cost of such animation which is natural to the computer is much less than conventional animation, it is not difficult to foresee that this method will have a tremendous impact on the animation industry.

Smoothness of action, technical competence, continuity of colour, creation of the right mood and accurate photography obviously matter a great deal in a feature length animated film, whichever technique is being employed. Large studios, like

figures made of bendable wire and papier maché. These figures were dressed simply, sometimes using textiles and, in the case of birds, real feathers It is remarkable that these simple characters were manipulated so well when chances of error under the camera were so pronounced.

In the mid-1930s, Hungarian-born George Pal used wooden puppets with the faces and clothes painted on the actual puppets. They were carefully sculpted, their features stylishly exaggerated and, for the first time, each part of the body could be detached and replaced. A walking cycle of a figure or a gesture demanded several dozen separate parts which could be changed between camera exposures.

By 1940 when Pal went to Hollywood, he dressed up his wooden puppets and used sophisticated metal clips for the detachable joints. Although he never realised his ambition to make a feature length puppet film, his influence made a strong contribution to the technique. He also had in mind to use latex rubber for the limbs of the puppets, an innovation which the outstanding Czechoslovakian puppeteer, Jiri Trnka advanced much further.

By 1950 almost all puppet characters were made of bendable plastic material with flexible wire skeletons. This enabled the artist to move a figure at will since it stayed in position and responded easily to delicate adjustment.

Trnka's feature film, *Midsummer Night's Dream* (1959) can be regarded as the peak of this technique. It brought together three developments; well designed easily manipulated characters; excellent use of soft materials on the figures for their clothes; expert animation of the characters under the camera.

By the time of the production, 1958/59, a similar

those in the USA and Japan, with a considerable staff, are obviously more able to carry out polished techniques than the smaller studios, but on the other hand the smaller studios in Europe maintain a more individual approach in their feature films.

In any efficient studio producing animation, good teamwork is essential between the creative side involving conception of the story, design of characters and storyboard, invention of ideas and graphic visualisation, and the technical side which is concerned with preparation of the work for stop-motion photography, charting the cels for the camera department and defining the relationships between the individual drawings and backgrounds.

The art and craft of animated film making is a balanced combination requiring technical knowledge of the medium as well as creative ability.

John Halas
London 1976.

INTRODUCTION

Over the last few years the Animated film has been undergoing a new phase of development, stimulated to a large extent by the increased use of animated cartoons and puppet films among the various television channels of the world.

This development is not only aesthetic but also technical. The most firmly established rules of the frame-by-frame method are undergoing striking modifications. The market for films, too, is changing its nature. The public throughout the world is better informed about the possibilities offered by the animation cinema, is interested in it, and understands the different forms of what some people call the "Eighth Art"—an art largely dependent on timing. The American animation empire is now facing serious competition from smaller countries; since the death of Walt Disney we are witnessing, particularly in the field of the full-length film, the emergence of several new names among producers and directors. This new situation has tempted me to devote a study to a particular type of film which, perhaps more than any other, reaches a very wide public, yet has a background that remains largely unknown. This type, which one too often tended to regard as the exclusive monopoly of Walt Disney, has recently exploded into a diversity of styles and forms, and the number of films produced in the field has been far larger than has been thought. The work of Walt Disney alone comes to more than twenty films and it is generally assumed that world production of full length animated films totals about fifty; these are statistics which can still be found in various works on the cinema.

However, looking into the matter more closely, one finds that the list reaches the impressive figure of nearly 300 films, and even then one cannot be sure that the list is complete.

The first example of the genre was made in 1916. The number in production in 1974 was at least 20, and they show a potential richness and variety which calls for a new kind of film criticism, a kind which recognises more fully than hitherto the peculiar talents in graphics, timing and structure which are manifested by those who create in this relatively rare film medium.

These artists have not yet been given the recognition they deserve, mainly because of the paradoxical situation that though a few films (e.g. *Snow White*) are among the most famous films ever made, yet the majority of them were distributed on a very limited scale and tend to be completely unknown outside their country of origin.

Historically, animation preceded the live action cinema by a few years [Emile Raynaud's Praxinoscope Theatre), but its spectacle was quickly eclipsed by that of the live cinema, and it has been on the whole relegated to the role of programme filler or special effect within a live action feature film.

As early as 1920, the animation of models allowed the presentation of apparent miracles in normal films; the film *The Lost World*, which took 7 years to make, illustrates the time and patience spent in producing a long film by these means. Unfortunately the names of the animators rarely appeared in credits, and the tradition of obscurity has continued ever since. Moreover, the patience and craftsmanship involved in producing a full-length animated film means that this medium is still a rarity and it takes on the appearance of the 'noble production' among animated films. The great dream of most directors is, in fact, to make a full-length film, and the current development in this type allows legitimate hope for most of them.

If it is sometimes a dream, it is also frequently for the general public at any rate, a sacred office—it is in fact that a director who has made a full-length animated film achieves with it a great reputation in this particular section of the cinema. At the present time there are many animation directors famous or unknown, working on full-length films. Some have already abandoned the attempt, while others are still pursuing and have been for many years, what is probably a unique experience in the world of cinema.

Because this form of cinematic art is so little known I have preceded my history of the development of full-length animated films with chapters which attempt to define the medium, and describe the aesthetics, and the financial aspects of production and promotion which it involves. My main interest, however, is to bring to attention the range and diversity of full-length animated films which have been produced in the last half century. The present study should throw some light on this type of activity, thereby filling a gap in the study of the cinema, and particularly animation cinema.

DEFINITIONS

There is no ideal running time for the animated film, just as there is none for the conventional type. Running time is dependent on the subject and the form of animation used.

Thus, there is no strictly observed norm for length; types are, however, defined by the forms they have customarily adopted.

Recently one has been able to distinguish in the animated film five fairly clearly defined types or categories:

(a) *Spot*
This is 10–60 seconds long and is used above all in cinema and TV commercials and for continuity spots or credits. The spot is sometimes enough to tell a gag or a very short story.

(b) *Pocket Cartoon*
Usually 50 seconds to two minutes long. This term, recently adopted, defines a new type, the 'fable' film, by means of which some film makers manage to say a lot in a very short time.

Per Åhlin, Sweden, the director of *Out of an Old Man's Head* and *Thundering Fatty*.

Osamu Tezuka, Japan, the director of *Thousand and One Nights*, *Cleopatra, the Queen of Sex*, *Pictures at an Exhibition* and *Jungle Emperor*.

Jose Antonio Sistiaga, Sapin, the director of *Ere Erera Baletba Icik Subua Arvaren* (Scope, Colour, Muda 75).

(c) *Short*

This is between 2 and 20 minutes long, 6 minutes however, being generally thought the ideal running time for cartoon animation, and 10 minutes for puppet films.

(d) *Medium length film*

Approximately 20–50 minutes long. (See Appendix)

(e) *Full-length film*

A minimum of 50 minutes long, the 'feature' in a film show. It reaches a very wide public, as children are usually admitted to such films, and cinema managers try to arrange their schedule so as to show this type of film during various national holidays.

All the films in this study are a minimum of 50 minutes long, although many of them are not designed for a general audience.

THE COMPILATION FULL-LENGTH FILM

Before getting on to the actual subject of this book—the full-length animated film—a little must be said about the various situations in which an animated film comes close to being a feature, without strictly speaking, constituting a feature-length animated film.

For some time companies which distribute short films produced by certain large studios (sometimes the same organisation produces and distributes such films) have been issuing complete programmes of 50 to 120 minutes. These programmes consist of a number of short films which sometimes have a common theme, and are distributed in the same way as a normal feature—with commercials. The uninformed public may expect a feature film and is sometimes in for a disappointment, as for instance in the programme of *Donald King of the Cowboys* we are led to believe that this is a full-length film whereas it is in fact a montage of 11 shorts: *Two Gun Goofy*, *Don Donald*, *The Legend of Coyote Rock*, *Californy or Bust*, *Donald's Gold Mine*, *Pests of the West*, *A Cowboy Needs a Horse*, *Wide Open Spaces*, *Up a Tree*, *Dude Duck* and *No Hunting*.

There are several other cases of this kind, for example: *Mickey Mouse Parade*, consisting of

Jiri Brdecka, Czechoslovakia, principal cooperator of many Trnka
features.

John Wilson, USA, the director of
Shinbone Alley.

Donald's Diary, Fathers are People, Goliath II, Hooked Bear, Pueblo Pluto, For Whom the Bulls Toll, Racoon Dawg, Symphony Hour, Pluto Jnr., Donald's Double Trouble, and *The Simple Things; Mad Adventures of Donald* including *Donald's Crime, Donald's Dilemma, Drip Drippy Donald, Home Made Home, Tiger Trouble, Mickey and the Beanstalk, Three for Breakfast, Social Lion, Frank Duck Brings 'em Back Alive, Two Chips and a Miss, Goofy and His Friends;* and *Donald the Sunday Hunter,* which consists of *Hooked Bear, Rugger Bear, Winter Storage, Tea for Two Hundred, Bee at the Beach, Donald's Vacation, Hook Lion and Sinker, Lion Around, Grand Canyonscope, Beezy Bear, Bearly Asleep.* These compilations are still being produced by the Walt Disney Studios and have been particularly successful on American tele-vision.

There also exist a good half-dozen compilations of other companies' animated cartoons: e.g. *Tom and Jerry* from M.G.M., which appeared as early as 1939; the *Woody Woodpecker* films by P. J. Smith and Alex Lory, produced by Walter Lantz; the *Bugs Bunny* films; *Titi and Sylvester* from Warner; and several others.

FULL-LENGTH ENTERTAINMENT FILM WITH ANIMATION

Many live-action productions of a fictional type include credits or bridges made by animation and it sometimes happens that we are told to go and see such and such a film "above all for the interest of its animated credits"

With the traditional film, animation can play an important role in special effects—especially for a large number of science-fiction films, fairy tales and extravaganzas, adventure and fantasy films, and even war films (with reconstructions of sea and air battles). But here the audience should not notice the difference between the live-action and the animated sequences—except when there is an intended combination of live-action characters in an animated background or vice-versa. This is the case, for example, in Walt Disney's *Mary Poppins,* or in *The Charge of The Light Brigade,* in which Richard Williams intentionally brings about such effects.

NON-FICTION FEATURE FILMS WITH ANIMATION

There are a large number of full-length films, some consisting entirely of animation, on which information is hard to collate—scientific, technical educational and military films. Most of these have been omitted from the present study, as they are usually important only for a limited audience, but there are a few titles which do have an important effect on the development of a studio or a country —for instance *Victory Through Air Power, Handling Ships* and *A Vida Do Solo*—and one, *Of Stars and Men*—which deserves the status of a work of art.

On the whole, however, animation in non-fiction films is confined to explanatory diagrams and models. A recent example of the use of simplified animation in an educational film is *Le Traite du Rossignol* by Flechet (France), a film of 1 hr. 40 mins., in which the linking material is in animation, giving the information necessary to understand the live-action scenes. The animation accounts for about twenty percent of the film.

FILMS IN MIXED MEDIA

Several directors are now working with new modes of cinema which combine animation, special effects and various other techniques, including scenes with live actors. Films of this type are only included in the catalogue when they consist primarily of animation or because they are the work of animation film makers, unlike live action films which include sequences of animation. In these directors' films, animation plays a dramatic role equalling that of the actor, even if their designation as full-length animated films can sometimes be contested. These films are one of the fringe activities of the category, and will be considered as mixed full-length animated films. Almost all of Karel Zeman, the Czech artist's films are of this type, and they will be examined later.

Three recent films which fall into this category are *Germany Dada, Le Socrate, Je, Tu, Elles* and the Swedish production *'Dunderklumpen'*; *Heavy Traffic*; *Coonskin*; (from Bakshi) *Daphnis and Chloe* (from Foldes and the Brizzi Bros.) mixed animated design and computer techniques. These will be referred to in the chapter on new directions.

A FEW WORDS ON MEDIUM-LENGTH FILMS

The medium-length animated film is a product with which we are unfamiliar for the very reason of its length; it is not always suitable as a programme filler because it is too long, yet it cannot alone constitute a programme.

There are, however, in this category, a number of films which are worthy of note since they are of marginal relevance to the present study.

25,000 frames (at a rate of 16 images per second)

Hanna and Barbera, heads of the largest USA studio.

Francisco Macian (on the right), Spain, the director of *Cinderella* and *El Mago de los Suenos*.

Walt Disney Studios, Burbank, Los Angeles. On the left sound stages, on the right editing buildings, in the background, the animation building.

is the impressive sum of the first of these films *The Sinking of the Lusitania*, made in America, by Windsor McKay as early as 1918.

In the United States, Walt Disney made some films of this type including *Pity Your Husband* (47 mins.), *Saludos Amigos* (42 mins), and *Winnie the Pooh and the Honey Tree* (30 mins), Another director, Jay Ward, produced *Fractured Flickers*. In 1923 the veteran Max Fleischer made a 47 min. film on *The Einstein Theory of Relativity* (Premier Productions Ltd.), employing already advanced graphic design.

The M.G.M. group made *The Pogo Special Birthday*, written by Walt Kelly for a television programme, and a cartoon by Dr. Seuss entitled *Horton Hears a Who*—each film being 30 mins. in length. Dr. Seuss also completed with Freelang and de' Petie a 40 min. film on pollution called *Lorex* in 1972.

In Canada Bill Petigrew and Chuck Jones made a 30 mins. film entitled *Animated Cartoon* and with Richard Williams Dicken's *Scrooge*. While this type of film has not been widely used in the United States, except in TV series, it does seem to be popular with film makers in Asia.

In China a large number of films of about 30 mins. in length were made after the 1949 liberation. These involve puppets, cartoons and paper cut-outs.

Thus we note, in the puppet category—*An Orphan on the Street* (by Chang Chao-Chun) 35 mins.; *The Gold Earring and the Iron Hoe* (Hsu Ping-to) 28 mins.; *Who Sings Best* (by Chin Hsi, 1958) 36 mins.; *The Mountain of Fire* (by Chin Hsi, 1958) 31 mins.; *The Carved Dragon* (by Yue Lou, Tchang Tchao-Tchiun and Wan Tshao-Tchen, 1959) 34 mins.;

The Cowherd and the Princess (by Yueh Lu, 1960) 32 mins.; *The Cock Crows at Midnight* (by Yeuo Lei). And in the category of paper cut-outs—*The Fisher Boy* (several directors in collaboration, 1959) 24 mins.; *Chi Kung and the Cricket* (by Wan Ku-Chan, 1959) 24 mins.; *Pigsy Eats Watermelon* (by Wan Ku-Chan, 1968) 23 mins.; *The Spirit of Giseng* (by Wan Ku-Chan, 1962) 26 mins.; *The Golden Conch Maiden* (by Wan Ku-Chan, 1965) 37 mins. In the category of animated cartoon—*The Conceited General* (by Teh Weî, 1956) 25 mins.; *The Wooden Maiden* (by Ho Yu-Men, 1958) 23 mins. *Pretty Little Goldfish* (by Wu Chiang and others, 1958) 23 mins.

In Japan we find *Polon Guitare* (30 mins); *Monster Prince* (25 mins.); *Ultra Seven* (25 mins.); *Kitro* (44 mins.); *Sally the Witch* (24 mins.); etc.

Likewise in Russia, we find *The Land of Toys* (30 mins.); *On the Way to the Moon* (30 mins.); *The Magic Shop* (30 mins.); *Kashtanka* (40 mins.); and above all *Le Gaucher*, by Ivan Ivanov-Vano, which is a fine attempt in creating a new style. Boris Stepancev's *Nutcracker* (25 mins.) which was completed during spring 1974, also belongs to the category.

In Czechoslovakia, Trnka has produced *Grandmother Cybernetics* and *The Archangel Gabriel and Mother Goose;* while from Poland we have *Opowiesc Michalkovicka; Janosik; Ballad of the Dentist* and *Wio Minut Dookola Swiato.*

In East Germany, the DEFA Studio in Dresden has produced *Das Tapfere Schneiderlein* (33 mins.); *Frau Holle; Pinocchios Abenteuer* and *Nobi;* from West Germany *The Ungerad She-Mule* (32 mins.), an animated cartoon made by the Bayerische Rundfunk; from Great Britain, *Ivor Pittfalks* (30

15

mins.); *Diary of a Madman* (30 mins.) and *The Little Island* (30 mins.)—all three by Richard Williams; from Italy *Lalla Piccola Lalla* by Friulani, in 1947; *Anacleto e la Faina* by Roberto Sigrilli; *La Pentola Miraculosa* by the Gavioli brothers in 1956 and *La Lunga Calza Verde* (20 mins.); while in France Mima Indelli directed *La Devouverte de l'Amerique* (1934) and Paul Grimault *Les Passagers de la Grande Ourse;* and just recently the ORTF produced *Perault 70* (30 mins.), combining live action and animation, directed by Jacques Samin and animated by Henri Lacam.

While medium-length films are few in number (though the above list represents only a tiny proportion of the total), a phenomenon has nevertheless arisen over the past five to eight years which merits a separate study as it is so characteristic of our time.

This is the phenomenon of the TV Serial—series of 13, 26 or even 52 episodes of animated film, usually made with very simple means. The length of each episode is approximately 26 minutes. The reason for the division of these serials into 13 parts as the most usual number is that this makes a weekly show run for exactly a quarter of a year.

The production of the serial established a whole new industry. Both cinema animation studios and television companies are producing so many TV series at the moment that this activity not only absorbs all the redundant animators but opens up the field to a great number of newcomers.

The reason for including examples is that several of the companies producing such series also make full-length animated films, and quite often the subjects of serials have been borrowed from full-length films, or vice versa.

In this field an impressive struggle is going on to capture the markets of great commercial potential—especially between the American and Japanese production companies.

In the United States, to quote but a few examples there are: Hal Seeger with *Batfink* (1956) and *Milton the Monster* (1965 for ABC TV); Seven Arts TV with *Marine Boy*; Hanna & Barbera, who in 1967 were making eight 30 mins. episodes a week of their various series; U.P.A. with a series of twenty-six *Mister Magoo*; C.B.S. Films with twenty-six episodes of *Astronut* (1965); Al Singer and Fred Ladd with fifty-two 30 mins. episodes of *Gigantor;* the Oriolo Studio with *Eight Man* and *Speed Racer* programmes; and lastly the recent extremely successful series by Bill Melendez and Lee Mendelson for C.B.S.—six 30 mins. episodes about the famous characters of the cartoonist Charles M. Schultz—*Peanuts*. Yet all these directors cannot satisfy the domestic market and there is still a demand for Japanese and a few British & Australian series in the United States.

These series are sometimes made in such a way that a 30 mins. film can easily be broken up into several 'sub-episodes', or alternatively one is presented with several small films of less than 10 mins.—put end to end to make a half-hour show.

William Hanna and Joe Barbera, for example, the great specialists in this field, make series which are well adapted to the needs of television, in which films conceived as 30 mins. programmes are really short features—likewise some of the *Mister Magoo* films such as *The Count of Monte Cristo*, *Cyrano* and *Snow White*, which is in two parts, each 25 mins. in length.

The Hanna & Barbera series are so numerous that it is hard to make general observations about them; but we must note that, apart from the series of 30 mins. films based on books for children, such as *Linus the Lion* (39 episodes) and *Moby Dick and the Mighty Mightor* (18 episodes), original treatments are sought in the subjects and in the animation, which nowadays come close to a real, adventurous interpretation of the strip cartoon style. Thus we have recently seen created *Frankenstein Junior* (18 episodes), *The Herculoids*, *Space Ghost*, *Huckleberry Hound*, *The Flintstones*, *Yogi Bear*, and *Top Cat*. Then there is the Western: *Depity Dawg*, *Quick Draw McGraw*, and *Lariat Sam*. Lastly the *Alvin Show* programmes, which are repetitions ad nauseum of a formula which also has its success in Europe—a mixture of grating voices and harmonicas.

This onslaught of the series is also very significant in Japan, and two studios in particular are bringing out large numbers of episodes, again 30 mins. in length. The success of a production by the Mushi Studio in 1962—*Astro Boy* (52 episodes), and another from the Toei Studio—*Ken the Wolf Boy*, stimulated several TV channels to set up animation studios. Recently these series began to appear on European screens, and the European market will probably soon be saturated with them. Some of their titles are—*A Squad of Milky way Boys*, *Wonder 3* and *Junior Emperor* from Mushi; *The Samurai Boy*, *The Cosmos Boy*, *Sally the Witch* and *Cyborg 009* from Toei.

In Great Britain John Halas has just directed a series of seventeen 30 mins. episodes for National Broadcasting Corporation of America, called *Tomfoolery*, and based on Edward Lear and Lewis Carroll nonsense poems. These television programmes were produced for Rankin & Bass Co, in New York, and were followed by two other series, *The Jackson Five* and *The Osmond Brothers*, also produced by Halas & Batchelor for Rankin & Bass, and animated from a pre-recorded American-made soundtrack.

In the realm of the TV serial there exists a production potential whose possibilities are as yet unknown. This is the case, for example, with computer animation—this specialised art which is developing so rapidly in the United States, Great Britain, Japan and several other countries. The advent of this method will certainly have a great effect on feature-length and other animated films.

At the Walt Disney Studio, USA. The animator is shown working with a mirror which helps him obtain the right expressions which are then translated to the drawing.

At the Walt Disney Studio, USA. Colouring celluloids for the film *Song of the South*.

Although until quite recently the full-length animated film was regarded mainly as family entertainment, it is finding recognition as a new art form. However, there will always be the traditional type of film production in existence, and these productions should also be considered on their artistic merits, an aspect which the critics do not generally take into account, but essential in order to evaluate this medium in its proper context.

In a culture of popular tradition the medium can be regarded in parallel with the first contact experienced by most children with an imaginary world—the illustrated storybook or comic. These books come at an important stage of a child's development, when the subconscious impressions of ideals are formed. The symbolism of, for instance, the quiet and weak character triumphing over the strong one, satisfies a psychological need in the child himself (weak and ineffectual) triumphing over the adult. Ideological archetypes are acquired by the children and the quality of the illustrations in books has a significant role to play, which is not felt by adults reading and looking at the same material. For this reason an adult cannot truly judge a film from the child's viewpoint; a fact which should be taken into consideration in order to gain a more objective opinion of the feature length cartoon.

Another problem is that this medium depicts present-day problems very largely, and so calls for a more imaginative kind of judgment than other media which are an imitation of normal life.

In all forms of art there are a number of important contributory factors to success. These include the qualities of the medium, the cultural background of the spectator, and the personality of the creator when he is actually envisaging his work, whether he is an author, painter, sculptor, or when there is collective effort (e.g. of musicians, actors, dancers, and choreographers).

All these elements apply to the animation cinema, but the authorship of a full-length film is nearly always collective. There are a few cases of a film made by a one-man unit, and bearing his personality. Here the critics' evaluation will be of the man as well as his work. Even in this case the work must be seen from a number of different angles, including the design, the technique used, the music, the commentary or dialogue and the meaning of the narrative.

With a film in which many people are involved the same criteria apply but it is much less easy to identify a particular experience with a certain artist, and this type of film calls for another dimension of understanding. Though it is akin to live films in that respect, the animated film, which does not have to copy nature, is closer to artistic creation than live action, and is in fact, a combination of several art forms. Therefore, it needs to be placed in a special category marginally allied to cinematography as well as to other forms of art. Looking at animated film in this way, the full length animated film is seen to be a special category within a category, calling for particular insight in the critic.

The main difference between film and the more traditional visual art form is, of course, that the onlooker can study a painting or sculpture at his leisure, whereas in animation (animated drawings and puppets), the equivalent elements are constantly moving, having a rhythm for which he is not necessarily prepared. This is why animation can be tiring to watch for the eyes and brain, and why children make better audiences than adults, who usually no longer have the keen interest and ability to give the film their full attention. The animated film can be described as art in motion. Whenever anyone finds pleasure in seeing a full length animated film, whether in its entirety or just an extract, the creators of the film have succeeded in transmitting their emotion to the audience, so something more has happened than the simple acceptance of a film fact. Here lies the true fulfilment of the term cinematographic art—communication has been made between transmitter and receiver. This in itself is definable in two stages; firstly there is the condition for the receiver—see —hear—understand—which leads to the second stage, the transmitter's statement using certain means by certain methods. In these two stages are contained all the theories of audio-visual communication.

As with other art forms, again, the full length animated film is judged according to its age. We are now at the 'second generation' since the conception of the medium, given that there exists an 'academic' form undeniably linked with the name of Walt Disney. The term academic is justifiable as it means that it is a style in which there is felt a need to apply principles of formal art.

All these vary according to the culture of the country or region under consideration—the social status of the audience and their outlook. As the art of the animated film is still in its infancy definite judgments should be avoided, particularly as currently artistic values are being reappraised, as are methods of working, and even philosophical concepts. Things that this generation regard as revolutionary will probably be forgotten in twenty years' time, and what is now regarded as affected and valueless will possibly be of value in the future.

The full length animated film is running the whole gamut of ways and means open to it, and it is now a question of making a summary analysis of what it is and its present aesthetic status.

First the elements upon which judgment may be based must be defined. These are:

1. *The Public*
Animated films can be classed for four categories of audience as follows:

(a) solely young children
(b) children accompanied by parents
(c) adolescents (the so-called 'difficult' audience)
(d) solely adults

For each category a different film is relevant.

2. Subjects (or sources of inspiration)

Ideally anything can come into a full length animated film, but the following categories can be pinpointed:

Fantasy adventures	Science fiction
Fables	Political caricature
Melodrama	Old or new legends
Strip cartoon	Modern events
Musical scores	World of experiment
Bible stories	Folklore
Surrealism	Original stories
Education	

3. Techniques and types

By type it is to be understood that a film produced using various techniques can be placed in two classes:

'Flat' technique	cartoon, cartoon with real actors, animated silhouette, animated cut-out drawings etc.
'Dimensional'	puppets, puppets with real people, animated objects, etc.

4. The sound track

It is many years since silent films were made, except for one made recently, the Spanish feature film *Scope, Colour, Muda 75* and in the majority of cases the sound track is more important than is usually appreciated—it only makes itself really known when it is too loud and spoils the film. The sound track has three elements— the dialogue or commentary, the sound effects, and the music ranging from old traditional songs, classical music, experimental and electronic music, to pop songs.

5. Location

The geographical and historical location of the action is most important. Although it is often set in an imaginary place and time, it still draws on real places and periods for inspiration.

6. Length of the film

This is a most essential factor and can decide the success of the film. It must be neither too long nor too short and the sequences must be well timed so that the audience should not become bored at any time.

7. Colour

It is not important, in my opinion, whether the film is black and white or in colour, but the way in which tones and hues are combined affects its message to a large extent.

These criteria are the basis from which any aesthetic criticism of the full-length animated film should arise. Bearing this in mind, in most cases it will seem that the treatment of the characters and narrative is the most important creative work involved in the film, and when comparing them to the characters and stories of live films it is easy to feel that they are over simplified and even trite.

There are many reasons for this impression, too tedious to detail now, although the financial conditions of production play an important part, but there is a strong hope that as the public becomes more aware of the experimental work which has been done (ever since 1916) and, more important, of the work which many directors are now undertaking, that the full-length animated film will be seen to be the supreme example of the Eighth Art, and it will become one of the most valued art forms of the late twentieth century.

**PRODUCTION
& PROMOTION**

PRODUCTION TIME

The production period for a full-length film can vary between one and four years, depending, among other things, on the number of animators the director has at his disposal. The number of staff working in some of the studios will be considered later.

There are differences too, in working hours. In the United States, animation as a profession is more specialised. Each area of activity is clearly defined. The staff work for 35 hours a week, whereas in Eastern Europe where the industry is nationalised the work might proceed at a different speed. In Western Europe the staff work between 40 and 50 hours a week and, as in Eastern Europe, employees may be called upon to do various jobs.

In the case of a full-length film the production team should be stable throughout the whole production period. But the same people do not always work on a film from beginning to end.

The number of people working on a large animated cartoon varies between 3, the lowest limit which is economically viable, to 150 and 250 which is the maximum practicable for work purposes.

The essential factor which makes the full-length animated film different from live film is the length of time it takes to make. A full-length animated cartoon, whether made by four or five to 100 or 250 people, takes a minimum of over a year to make.

COSTS FOR ANIMATED CARTOON

This can obviously vary according to the technique used.

Costs vary greatly from film to film. However, it is interesting to note that eight minutes of computer animated film can cost as little as $4,000–$6,000 which would be only just enough to make 30 seconds of normal TV animation and barely 10–15 seconds of the traditional, Disney-style animated cartoon.

It is also interesting to note that the revenue of the American animation industry in 1965 totalled about $15 million, in 1968 $25 million, in 1969 about $40 million and that in 1972 it might well earn as much as $100 million and $150 million by 1975 (statistics from Entertainment World). There are many more optimistic estimates regarding work for the cinema and, above all, for TV. These figures make the field of animation one of the quickest growth areas in the world of cinema.

Another new vehicle for animation is now making its appearance, which will be in the 1970s a medium whose precise evolution it is now difficult

At the Walt Disney Studio, USA. The Multiplane Crane camera with full camera crew.

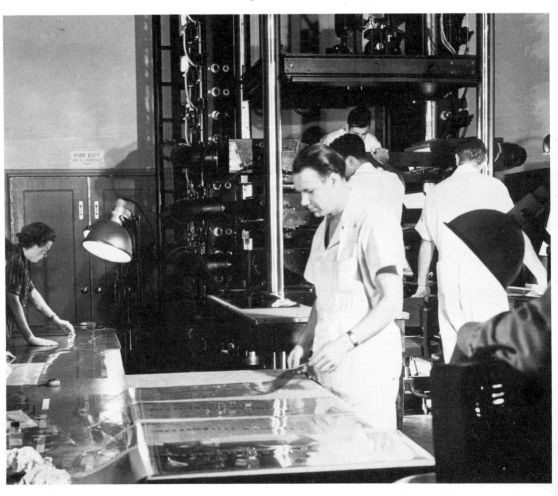

to calculate. This is the "video-cassette"—the mini-television tape—by means of which one will be able to hire sizeable programmes for fairly small sums of money for home entertainment.

MANPOWER AND COST

Europe (Belgium):	50,000 B.F. per minute for T.V. film rising to 100,000 B.F. per minute for cinema film.
United States:	Up to $90,000 per minute for cinema film and $10,000 a minute for T.V. serials.

Budget for the film *The Aristocats*	$4,000,000
Budget for the film *The Jungle Book*	$4,000,000
Budget for the film *Robin Hood* compare with budget for	$4,000,000
The Reluctant Dragon (1941)	$500,000

Breakdown:

The Jungle Book	250 people/322,000 drawings 760 backgrounds.
Animal Farm	60 people/225,000 drawings/ three years' work.

At the Hanna and Barbera Studio, USA. The mechanised tracing department with Xerox machine.

Asterix le Gaulois	50,000 drawings on paper and 50,000 on cels/300 back-grounds/1,000 brushes/500 Kg. of paint/200 pairs of gloves/120 people.
Pinocchio	in production at present in Italy. 30 people. Planned for three years of work.
Phantom Toll Booth	100 people. 2 years in production.
West and Soda	400 backgrounds / 120,000 drawings/100,000 hours of work.
Adam II	By Jan Lenica: 3 people (himself, a cameraman and the musician) 3 years.
Scope, Colour, Muda 75	by J. A. Sistiaga. In 17 months, absolutely alone, drawn on to the film.

These figures show both sides—the monumental aspect of a work or the remarkably small size of the team.

The staff of some animation studios (making short films as well as full-length during 1974)

Defa (East Germany)	200 people
M.G.M. (U.S.A.)	100 people in 1955.
Walt Disney (U.S.A.)	750 people in 1937 (of whom 200 were working on *Snow White*). 1,300 in 1965 (all staff). 40 people in 1974 on animation only.
Halas & Batchelor (G.B.)	100 people.
Zagreb Film (Yugoslavia)	About 100 people.
De Patie Freleng (U.S.A.)	110 people.
Soyuzmultfilm (Moscow)	625 people.
Toei (Japan)	About 550 people.
Hanna-Barbera (USA)	About 400 people.
Belvision (Brussels)	100–120 people.
Idefix (Paris)	50 people (1975).
Shanghai (China)	About 400 people.
Bruno Bozzetto (Italy)	30 people.
Kratki Film (Czech)	150 people.
Pannonia Films (Hungary)	200 people.

American rates for animation specialists (weekly during 1974)

Director	Just over $600
Animator	$220–350
Lay-out	About $300
Apprentice	About $120

DISTRIBUTION AND RELATED MATTERS

The distribution, within a country, region or town, for a full-length animated film is governed by an economic system which differs greatly from that of a traditional film. Marketing plays an extremely important role.

Advertising takes place in two separate spheres before the audience pay for their tickets, and the efforts of the two advertising campaigns are of mutual benefit.

Firstly, before the completion of the film, the distributing organisation gives early warning of the release of the film in question. This gives book-shops and publishers the opportunity to bring out extra copies of the book on which the film was based, or to bring out new books on the subject.

Then the larger shops combine, paying for the right to do so, and launch a campaign to stir up advance interest, especially among children. Even some time after the release of the film, signs of this campaign remain.

The machinations of a launch campaign and its consequences alone would be enough for a very detailed study. In the context of this book, a few more characteristic examples should be mentioned illustrating this publicising and commercial aspect which surrounds a full-length animated film, for it is a commodity for sale.

This is true particularly of Disney films, but not only with these. The same process applied in Spain, when Macian brought out his *El Mago de Los Suenos*, and in France with *Fablio le Magicien*. It usually begins on the radio and T.V. Then records from the film are put on the market and books follow. Gradually the rights to certain characters are sold to manufacturers and shop windows begin to fill up with pictures of the hero.

It goes from the record to the "de luxe" version of the book, and can go as far as puzzles, colour-ing books, carnival masks, comics, cartoon strips, to the simple embroidering of the hero on a handkerchief and on to the full panoply, via jerseys, T-shirts and mounted photographs.

BOX OFFICE FIGURES

According to the 1974 anniversary issue of 'VARIETY', the box office takings of *Snow White* made in 1937 amounted to $16 million. The partly animated *Mary Poppins* (1964) took, so far, $40 million. *The Jungle Book* (1967) earned $13 million in 13,600 cinemas, so far.

The Belgian-French made *Asterix le Gaulois* (1967) had an audience of 2,500,000 in France alone and earned its negative cost back within one year.

Fantasia (1940) is up to $8,350,000 and *Fritz the Cat* (1972) just past the $6 million mark. Who said that there is no money in feature length animated films?

At the Toei Studio, Tokyo, Japan. Animation department.

At the GAMMA Studio, Milan, Italy.

At Halas and Batchelor, London, UK. Tom Bailley in the background department.

At the TRNKA Studio, Czechoslovakia. Dressing a character for a puppet film.

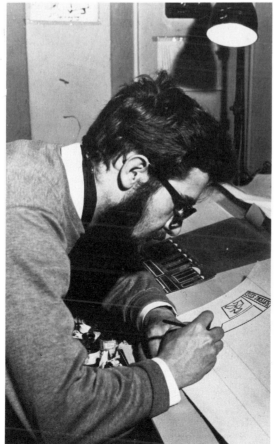

There are not, as yet, many works on the history of the animation cinema, but since the creation of the International Animated Film Association (ASIFA) several specialists have turned to this problem; so that there now exists a valuable literature on the frame by frame cinema for almost all the countries of the world, defining types and techniques.

The works of Georges Sadoul, Robert Benayoun, Andre Martin, J. M. La Duca and Marie-Therese Poncet in French, of Walter Alberti, Gianni Rondolino and Piero Zanotto in Italian, of John Halas, Walt Disney, Robert D. Field and Roger Manvell in English, as well as other specialists in other languages, form a very valid and authoritative source of reference which, for more than fifteen years, has provided a reliable basic documentation for the animated cinema on a world-wide basis.

In the sphere of full-length animated films, references are harder to come by. Very few works are devoted to this particular subject, especially to the period between the early days of the cinema and the end of the Second World War in 1945.

In compiling a precise catalogue, one comes up against considerable obstacles, particularly in countries where no historian has ever considered the animation cinema within its own terms of reference. However, because of its specialised nature, the full-length animated film cannot be completely left out of any account by cinema historians. This present chapter should not be missing many titles. Of course, there does always remain a doubt, which sometimes takes the form of a hope—the hope of discovering, after the event, films which have been forgotten, or references to works begun but never finished.

While it is possible that this work may not reveal, with absolute precision, everything which has been done in full-length animation, even so the margin or error will be minimal, since most films of this kind (with the exception of the total failures) are distributed and shown on a large scale. By definition such films are made to be widely shown. Apart from this factor many animated feature films are periodically re-released, even if they are more than twenty years old, and as we are currently facing the end of a most difficult period for the distribution of new films, it is possible that even older films maybe re-released over the next few years.

If it is possible to see at regular intervals, films like *Snow White*, *Fantasia*, or *Pinocchio*, then we may also hope to see again the films of the Fleischer brothers or the Russian, Chinese, British and Italian feature films.

The Americans understood the market value of an animated film very well indeed, and this is probably one of the reasons why this type of film blossomed first in America and was successfully exploited by American organisations throughout the world. The animated feature film as Walt Disney conceived it, was specifically aimed at children—an audience at which, in fact, not many other films were aimed. This means that success was assured for an animated cartoon such as *Snow White*, before it was even made. By means of a distribution network, with world-wide ramifications and a cleverly orchestrated publicity campaign to launch the film, it was guaranteed a large audience, of which it was indeed possible to calculate the minimum size. In addition, somebody making a children's film knows that parents will, perhaps, accompany their children to the cinema, which thus assures him of a fairly large adult audience as well. This is why until less than five years ago, animated features, apart from rare exceptions, could be considered as commodities in the film market which were almost certain to be box-office successes, and whose contents, where possible, were aimed at a family audience. Walt Disney grasped this at a very early stage, and it is not surprising that this type of film should still be considered by the public and even by certain critics as a lesser area of cinematographic art.

But paradoxically, this essentially commercial factor, while bringing success to Walt Disney, probably hindered the initiation of other productions for many years. While the number of Disney features produced up until 1945 was large, few other productions were attempted and have now mostly drifted into obscurity. Walt Disney had contrived so successfully to touch the infant soul and the good mothers and fathers, and to attach a mythical value to his early works, that he achieved a monopoly of the market, against which few producers were tempted to set up in competition. The public were so favourably prejudiced towards Disney's work and awaited with such impatience each new film that other producers were relegated to the pale role of imitators with the prospect of more or less inevitable failure. But we should not exaggerate this rather disagreeable aspect of the productions of the Burbank Studio. We must recognise the fact that these films were of high quality and represented a quest for perfection which it is even now difficult to imitate. By setting his sights on the junior public as the target for his animated feature films, Walt Disney cast this film medium into a well-defined category of cinema where it remained for many years.

Walt Disney is usually thought of by the public at large as the pioneer of the animated feature. This is, however, far from the truth. By the evidence now available to us, it is possible to trace the history of the genre back to origins which pre-date the appearance of *Snow White* by twenty years.

Among the pioneers of the silent cinema we find two famous names associated in what must be the first full-length animated film in the world, *La Guerra e Il Sogno di Momi*, a film combining puppets and live-action made in Italy in 1916 and produced by one of the largest production companies of the time, Itala-Film. The script was written by Segundo de Chomon and Giovanni Pastrone, the latter taking the credit for producing the film. Giovanni Pastrone was born in 1882 and died in 1959. He began his career in the traditional live cinema in about 1910 at Itala-Film, where he later became a director. There he produced numerous films of all types and particularly in 1912, 1913 and 1914, several epic productions, of which the best known is *Cabiria.*

Segundo de Chomon was born in 1871. In 1902 he established a film-colouring workshop in Barcelona and worked for Pathe. He is often cited as one of the inventors of the hand-cranking photographic method. He was very interested in special effects and animation, and in 1905 made his first comedy film, and then his first special effects film *El Hotel Elettrico*, with animated objects. In 1906 he went to Vincennes, near Paris, to work for Pathe and then on to London in 1908 where he made, among other things, a film of animated shadows, *Aunt Sally's Outing*. In 1910 he returned to Barcelona for two years, then went to Italy and Itala-Film, where he made use of his knowledge of special effects and animation. However, because his work was not exclusively in animation, he has not always been considered by the specialists to be a true pioneer. He left Italy in 1919. Although Giovanni Pastrone undertook no other experiments in animation, the list of films into which Segundo de Chomon inserted frame by frame scenes amounts to about twenty titles.

ARGENTINA

As with traditional live cinema, one is sometimes surprised to discover that it is not necessarily the countries with the largest output where the most interesting or significant events occurred. Thus, in Argentina, we find that three full-length animated films have been made, one of which was the first cartoon film in the world, *El Apostol.* Unfortunately these films were burnt in the fire at the Argentinian Cinematheque in 1969, together with all the material concerning them.

The film-maker Don Federico Valle had, since 1916, felt a need to do something new in the cinema world, and undertook the production of a full-length animated film, something which had never been done before. Ten years after the presentation in Paris of Emile Cohl's *Fantasmagorie*, there was in Argentina, very little information available about animated cartoons and the techniques used in this new art form. There had been some attempts to make sequences by taking single shots, drawing by drawing, in the open air with live-action cameras, but these were fruitless failures owing to the interference of strong light and mechanical difficulties. Instead of wasting his time with this approach, Valle constructed a

vertical multi-plane set-up of a type which was just then being adopted for animation, though of a primitive type compared to Disney's "Multiplane" system. He worked out an efficient system for taking camera shots frame by frame, stopping the camera for every single shot. The theme for his first film was chosen from a book by Alfredo de Laferrere, containing a political caricature of the then President, Irogoyen. The key drawings and the faces of the main characters were done by the popular caricaturist of the time, Diogenes Tabora. The task of completing the (approximately) 50,000 drawings (at the time of silent film the camera worked at 16 frames per second) and the models needed in the film were entrusted to two of Federico Valle's collaborators, the designer Quirino Cristiani and the French technician and craftsman, Andre Ducaud. The latter made, specially for this film, a 21 ft. high model representing different locations—streets, houses, avenues, monument, Town Hall, and objects like cabs and coaches, all moved by invisible wires. With this minutely detailed decor, Valle created a Dante-esque spectacle. But in spite of the richness of the idea, *El Apostol* did not have the success it deserved.

In 1931 another satire on Irigoyen appeared, but this appeared after his dismissal from the presidential seat. The film was made with sound provided by the Vitaphone records system, the first in Argentina. It was produced by an old member of the *El Apostol* team, Quirino Cristiani, and was entitled *Peludopolis*. Unfortunately this film was also an economic disaster. Lastly, in 1942, an experiment took place which should have resulted in a full-length film, for which 30,000 drawings and 250,000 "bocetos a lapiz" (cels) were used. Approximately 15,000 ft. of film was shot, of which only 1,800 ft. was eventually used.

Dante Quinterno, the director of the film, *Upa en Apuros*, gained his experience by contacts with Max Fleischer and Walt Disney. The production was supervised by the artist Gustavo Goldschmidt. It took over two years to make, and it is the best Argentinian animated cartoon ever made. The actual materials for filming, since agreements had not yet been reached with the United States, came from Germany. But with the beginning of the war, deliveries were interrupted and some sequences had to be cut out. This film, so well planned and executed, was consequently reduced to a short, which was not distributed until 1950. Only four copies of this film were printed for distribution. This bad experience brought about the premature end of the Argentinian animation cinema, even though it had, before the war, progressed along original lines.

Several years after Valle's first experiment, some interesting attempts were seen in Germany, such as *Max and Moritz* (1924) an animated cartoon in seven acts presented in a single programme. Though the film was not full-length it did foreshadow the film series, which was at that time known only in the United States, and proved that there was some worthwhile activity going on in the stop motion cinema in Germany at that period.

LOTTE REINIGER

The climate was crystallised in 1926 by an ambitious work which excited world-wide interest. *Die Abenteurer des Prinzes Achmed* brought world-wide success to an animation form midway between the animated cartoon and the puppet film—animated shadows. Because of its sobriety and respect for the oriental style this tale from The Thousand and One Nights necessitated 250,000 frames in a running time of 65 minutes. The film, produced by Comenius, Berlin, was made by Lotte Reiniger and her husband, Karl Koch, between 1923 and 1926, at the U.F.A. Studios in Berlin, on an antiquated titling bench with a few collaborators who later became famous pioneers in animation—Walter Ruttmann, Alexander Kardan and Berthold Bartosch. The musical score was by Wolfgang Zeller. The fact that this film could be made at all was due, to a large extent, to the feeling in Germany at the time, a climate of research into the arts, and cinematography in particular. The animated shadow, a technique dear to the German and the Japanese, exemplified a form of aesthetic research which had parallels in several spheres. Lotte Reiniger began in the cinema in 1920, and had already done six shorts with animated shadows when she started *Prince Ahmed*, her major work. She made 22 films during her career in Germany, left the U.F.A. Studios in 1928, and continued production in Italy and then in England from 1934 when she joined the famous G.P.O. film unit.

Among the many highlights of her distinguished career, it is worth noting that Jean Renoir commissioned an animated shadow sequence from her for a part of his film *La Marseillaise* in a scene taking place at a famous shadow theatre, the Caran d'Arche. And, as a postscript to her achievement in the feature film (with the help of a British production company, Primrose Films, London and the British Film Institute) a new version of *Prince Ahmed* was made in 1954, following the instructions of Lotte Reiniger herself, and was shown on television in six episodes. This version was hand-coloured and scored with new music by Freddie Phillips, as W. Zeller's score had been only an accompaniment to the original film.

In 1955 she won the Venice Biennale Television Film prize for her *Tapfere Schneiderlein,* and in 1970 she published a book on her career and shadow technique.

EARLY RUSSIAN WORK

A pioneer of animated puppet film, Ladislas Starewitch, was the creator of the most titanic work of the full-length animation cinema—*Le Roman de Renard*, which came out in France in 1940. He died in 1965 almost completely forgotten, like many other pioneers of stop motion film—Emile Raynaud, Emile Cohl, and very recently Berthold Bartosch. Starewitch, born in Russia in 1882 but of Polish origin, first worked as a teacher of natural history. From 1909–1910 he used films as a pedagogic medium. He left teaching at this point to devote himself to a career in film, starting off as a camera operator. Then he became a director in live-action directing, for example, Mosjoukine and Toujanski, two great actors of the silent screen in Russia. He also carried out experiments in animation, made educational films, and directed the first Russian film to pass the frontiers of the country, *The Grasshopper and the Ant.*

The film was seen by Tsar Nicholas II and rewarded by him. It was made in the Khanjoukoff Studio, Moscow.

When the studio moved to the Crimea in 1917, Starewitch left traditional direction, settled in Paris and organised at Joinville-le-Pont a studio for the exclusive production of animated puppet films, where he made several hundred dolls. After making a number of shorts, he needed to expand and moved to Fontenay-sous-Blois in 1924. Here he built a larger studio in which to undertake his feature film, and worked on it from 1925 to 1936.

Unfortunately the film was not as good as it should have been, and some scenes are rather insipid. The dangers of the puppet medium and the long time-lapse between the beginning and end of production seem to have contributed to its failings. However, it does have the merit of having a soundtrack well in advance of its time, and it has, fortunately, been preserved to the present day.

Starewitch left his successors a large store of knowledge and experience which it was hard to better. For example, he created his own system for animating his puppets. They were larger than those used in contemporary animation, and controls at the back of their heads enabled their facial features to be moved.

While Starewitch was making his short films in France, Russia was the scene of many developments in the experimental cinema, and Starewitch benefitted much from them. The unit responsible was the Mosfilm Studio. Following a reorganisation of the Russian animated industry in 1924, there was a lively period of production both in the field of experimental films and those aimed at cinema audiences.

One of the prime movers of Mosfilm was Alexander Ptuschko, who worked at Mosfilm from the early days. Ptuschko had a long-lasting partnership with Merkulov, the puppet-maker. They worked together on various films, notably *Interplanetary Journeys*. Then in 1935, after three years of production, their famous feature film *Novii Gulliver* (New Gulliver) was born.

The Novii Gulliver is a film with a mixture of live characters and animated puppets. There are three thousand puppets in the film, which were made by Merkulov, while Ptuschko directed the film. There were some impressive experiments with puppets and actors appearing in the same scene. The superimposition was carried out in the camera, although at that time it was a very little known technique. It was so effective that the puppets seem absolutely human and this realism, together with its versatility, creates a universe where only the proportions of the characters seem fantastic. Ptuschko's is the most realistic of animated films and occupies a position at the opposite end of the scale from Disney's *Alice in Wonderland*, where every trick divorces the film from normal experience. *Novii Gulliver* is one of the most successful adaptations of Swift's novel.

Apart from *La Guerra e il Sogno di Momi* (which had a number of live-action scenes), this film of Ptuschko, and Starewitch's *Le Roman de Renard* are the only full-length animated marionette films made during this period (1916–1945). In fact, in the whole history of the animated film, there have been very few productions in that distinctive Russian style, although following Starewitch's residence in Europe, the style did become established there.

Animated cartoons were, however, the main area of production in Europe at this time. One of the most interesting attempts was an Italian full-length film of Collodi's *The Adventures of Pinocchio*. Started in 1936, this film was produced by C.A.I.R. (Cartoni Animati Italiani Roma) and directed by Raoul Verdini (several histories of the cinema mention Umberto Spano as director, but this seems to be incorrect). For this, 150,000 drawings were produced and it was filmed in black and white. But, before completion, it was decided to make *The Adventures of Pinocchio* in colour instead. As there were no colour processing laboratories in Italy, the work was done in London.

At this point, disaster struck the production. As well as political troubles, there were copyright difficulties (and perhaps some unfriendly activity by the Disney organisation). By 1940, when the film was scheduled for release, work was entirely abandoned.

The artists on this film were famous at the time for their cartoons in childrens magazines, and people who have seen sequences from it maintain that the animation is extremely fine, and aesthetically very pleasing.

We must conclude that there was a desire in Europe to produce full-length animated films and that the first twenty years of activity in this field (1916–1936) did produce several interesting works, while in the United States nothing had been attempted in spite of the remarkable success of short animated films. The success of *Prince Ahmed*, *New Gulliver* and *La Guerra e il Sogno di Momi*, and the fact that the trade press spoke of Starewitch's and Verdini's works, show that there was a climate of interest. But something was missing, and nowhere in the world had anyone found what it was. Then in 1937 Walt Disney relegated all previous efforts to oblivion.

DISNEY ERA

In the United States, the golden age of the animated cartoon was now in full swing. Scores of studios were bringing out films regularly, and several were released every week. The industry was getting into good shape and the jovial Walt Disney had acquired a good status in the American and world market. The appearance of *Snow White and the Seven Dwarfs* (1937) opened the way to his enormous commercial success.

The high quality of *Snow White* assured Disney of an unprecedented popularity. He initiated the public to the pleasures of the full-length animated film while paradoxically preventing all other studios from producing their own. The name Disney became synonymous with fantasy, eclipsing the names and aims of all competitors.

The Disney era gathered momentum with further feature films. In *Fantasia* (1939), Disney visualised, in his own particular style, eight works of music by famous composers (see catalogue for full details). Recently, re-released in Superscope, it remains like *Snow White* a major work of full-length animation. It is Disney's only film of this length which allowed his individual artists to express themselves in their own way, each section of the film being undertaken by a different director. It also represents the major initiation of "multiplane", the famous technical creation of the Burbank Studios, which is a camera set-up designed to allow change in focus between different parts of the same scene, and which creates a realistic impression of three dimensions. The soundtrack, too, was constructed with the maximum technical virtuosity. The orchestra of 103 musicians, directed by Leopold Stokowski, was recorded on nine separate tracks, in stereophonic sound, using 450,000 feet of soundtrack.

Then in 1940, Disney's *Pinocchio* was produced. It was better made than *Snow White*, but a less poetic subject. The very expressive characters can even now serve as examples of outstanding animation. *Dumbo* (1941), *The Reluctant Dragon* (1941) and *Bambi* (most of which was produced in 1942) are part of the gradual rise of the Masters of Burbank. With *Bambi* "Walt Disney has perfected his style of an even greater degree. His sense of observation has become even more refined, if that is possible, and the excellent technique of the film frequently gives a real impression of three dimensions. Lastly, the colour is never violent.

The musical score contains no hackneyed, jarring melodies. It would be very hard to find a more suitable show for children, who will love the peevish frog and Thumper, the shrewd rabbit. Adults will be no less sensible to its charm, though they will feel that the plot is rather slim."*

Released again in 1969 and 1971, this film had yet more great box-office successes.

While Disney was building up his empire, there was an attempt by Max and Dave Fleischer to reach a wide audience with their own full-length animated cartoons. Max Fleischer's character, Popeye, was nearly as popular as Mickey Mouse and with *Gulliver's Travels* (1939) and *Mr. Bug Goes to Town* (1940), the brothers attempted to carry their success over to feature films. *Gulliver's Travels* was closer to the spirit of the first book of Swift's satire than any other animated film adaptation has been, and the film evokes an atmosphere of colourful fantasy. It also has great technical merit. *Mr. Bug Goes to Town* is the story of a colony of insects which lives forty-five inches off Broadway, and is sensitive, humorous and well-visualised. Both films were made at the Miami Studios, which at that time had a staff of four hundred. However, the films were commercial failures. Although this period was still a time of experimentation on the organisational and technical level of animation production, the commercial aspect of the full-length film was already giving rise to cases of sharp business practice. The Disney organisation had a stranglehold on the market and the advent of World War II severely curtailed all production.

In other parts of the world, the Disney monopoly did not so much affect production, but the war did. Before the modern period, only two full-length animated films of any note were made during the period of Disney's first five. The first is Alexander Ptuschko's *Solotoj Klujutschik* (translated as *The Little Golden Key or The Adventures of Buratino*). This was another puppet and live action film from the Mosfilm Studio, based on Alexander Tolstoi's book of the same name, a Russian version of the Pinocchio story. It does not have the same charm as *New Gulliver*, perhaps because Merkulov was no longer making the puppets, and this could be what prompted Ivan Ivanov-Vano to make his cartoon version of the same story twenty years later. *Solotoj, Klujutschik* marks the end of an era in Russian animation, which has since in many ways failed to live up to its early promise. The second film which we must mention here is, however, a true pioneering effort. It was produced in China in 1940 and set the foundations for what is, between political troubles, a fairly flourishing animation industry. The film is called *The Princess with the Iron Fan,* and was made by Wan Lai Ming and Wan Kou-Tcan, as a cartoon version of the book *Journey to the West*.

*From Index la Cinematographie Francaise.

Films of the Walt Disney Studio. By courtesy of Walt Disney Studio.

Snow White and the Seven Dwarfs (1938) (C).

The Reluctant Dragon (1941)

THE SUPREMACY OF WALT DISNEY

Of the eight feature films produced by the Walt Disney studios up to the end of the Second World War, four have become part of our heritage of children's films (*Snow White*, *Pinocchio*, *Dumbo* and *Bambi*) while three others were already directed towards a much wider public (*Fantasia*, *The Reluctant Dragon*, and *The Three Caballeros*). The eighth *Victory Through Air Power*, was a propaganda film distributed only on a limited scale. *Fantasia* and *The Three Caballeros* can be considered as musicals in which the continuity of action is provided by the soundtrack rather than the subject. This formula was to be used for half a dozen films made between 1946 and 1949.

The output of American films was characterised by the large number of musical comedies which were sweeping the cinema screens of the world. This type of film, coming immediately after the war, corresponded to a general need among the public for escapism. It is therefore not surprising to see Disney influenced by this need for a fairly long "musical period". The importance of the story was drastically reduced, and his films consisted of pieces of music with pictures added. Full-length films became a succession of episodes held together by a slim story line which was usually shot in live action.

The target audience for these films was not only children, but the whole family; just as with the ordinary cinema of the time, the object was to entertain through song. It seems that this period in the production of the Disney Studios was, as far as features were concerned, its worst, as none of the films earned a particular place in the memory of the public and they are never revived. This fact is paradoxical, however, for it was at the time of the worst feature films that the name of Walt Disney came to world-wide fame by the success of his short animated cartoons.

Reality or legend, the Disney myth is well and truly established today, though we must to some extent de-mystify it by admitting that everything did not happen as easily in all Burbank productions as we are led to believe—they had their ups and downs and this the immediately post-war period, does of course figure among the downs.

There have been numerous studies of Walt Disney. At the beginning of 1968 a young American journalist, David R. Smith, completed a biography and filmography in which he listed 585 books, 700 films, 335 T.V. shows and more than 600 articles on the subject. Since then the numbers have increased considerably.

One of the most recent authoritative books on Disney is "The Disney Version" by Richard Schikel, where we read that the immediate post war period is castigated as a slump between the "golden ages" of Disney production. We must have a brief look at the history of the Disney organisation to explain how such a slump was nearly inevitable.

Walt Disney became famous initially through nearly fifteen years' activity in producing short films. Then, on top of his work of this nature, which

Victory Through Air Power (1943).

was already enormous, he threw his energies into features with *Snow White*. At this time 750 people were working in his studio. Even so, this was insufficient for the production of a full-length film. *Snow White*, which should have taken two years, in fact needed more than five years' work.

Before the war, the number of employees had already passed the 2,000 mark, and a re-structuring of the studios and administration became necessary. Bureaucracy moved in, with all the usual attendant difficulties. Great damage was done by the increasingly demanding organisational needs, and the jovial atmosphere which Papa Walt wanted to preserve very soon disappeared to leave a disastrous artistic and social climate which led, in 1941, to the most serious of the strikes at the studio.

After these troubled years, the free-lancers left and the Walt Disney Studio enjoyed a highly productive period up until the end of the war. Traditional productions were supported by government propaganda films which offered financial security and richly adequate distribution. This resulted at length in a certain amount of stagnation in the organisation. When the war ended, it became necessary to predict and adopt new tendencies in audience taste, and to become financial self-supporting once again. In such a climate, the laborious and hazardous preparation of a full-length feature could not be expected. More films had to be produced in a shorter time, and up to about 1950 ease of production was the paramount concern. The five feature films of the period scarcely deserve the name, for all consist of short episodes linked together by a tenuous story-line.

This period of intensive production left little to posterity. *Make Mine Music* is the only full-length film to consist entirely of animation, and is a series

Fantasia (1939).

Fantasia (1939).

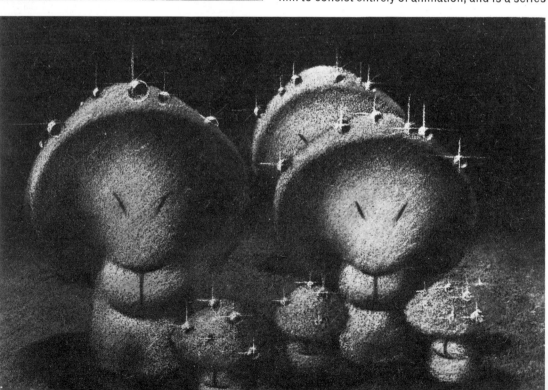

Pinocchio (1940)
Dumbo (1941)

of illustrations of pieces of music or songs. *Song of the South* has live action characters to represent reality and cartoons to represent dreams and stories. In *Fun and Fancy Free* we meet Mickey, Donald, Pluto and Jiminy Cricket in rather unsuitable juxtaposition with a new character, Bongo the bear cub. *So Dear to my Heart* is a story of a little boy and a black lamb, which tends to exploit the innocence of childhood. *Melody Time,* the last of the series, is perhaps the best constructed of the films of this musical period and uses the singing stars of the day, Ethel Smith and Roy Rogers, the singing cowboy.

The success of these films did not spread

Make Mine Music—After You've Gone (1946).

beyond the English-speaking countries, but the theme tunes of several became popular elsewhere and this brought in some copyright fees to the Disney Studios. But the success of the American musical comedy began to diminish about 1950 and in the Disney Studios new features were being prepared which no longer used the formula of the moment and heralded a return to what had made *Snow White* so successful—the presentation of a good story, with narrative unity and a high level of technical and graphic skill.

The first sign of the new departure was in 1949, with the appearance of a new animated cartoon that ran for sixty-eight minutes without live action. *The Adventures of Ichabod and Mr. Toad,* though not very well known, represents a new attempt to achieve a unified film. It consists of two separate stories, cleverly linked by a debate between the narrators. The smoothness of the production, the creation of new characters, the good dramatic construction, and the relatively complex animation show the way to a new sense of values.

The crystallisation of the return to good quality productions was a film which will become part of our cinematic heritage—*Cinderella* (1950). For the first time since *Snow White*, the human figures are not caricatures, but include an ideal hero and heroine. The animation is once again more carefully finished, the backgrounds are excellent, the adaptation of the story is meticulously carried out,

Bambi (1942)

The Flying Gauchito. From *The Three Caballeros* (1945).

Peter and the Wolf. From Make Mine
Music (1946).

Ichabod and Mr. Toad (1949).

Peter Pan (1953).

Sword in the Stone (1963).

Mary Poppins (1964).

The Jungle Book (1967).

Left, top and bottom. *Cinderella* (1950)

and the plot is not diluted by live action or static sequences. There is also a fine mixture between well-staged gags and poetic atmosphere. *Cinderella*, taken from Perrault's tale, was the first animated cartoon to enjoy world-wide success, and for many people it constitutes one of the first film memories of the post-war period, notably for those who were children when it came out.

On the purely professional level, *Cinderella* signals the return to films which need much more time and work spent on them but which, in the long run, are commercial successes, regularly re-released. By concentrating on high quality, Disney was able to make the frustration of his early plan to produce a feature every year turn to his advantage. His aim had been thwarted by strikes, complications in studio procedure, the wartime need for sponsored films, and the economic problems of the immediately post-war years. So he launched into live action production, television series, and the construction of Disneyland, which meant that the production of animation films became more leisurely. After *Cinderella*, there is no more than an average of one full-length cartoon every two years.

In 1951 a free adaptation of Lewis Carroll's *Alice in Wonderland* was made. The nonsensical situations are depicted in an attractive dream-like sequence, and details such as the disappearing Cheshire Cat contribute to the atmosphere.

A new box-office success appeared in 1953, *Peter Pan*. The title character is hero of several generations of Anglo-Saxon children, thanks to James Barrie's books about him, and in Walt Disney's adaptation there is a new element of his story-telling craft. Whereas in *Cinderella* or *Pinocchio* or *Snow White* or *Alice in Wonderland*, there are few characters in human form and many animals, in *Peter Pan* the majority of characters are human and the animals are few. There is an approach to plausible reality which makes the magic scenes all the more charming, and with the contrast between the fresh gaiety of the nursery and the mysterious confusion of Never-Never Land, this can be considered as the most ethereal of Disney's films.

A return was made to the personification of animals in 1955 with a film, which though it contains human figures, is centred on the amorous adventures of two dogs, *Lady and the Tramp*.

A new method was evolved for the film that followed, *Sleeping Beauty*. In order to obtain the closest possible approximation of real movements, several scenes were actually shot in live action before being drawn. In addition, the use of Technorama and the wide screen demanded a perfection of drawing rarely matched before or since. Despite its high cost and the perfection of its

Left. *Aristocats* (1970).
Far left. *Bedknobs and Broomsticks* (1971).

Right. *Robin Hood* (1973).

Far right, top. *Gulliver's Travels* (1939) by the Fleischer Studios, USA.

Far right, bottom. *Mr. Bug Goes to Town* (1940) by the Fleischer Studios, USA.

execution, however, this film did not have the commercial success of the far less ambitious *Peter Pan*.

In 1961 *One Hundred and One Dalmatians* had a fair degree of success. It was made by traditional techniques, and had nothing new to offer aesthetically, but it had the merit of being the first film to make primary use of the wax crayon instead of pen and ink. It also introduced the Xerox method of image duplication in this area, a technique whereby original drawings are photocopied directly onto the cel, and much of the work of tracing these pictures is no longer necessary.

Two years later, *The Sword in the Stone* used the same technique with a more highly developed artistic sense. After this film, the Disney studios produced no more full-length animated cartoons for five years. *Mary Poppins* (1964) used a mixture of live action and drawing at times, but not enough to be considered an animated feature. The same applies to the later feature *Bedknobs and Broomsticks* (1971).

The next full-length film was released in 1967. It was the last to be made in Disney's lifetime. *The Jungle Book* from Kipling's novel is probably the most successful of the long animated cartoons by Disney. It was also a rapid box-office success, as these figures from "Show Business Magazine" show.

Back on May 1st 1970, three Disney films were in the top eighty box-office champions of the USA and Canada. *Snow White* was at No. 32 earning $15,650,000. *The Jungle Book* was at No. 62 with $11,500,000 after only three years' distribution, *Peter Pan* was at No. 72 with $10,500,000. But the September 1970 figure shows *The Jungle Book* with takings of $23,795,000 overtaking all other Disney productions.

Thus, from 1937 to 1967, the giant Walt Disney imposed his supremacy in this particular type of full-length animation. Towards the end of his life he only supervised a collective effort, but it is notable that *The Aristocats* (1970) and *Robin Hood* (1973) which his veteran animator Woolie Reitherman directed, still keep entirely to the Disney style

which was basically set in the thirties, forties and fifties. It will be interesting to see what happens during the next productions from the Disney studios.

THE OTHER AMERICANS AND CANADA

While the Walt Disney studios were solving their economic problems with the episodic films of the "musical period", production of full-length animated films was rather limited in the United States and on the rest of the American continent.

In the face of the "giant" it seemed even harder

to attempt this adventure, already delicate even in the field of shorts, and the experience of the war period had shown that it was not enough just to put on the market films which offered reasonable competition with Disney, but an efficient commercial organization was needed, with outlets outside the USA.

Dave Fleischer had separated from his brother Max in 1941 after the closing of their Miami studios (where there was a serious strike in 1937), and he left for Los Angeles while Max returned to New York. In spite of the limited success enjoyed by his two previous feature films, Dave started on a new one with Popeye as the main character. *Sinbad the Sailor* came out in 1946 and was a comparative failure. This seemed confirmation of a situation

Alice in Wonderland (1948) by Lou Bunin, USA.

Mr. Magoo—A Thousand and One Arabian Nights (1959) U.P.A., USA.

Bunin directed it, and it appeared in 1948.

It was not until the sixties that the dominating influence of Walt Disney began to diminish, and that there began to be a place for other productions in the sphere of full-length animated films. The first studio to undertake the serious production of competitive films was UPA (United Producers of America), and their studios at Burbank were nearly as successful as the neighbouring Disney studios. Mr. Magoo, a long-established character in short films, was the star of UPA's first full-length film, *A Thousand and One Arabian Nights* (1959), which was produced by Stephen Bosustow, directed by Jack Kinney, and had Abe Levitow as head animator. This production brought in a good deal of money and was shown and well-received even in Europe. The comic character of Mr. Magoo was a new type in the full-length animation cinema, and his blundering activities as an Arabian lamp seller trying to make himself the hero of the film were conceived in a style refreshingly different from Disney's.

Gay Purr-ee (1962) UPA's next feature, has an even more distinctive approach. The subject, a musical about night life in Paris at the beginning of this century, involves character types which owe little to previous cartoon animals. The director was Abe Levitow, who started in animation in 1940 and joined UPA in 1958. To date he has directed 130 Dick Tracy shorts, 130 Mr. Magoo shorts, 26 Mr. Magoo half- hour programmes, and five features. His perennial partner, Chuck Jones, has been just as productive. He directed many *Tom and Jerry* films, and created characters like *The Road Runner, Wile E. Coyotte, Daffy Duck* and *Bugs Bunny*. When the MGM animation team suspended activity for a time, Chuck Jones worked on *Gay Purr-ee* for Warner Bros. and helped UPA to take a new direction in the full-length animation cinema. Much of its reputation rested on the voices in the film—Judy Garland, Robert Goulet and other Broadway stars—and it could be called the first cartoon operetta.

In the same year 1962, at Christmas, the first television cartoon of as much as an hour's duration was presented to the public on NBC TV and it brought enthusiastic reactions from the specialist critics. This was another UPA production, again featuring Mr. Magoo who, this time, aspires to plan the role of Ebenezer Scrooge in Charles Dicken's famous story A Christmas Carol. The film was entitled *Mr. Magoo's Christmas Carol*, and was also directed by Abe Levitow. UPA now stopped making features until 1969, as they were occupied almost entirely in setting Mr. Magoo in short adventures for TV series.

But in *Uncle Sam Magoo* (1969), Mr. Magoo was again allowed to entertain TV audiences for an hour. Abe Levitow's second TV Special, it was produced by Henry G. Saperstein (President of UPA) and it is a revue-type version of the history

in which no American would dare to try his luck, although there were many large studios in operation at the time. Because of this feeling that Walt Disney was too strong a competitor, and that his distribution system was too well organised, more than ten years lapsed before a new non-Disney full-length animated cartoon appeared. However, there was film produced in the meantime which merits attention. The only puppet feature from the whole of the American continent, it was an adaptation of the famous book, *Alice in Wonderland* of Lewis Carroll, and according to Robert Benayoun, the French critic, it is much closer to the spirit of the story than Disney's version. Lou

of America as told by Uncle Sam Magoo, from the discovery or discoveries of America to the time of the hippies. The idea was Saperstein's and it was broadcast in 1970 along with *The Phantom Toll Booth,* which Abe Levitow co-directed with Chuck Jones. This was co-produced by Les Goldman, made for MGM, and broadcast by NBC television.

The Phantom Toll Booth is based on a book by Norton Juster, published for the first time in 1961, which became a classic of fantasy literature or science fiction, worthy of a place beside "Alice in Wonderland" and "The Wizard of Oz". The story is, at first sight, aimed at children but bears in fact the imprint of an adult and modern philosophy. This film is the first full-length animated film from MGM. The beginning and end of the film is done in live action (20 mins. altogether), but all the rest is in animation (70 min.). The outside live sequences were shot in 1967 in San Francisco, while the interior live sections were done in the MGM studio in Culver City. As for the animation itself, several sequences constitute interesting visual experiments.

In America, the decade 1960–1970 presented an unusual situation in the animation cinema. The "giant", Walt Disney, produced few animated films. More than eighty percent of his production concentrated on documentary or live-action films. Shortly after 1960 several large animation studios closed down, putting many technicians and artists out of work, and reflecting a real climate of crisis

Mr. Magoo's Christmas Carol (1962) USA.

The Phantom Tollbooth (1969) by Abe Levitow and Chuck Jones, USA.

in this specialised sphere, a crisis which could be explained by many factors, too lengthy and complex to detail here.

But when we speak of crisis in the cinema, in animation particularly, the state of affairs is not definitive. Animators with patience and faith in their profession did not let themselves be beaten by the almost catastrophic situation of the early sixties. The animation cinema had a difficult recovery but, on the other hand, a new structure was being built in this field. Small independent teams were formed, and from their research sprang many films of importance to the evolution of the contemporary animation cinema. Thus, from 1965, a regeneration took place and, in 1968 there was again full employment in this field whereas in 1963 there was about forty percent unemployment. According to a study, quoted in "Entertainment World" (October 31st 1969) by Art Harger, entitled "The Hyper-animated Animation Industry" it appeared that revenue from animation in 1965 was 15 million dollars (for the USA) 25 million dollars in 1968 and nearing 40 million dollars in 1969. The predictions for 1972 were as much as 100 million dollars.

In fact since 1960, two opposing tendencies, quite clearly defined, are appearing in the animation cinema, and they meet but rarely. There are, firstly, those who have confidence in the cinema, and who carry on making films for cinema audiences; these are few, for it is true that profitability is not necessarily calculable in advance. According to the above mentioned article on animation, films for the cinema pay back only 65% of cost in American cinemas and 35% in other countries. On the other hand, there are those, more numerous, who hang all their hopes on television. There is more security in this sector for the sale of films, and a good organisational system which can ensure the profitability of an animated film. There are, however, certain conditions which do not allow work to be as polished as it can be for the cinema; the serial especially has become a conveyor-belt industry. Since television is a large consumer of animated film, it was thought at one time that it might completely stifle the USA production of animated films for the cinema, full-length films in particular. But this was to reckon without individuality. At the beginning to the sixties Disney and the other studios, including UPA, made few films for the cinema. However, apart from "bread-and-butter" work, small teams were working on research which brought about the blossoming of modern animation. In the field of full-length films, several attempts are worthy of mention.

In 1961 one of the first works was produced which admitted a belief that full-length animation had a chance of escaping from the well beaten tracks of Walt Disney. If all the films quoted so far were industrial products (even those of UPA, though

Of Stars and Men (1961) by the Hubley Studio, USA.

these offered a new conception), made with large teams in an unchanging quest for the key to public taste, one film is clearly distinguished from the rest: *Of Stars and Men* by John Hubley.

Of Stars and Men, both by its subject (the condition of man in comparison with the infinitely great and the infinitely small), and by the way in which it is treated (in rough animation), opened up new perspectives for full-length animation, shaking the basic concept of the full-length animated film, just as he had already shaken firmly anchored basic concepts with several of his shorts.

John Hubley was not a newcomer to the world of animation. He had taken his first steps in the studios of Walt Disney, where he was assistant art director on *Snow White* and associate director on *Pinocchio*, *Fantasia*, *Bambi* and *Dumbo*. He then went to UPA where the first films on which he collaborated were successes, and where he had the opportunity of directing several important shorts, among which were *Rag Time Bear*, the first in the Mr. Magoo series, *Robin Hoodlum*, *Magic Fluke*, *Gerald McBoing Boing* and *Rooty-Toot-Toot*. Together with his wife, Faith Hubley, who was a scriptwriter for some important directors such as George Stoney, Irving Lerner, and Sidney Lumet, he then set up his own studio, Storyboard Inc. The worldwide reputation of this pair came from films such as *Tender Game*, *Children of the Sun*, *The Top* and many others.

Hubley's great theory was that an animated film already has all its artistic value at the time of first considering the work and preparing the animation, that is, before the tracers get hold of the drawings to transpose them on the cels. John Hubley was, and is still, the great defender of animation left in its raw state, "rough animation", alone capable of transmitting on to the screen the true intentions of the artist-animator.

Of Stars and Men is 53 minutes long and is both a story and a didactic work; it is a philosophical dissertation on the condition of man among the stars—and the electrons. It was made by a very small group, in collaboration with the scientist Harlow Shapley, who was director of the observatory at the University of Massachusetts.

A specialist in cosmography and author of many philosophical treatises on this subject, he wrote the book on which *Of Stars and Men* is based. The objective of the film was to translate into simple and explicit terms the complexity of the universe in which we live, and it was achieved perfectly by the joint talents of the author, of John and Faith Hubley, and of the small production team, which included Bill Littlejohn.

The most remarkable fact about the whole film is undoubtedly the number of people who worked on it—six people, working for a production period of ten months, after two years of preparation. This economy of time and manpower was unheard of in American animation. Thus, *Of Stars and Men* occupies a special position among full-length animated films, and has the distinction of being made in Walt Disney's lifetime, well before any

Hanna and Barbera formed their own studio, which became one of the largest in the world, with 600 employees.

From the very beginning, they have directed their

Fritz the Cat (1972) by Ralph Bakshi and Steve Krantz, USA. By courtesy of Black Ink Films.

The Man from Button Willow (1965) by David Detiege, USA.

A Boy Named Charlie Brown (1969) by Bill Melendez, USA.

other individualist attempts of such an ambitious nature.

But there were to be three other feature animated films before Walt Disney's death on 15th December 1966. The first was a production from the Hanna-Barbera studio: *Hey There It's Yogi Bear* (1964).

William Hanna and Joseph Barbera are old friends from the MGM studios where they created many characters for animated shorts. They designed many films in the *Tom and Jerry* Series. In June 1957, when the situation in the American animation industry began to grow very difficult,

production towards television, and Yogi Bear is one of their television characters. Since he was universally known, his creators decided to use him, with several of his likeable friends, to make a full-length film for the cinema. Among the episodes in Yogi's adventures are a circus parade and a Venetian dream in the best of taste. So, *Hey There It's Yogi Bear,* was another film made by a relatively small team, and in a short length of time. It allowed use of a simpler technique than that of Walt Disney's films and since it depended in its essence on lively, active characters it could do without impressive backgrounds.

The second film to be undertaken before Walt Disney died has unfortunately not been finished. This was *Rainbow Road to Oz*—an animated cartoon which was to be 60 minutes long. It commenced production in 1965 at the Crawley Film Studios in Ottawa. Canada has produced several great names in world animation. But this is the only full-length cartoon to be attempted. The reasons why it was abandoned are not known.

The third of these films was by David Detiege, a strange experiment entitled *The Man from Button Willow*. Breaking with all conventions, David Detiege sought to produce something different and succeeded in doing so. Unfortunately his alm will not have a sequel for, since it came out in 1965, the style it inaugurated has become commonplace. Detiege's team of animators was formed in part from the Disney school, and included Ken Hultgern, Don Towsley, Don Lusk and George Rowley. The film was drawn so that two styles of imagery meet and mix. One is traditional, with the personification of animals as in Walt Disney, and the other, dear to the romantic American view of the 1860's, was the pure style of the wild west cartoon. The film can be considered as a ballad.

Since 1966 there have been many new developments in American full-length animation. Hanna-Barbera have continued in the style they set in *Hey There It's Yogi Bear*, with a theatrical feature

© 1969 by United Feature Syndicate, Inc.

Charlotte's Web (1973) by Hanna and Barbera and Charles Nichols and Iwao Takamoto, USA. By courtesy of Scotia-Barbera Distributors.

Right, top. *Nine Lives of Fritz the Cat* (1974) by Robert Taylor and Steve Krantz. By courtesy of Rank Film Distributors Ltd.

Right, bottom. *Heavy Traffic* (1973) by Ralph Bakshi and Steve Krantz, USA. By courtesy of Black Ink Films.

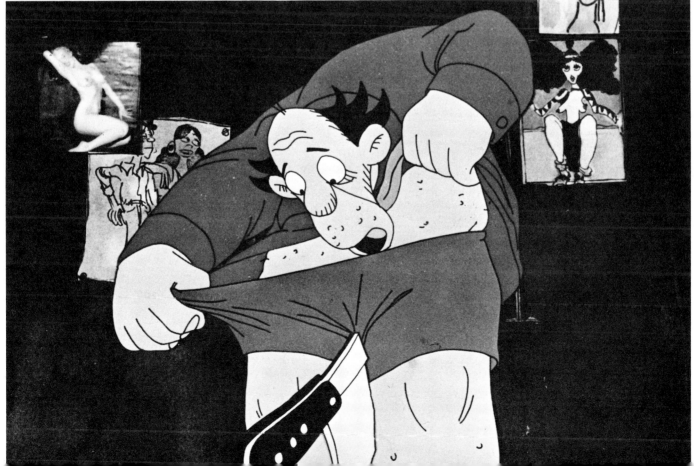

based on their television series, *The Flintstones*, and called *A Man Called Flintstone* (1967), and two TV specials, *Jack and the Beanstalk* (1967) and *Alice in Wonderland* (1968). These all use the simple style and animation associated with the television series.

Encouraged by the example of *Shinbone Alley*, *A Boy Called Charlie Brown*, *Fritz the Cat* and *Heavy Traffic*, which will be described in a later chapter, many new projects for theatrical features have been announced in the USA. It is not certain that the films involved will actually be produced, for they are mentioned in trade magazines well before production starts, but they represent a wide diversity of subject matter.

Fred Mogubgub, a New York film-maker, is working on a film entitled *The Day I Met Zett*. Lester Novros, of Grafic-Film, should soon finish *Space Survey*. Norman Prescott, of Filmation, has announced a film of *Return to Oz*. Fred Calvert intended to make *Don Quixote*. Finally, there is to

A Vida Do Solo (1968) by S. Mello, Brazil.

be a production with Rock & Roll music, *The Wizard of Oz*. There is no doubt that there will be a great flood of new features by the late 1970's—produced by old and new studios.

LITTLE KNOWN SOUTH AMERICAN PRODUCTIONS

The South American cinema is not world famous, yet it does exist. From time to time, at festivals or specialised film shows, a Brazilian, Cuban or Argentinian film is shown. If South American animation is badly distributed, this is primarily due to the importance in this part of the world of the North American cinema, and secondly to the influence of Spanish films which are, paradoxically, better distributed in Latin America than in Europe.

In the field of full-length films, one recalls the three films made in Argentina, *El Apostol* (1917), *Peludopolis* (1931) and *Upa en Apuros* (1942) which, mainly for economic reasons, had no follow-up. Now other countries have been proved able to compete with their North American neighbours. There is in Cuba an animation cinema of great merit, and it seems likely that we shall see the birth there of full-length films within a few years. Rumours confirming this impression have circulated despite the discretion shown by the National Cinema Centre. Brazil already has produced two interesting works, one of which is an animated cartoon from the hand of Anelio Latini Filho. He made this film over a long period of time and almost entirely alone—design, animation photography included. Based on the local legends of Amazonia, it is entitled *Sinfonia Amazonica*. It was finished in 1953. Made in a style reminiscent of Disney, with animals and characters of Amazonian folklore, this film was one of the great revelations of post-war South American animation. Filho, in very difficult conditions and uncertain of the eventual outcome, is currently working on a new feature film, though he is unable to guarantee regular work on it. He periodically has to abandon this project to work in bread-and-butter films.

It is strange that South America should not yet have found the means to maintain a regular production, since in its various countries, there are many artists who would be capable of undertaking valuable work in animation. There is also a mythological aspect and an atmosphere of fantasy which could be a great inspiration to producers, but up to now probably the main obstacle to this has been the cost of production, possibly too high for such countries.

However, a 78 minute film made in Brazil in 1968 does indicate that the principle of economic animation has been understood. This film, *A Vida de Solo* (The life of soil), has a practical and didactic aim, but nevertheless constitutes a full-length animated film. Made from animated cartoons and cut-outs, the object of this film is to explain how to look after and cultivate the soil.

The director was Orion Silva Mello, and it was sponsored by the Federal University of Santa Maria.

There is news also of a fourth Brazilian full-length animated film. It is to be a co-production with Czechoslovakia, directed by Geraldo Sarno, and it will involve animated puppets.

The only other important South American venture in the animation field is to be undertaken in Venezuela, where a group of Venezuelan and Cuban artists is to be aided by animators from Zagreb in a full-length cartoon about which little is yet known.

THE MIDDLE EAST, ASIA AND AUSTRALASIA

On the Asian continent only four countries (apart from the Soviet Union—see Eastern Europe) have, as yet, embarked on full-length animated films—Israel, China, Korea and Japan, which is at present the largest world producer of this type of film.

ISRAEL

The Israeli film industry is one of the youngest in the world, only ten years old, but it is of considerable commercial interest above all in the field of co-production.

In the sphere of animated films, the examples are few as yet, but there is one important studio created by Yoram Gross, who has since moved to Australia. But others have continued his pioneering work.

This studio produces shorts and commercials, mostly with animated puppets, but in 1961 after two years of hard toil, Yoram Gross helped by his wife Alina and a small team, finished an adap-

Joseph Sold by his Brothers (1962) by Alina and Yoram Gross, Israel.

tation of an episode from the bible entitled *Joseph the Dreamer* (80 min.).

The puppets in this film are remarkable in that their appearance is very different from European equivalent puppets and the whole film attempts to disengage the 'puppet style' from conventional tracks.

This effort, unique both by its subject since it is rare to choose a religious subject for animation, and by its aesthetic effect, deserves a place among films which open new horizons.

CHINA

Little known on our screens, the animation cinema of the People's Republic of China knew a definite Golden Age from 1950 to about 1956.

Historically, Chinese animation between 1926 and 1949 was relatively inactive, and we can count only a score of films made during this period—all shorts apart from *The Princess with the Iron Fan* by the Wan Brothers.

The Chinese animation cinema includes both puppets and various "two-dimensional" techniques of roughly equal importance.

Among the two-dimensional techniques, China possesses two original skills which the animators have mastered and used as a vehicle for their great talent. First of all there is the technique of paper cut-outs, coloured and engraved, which can create as fluid a movement as cartoon animation; many short and medium-length films have been made by this technique. Secondly, there is the animated washtint, which was used notably in two particularly successful short films, *The Tadpoles in Search of Their Mother*, and *The Coward's Flute*. Although only 20 films had been made before 1949, since the inauguration of the People's Republic, considerable effort has been put into the animation cinema, and the original pioneers were able to create schools and studios. The one at Shanghai was particularly well equipped for animated cartoons and puppets. They employed several hundred artists, and produced from 1949 to 1959, about a hundred new films, a number which increased continuously until 1967, when it was interrupted completely by political events.

The intellectual revolution has now ended, and the directors have returned to the studios, which have recently re-started their activity to a certain extent.

The present situation does not guarantee absolute accuracy of information on the Chinese scene.

The major works of Chinese animation are produced by teams in which older people and young people work together. This guarantees a continuity of style, a style which is fairly traditional in the sphere of full-length films.

The leading Chinese animators were three brothers, Wan Kou-Tchan, Wan Lai-Ming and Wan Tchao-Tchen. The younger animators are Chien Chiao-Chun, Chin Hsi, and Yue Lou.

Considering Chinese feature films made after 1949, there are two which cannot be included in the catalogue since they are not strictly animated films, but illustrate the use of certain fringe activities. In 1958 a Chinese film, made with hand operated shadows and puppets at the Shanghai animation studio by Hsu Ping-Touo, demonstrated the richness of these two essentially Chinese folk arts, from which the directors take their inspiration as much as from animation technique. This film was made with the help of the Chinese Puppet and Shadow Troupe of Hounan, and is called *Two Lotus Flowers* (52 mins.). The second is called *Little Bell*, made in 1964, 72 mins. long, directed by

A Chuang Tapestry (1959). Director Chien Chiao-Chun, People's Republic of China.

logical epic legend *Journey to the West* with the animal-gods, the monkey and the sacred pig.*

In the animated cartoon of classical type, the Chinese style shows great suppleness, giving an airy atmosphere to the battle scenes between the monkey and his enemies, for the story takes place partially in the sky.

The two full-length puppet films are also taken from ancient legends and were made in 1964.

The first is *The Peacock Princess*, directed by Tchin Hsi and taken from a Tai legend in South West China, telling of the valour of the King's son, who received a bow which took extraordinary strength to string. The second is *The Girl with Long Hair*, directed by Yue Lou, adapted from a folk tale from Tong, the mountain region.

Both films are productions of the Shanghai Studios.

With the renewed activity in the animation studios, during the early 1970's, It Is certain that we shall soon be seeing original films, for in China there are a great many talented animation artists, and the experiments which began during the sixties should result in the production of films with a brand new aesthetic quality.

KOREA, VIETNAM AND INDIA

A Korean director, Il Young, has made five full-length films in animated cartoon, but little is known of the subjects or titles.

The People's Republic of North Vietnam has also recently created animation studios which will quite possibly produce interesting feature films, and so has India, where medium-length educational films have already been made.

JAPAN

Since their first full-length animated film was shown in 1959, Japanese directors and producers have come to lead world production in this sphere.

Of course figures do not mean much, yet between 1958 and 1971 the Japanese have made more than 30 films, while even the United States has produced only 20 over the same period (previous American production having been as much as 23 films from 1937 to 1957).

In fact, Japanese animation including short, medium and full-length as well as TV films, has made the greatest progress in world-wide terms during the last 15 years. It is also among the oldest industries, dating back to 1916. Many Japanese directors have achieved international fame, though Europe is not yet familiar with the full range of Japanese productions. In America, however, Japanese work has been seen regularly for more

Hsieh Tien and Chen Fang-Chien. It is a mixed film of live action, glove puppets and marionettes, and the subject is the story of two children who become involved in the magic world of a troupe of puppets—the puppets come alive for them.

Chinese shadows, marionettes and puppets are pure folk arts which in the East, and particularly in China, enjoyed and still enjoy spectacular success and are as valid artistically as the traditional theatre.

The Chinese puppet show is essentially an art of spectacle, always with rich backgrounds, and very expressive. So it is only natural that the animation cinema of this country should have succeeded perfectly in assimilating the puppet technique. Czechoslovakia and East Germany are the only other nations with a tradition of presenting so many puppet films.

Since 1949 four full-length animated films, two cartoons and two puppet films have been made, as far as we can tell from the information we have.

In 1959 the Shanghai studio made an animated cartoon in the traditional Disney style with human characters. This film is taken from an ancient legend of the Chuang, a people from the South West of China, and tells of the courage and assiduousness of one son of three who retrieves a tapestry for his mother. It is directed by Chien Chiao-Chun.

Another animated cartoon much more ambitious with a running time of two hours was made in 1962 by the veteran Wan Lai Ming.

This was shown with great success at the Locarno '65 Festival under the title *Troubles in the Kingdom of Heaven*; it tells the famous mytho-

*This also provided the inspiration for the earlier Chinese film *The Princess with the Iron Fan.*

than seven years, both in the cinemas and on TV screens. The ties between Japanese and the American animation industries are close; some American producers have their films made in Japanese studios, and many of the longer films are American co-productions. The American animation industry and unions do not particularly approve of this activity. Japan can also support a large animation industry of its own through its home market.

As a consequence, Japan has several large studios for animated cartoons which have become among the most important in the world, and we are likely to see many Japanese names in the credits of full-length animated films in future years.

These films are mostly made in two versions—Japanese and English—or else with English subtitles. For the Japanese film industry, full-length animation has become of considerable commercial importance.

The pioneer of Japanese animation was Noburo Ofugi, who died a few years ago. He was the spokesman for Japan at the Cannes Festival in 1958—the first programme devoted to world-wide animation. Other well known animators are Yoji Kuri, most of whose films have been shown more or less everywhere in the last few years, Taiji Yabushita and Osamu Tezuka.

There are many other Japanese animators whose work is certainly as important as that of the well known European directors and whose names should be more familiar to the public.

The pioneer era in Japanese animation started in 1916 and continued up to the last war. It embraces several hundred interesting short films.

But frame-by-frame films were developed mainly since the war, stimulated by the rapid rise of tele-

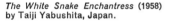
The White Snake Enchantress (1958) by Taiji Yabushita, Japan.

vision. The numerous television channels demanded a great quantity of animated cartoon and puppet film programme material and used many from abroad, mostly from the USA.

As this type of programme proved a success with the public, steps were taken to develop a national industry so that many studios, helped by a revived interest, were to set up a true animated film industry which during the next 12 years, developed at a rate never seen before. They assimilated the techniques of American production quite easily, adding this to their already highly developed artistic sense. The Japanese had inherited an instinctive graphic tradition and also possessed an acute sense of the commercial value of an animated film.

The field of full-length films has been entered forcefully by Japan's largest live-action studios, such as the Toei Company. With an impressive total of 18 full-length animated cartoons, the Toei Company is easily the largest Japanese producer, and its production is second in size only to Walt Disney. Disney animation production will soon however, be overtaken by Teoi, which is managing to produce between one and two full-length animated films per year in addition to TV series, one or two medium-length films, several shorts, entertainment or educational, and several hundred commercial and PR films.

Taiji Yabushita is often known as the Japanese Walt Disney. He has worked at the Toei studios since their creation, and is at the root of the formidable evolution of this type of film in Japan. He has already directed more than seven features in the Toei studio, which contains about 600 specialist staff.

While the stories and legends of Europe are of quite recent origin, there is much more ancient Oriental mythology in which Japanese animation almost always finds its subjects. This is the case with the first Japanese full-length animated film, directed by Taiji Yabushita in the studios of Toei. The film, entitled *Hakuja Den* (*The White Snake Enchantress*), 78 mins. long, was made in 1958. It is an illustration of a Chinese legend, comprising a delightful love story and including children, animals, a sorcerer and other characters.

Although the animal characters take their inspiration from the technique of Disney and are similar to the characters in American animated cartoons, they are much more refined, and the backgrounds are in a delicate style reminiscent of the great masters of Japanese art. This gift for design is innate in the Japanese, and cannot be found in films of other countries. *The White Snake Enchantress* won a special diploma at Venice in 1959, and did a great deal for Japanese full-length animation, especially since it has been shown in the USA and in many European countries. The second production of this studio, *Shonen Sarutobi Sasuke* (*The Adventures of Little Samurai Magic*

安寿と厨子王丸
© TOEI 1961

*The Adventures of Little Samurai
Magic Boy* (1959) by Taiji Yabushita,
Japan.

The Orphan Brothers (1961) by Taiji
Yabushita, Japan.

Right. *A Story on a Street Corner* (1962) by Eichi Yamamoto and Yusaki Sekamoto, Japan.

Far right. *The Life of Buddha* (1961) by Noburo Ofuji, Japan.

Centre, *Adventures of Sinbad* (1962) by Taiji Yabushita, Japan.

Bottom. *Touring the World* (1962) by Ryuichi Yokoyama, Japan.

Boy), 1959, won its director, Taiji Yabushita, the Lion of St. Mark at the 1960 Venice Festival. This, too, is a story taken from an ancient legend. Taiji Yabushita, together with another director, Osamu Tezuka, who since has opened his own studio, made a third film at Toei in 1960. It was called *Sai Yu-Ki* (*Alakazam the Great*), 88 mins. long, and was followed in 1961 by *Anju to Zushio Maru* (*The Orphan Brothers*), 88 mins., which was shot in Toeiscope and yet again illustrated Oriental legends.

Well known for his short films, *Phantom Ship, Whale* and *Legend of the Dragon*, Noburo Ofuji, in 1961, made a monumental film of animated shadows with a very ambitious subject—*Shaka No Shogai* (*The Life of Buddha*), 70 mins. long, which breaks away from the Toei studio type of film. The subject is a succession of scenes from the life of Buddha.

The first period, from 1958 to 1961, confirms the achievement of the Toei studio, the first to dare venture into this type of production and succeed. Noburo Ofuji's film is a contribution to the great art of shadow films, though it has not yet been rewarded with international recognition.

After 1962, apart from Toei, several other producers launched into animated features and since then new studios have been formed. Also some films of a slightly experimental nature have been ventured upon in Japan. Osamu Tezuka, one of the old collaborators of Taiji Yabushita, founded his own studio Mushi-Film in 1961. He attempted to create, in his first production, a graphic image different from the familiar American style—an artistic conception new to full-length films. The film is directed by Osamu Tezuka himself and entitled *Aru Machikado no Monogatari* (*A Story on a Street Corner*). The content of this film is a simple, everyday story completely without legend, which ends with a town being destroyed by bombing. One cannot help thinking of Japan's moral situation after the war.

During this time, Taiji Yabushita continued to direct new films, and in the same year, 1962, there was another Venice Grand Prix, this time for the film *Shindbad no Boken* (*Adventures of Sinbad*), another of the Japanese films which has gained a large audience on the American continent and in Europe. Of the numerous cartoon adaptations of Sinbad, this is probably the best.

Ryuichi Yokoyama who in 1955 had founded his own company, Otogi Productions, directed two long animated cartoons one after the other, in 1961 and 1962. These are *Hyotan Suzume* (*Sparrow in a Gourd*) and *Otogi no Sekai Ryolo* (*Touring the World*), which is in Toeiscope. Both seem to be aimed particularly at juvenile audiences. *Touring the World* is divided into seven parts, and is full of burlesque and enjoyable nonsense.

Lately, a new director, Yugo Serikawa, has appeared at the Toei studios. He has directed an adaptation, in a more modern style, of an ancient

Sparrow in a Gourd (1962) by Ryuichi Yokoyama, Japan.

legend *Wanpaku Ogi no Orochitaiji* (*Little Prince and the Eight-Headed Dragon*) (86 mins. made in 1963) which won the "Osello di bronzo" at Venice in 1963.

The Toei studio which had exerted an increasingly powerful influence made its mark on almost the whole world, with a film which one might easily take for a Disney production—*Wan Wan Chushingura* (*Doggie March*), 82 mins., directed by Daisaku Shirakawa. The subject, inspired less by legend than other productions, portrays several animals, who defend themselves against a tiger and a fox, in the type of adventures often found in Western stories. A little dog who sees his mother come to an early death, together with his friends— all stray dogs—takes revenge on a tiger and a fox, though not without having sniffed the air of the human's town.

The change in the type of subject becomes more accentuated with *Garibah no Ucho Ryoko* (*Gulliver's Space Travels*), (1965), directed by Masao Kuroda and produced by the Toei studios. This is a very free adaptation of Swift's tale, in which Gulliver is

shot out of a rocket with some companions and has space adventures with robots.

The marionette film has also attracted some directors. In 1966 Ichiro Michibayashi won a prize at the educational film festival in Tokyo with a feature film *Tatsu No ko Taro* (*Taro, the Son of Dragon*).

Two significant screen fiction films were made at the Toei studio in 1966 and 1967 *Saibogu 009* (*Cyborg 009*), 1966, 64 mins. long, directed by Yugo Serikawa, brings human and robot heroes up against the terrible Black Ghosts. This first film had such great success that a sequel *Saibogu 009 Kaiju Senso* (*Cyborg 009 Underground Duel*), 60 mins. was brought out in the following year. This was directed by Yugo Serikawa. This was actually the first animated feature cartoon to have a sequel. For Osamu Tezuka 1966 marks a new attempt to go off the beaten track with an interesting experiment in illustrating Mugsorsky's musical score, the famous *Tenra Ka No E* (*Pictures at an Exhibition*). This is, to some extent, the Japanese equivalent of Fantasia, made up of 10 parts, each having a

Little Prince and the Eight-Headed Dragon (1963) by Yugo Serikawa, Japan.

particular theme which matches the music. The same year Osamu Tezuka's Mushi-Film brought out another animated cartoon, directed this time by Shigeyuki Hayashi, Jungle Taitei (Jungle Emperor), whose international success has touched Europe. It is made in a style similar to Disney's.

A second full-length puppet film was made in 1967 entitled Kurohime Monogatari (The Kurohime Story). Like the first—Taro, the Son of Dragon—it was produced by Kyodo Eiga, directed by Miyogi-Ieki. This film is based on the famous Japanese legend of Princess Kurohime.

One experiment, though not strictly an animated film, is nevertheless worthy of note. It is Ninja Bugeicho (The Immortal Rebel) a full-length live-action film of a strip cartoon by Sampei Shirato, well-known in Japan, which re-tells certain events of the 16th century. The film's director, Nagisa Oshima, has thus made an 80 min. long, anti-animation film based on a cartoon strip.

In 1967 at Toei, after an absence of about five years, Taiji Yabushita returned to full-length films

and directed two animated cartoons of a fantasy and a science fiction story—Shonen Jack to Mahotsukai (Jack and the Witch), and Hyokkori Hyotan (The Madcap Island).

In 1968 a newcomer, Shinichi Yagi, was working for a production company, Nihon Doga, which was equally new in this field. The product of his direction was an animated cartoon with a remarkably delicate and "Japanese" graphic style, entitled Sessho-Seki (The Fox with Nine Tails), based on an ancient legend of the beauty and fidelity of a young couple.

It is very simple, apart from the human characters, and offers a beauty of style which only the first Japanese full-length films had been able to accomplish, due to the delicacy of the character drawing and the suppleness of the backgrounds.

As time went on, the production of animated feature films in Japan became an industry, just as in the United States. The quest for perfection of style, has for the most part disappeared, and given place to a much coarser line, corresponding to a

わんわん忠臣蔵

Left, top. *Doggie March* (1964) by
Daisaku Shirakawa, Japan.

Left, bottom. *Cyborg 009—Underground Duel* (1967) by Yugo Serikawa,
Japan.

Top. *Pictures at an Exhibition* (1966)
by Osamu Tezuka, Japan.

Bottom. *Jungle Emperor* (1966) by
Osamu Tezuka, Japan.

The Kurohime Story (1967) by Miyoji Ieki, Japan.

Jack and the Witch (1967) by Taiji Yabushita, Japan.

Right, top. *The Madcap Island* (1967) by Taiji Yubushita, Japan.

Right, bottom. *The Fox With Nine Tails* (1968) by Shinichi Yagi, Japan.

Little Norse Prince Valiant (1968) by
Isao Takahata, Japan.

The Mighty Taro (1968) by Miyoji Ieki,
Japan.

Right, top. *Puss'n Boots* (1969) by
Kimio Yabuki, Japan.

Right, bottom. *Flying Phantom Ship*
(1969) by Hiroshi Ideka, Japan.

much more expeditious and rational technique. *Sessho-Seki* is, however, a notable exception.

Since 1966, the Japanese animation industry has produced four full-length films a year (two from Toei and two from other studios). In 1969 there were six. These figures need no comment; in the United States 1967 was a record year, when three films were made. This rate of production is maintained today.

In 1968, the director Miyoji Ieki finished an animated puppet film—*The Mighty Taro*, with the same characters as the original *Taro, the Son of Dragon.* In 1969, *Hanoko the Elephant*, another marionette film, was made by Hiroshi Matsumoto at Toei. It is evident, therefore, that a number of new directors are now making their appearance. Kimio Yabuki directed *Andersen Monogatari* (*Fables from Hans Christian Andersen*), 1968, based on some of the most popular talks of the Danish story-teller, and *Nagagutsu Ohaita Neko* (*Puss'n Boots*), 1969. Isao Takahata made *Taiyo no Ogi,*

Horusu Daiboken (Little Norse Prince Valiant), 1968, based on the well-known adventures of the little Norwegian prince.

Iroshi Ikeda made Soratobu Yureisen (Flying Phantom Ship), a new science fiction fantasy by the Japanese author Shotaro Ishimori.

Nine Japanese films for adults have so far been completed. One Thousand and One Nights and Cleopatra, Queen of Sex (Mushi); Maruhi Gekiga Ukiyoe Senichiya (The Fantastic World of Ukiyoe) (Teoi), and the Kyojin no Hoshi series, directed by Tadao Nagahama for Toho. Toho is one of the big five Japanese producers and this, their first full-length animated film, was made in 1969. The development of this type of film, and the important role played by Japan in this respect is described in a later chapter.

Toei seems to be using materials from the European classics with increasing frequency especially since their film Chibikko Remi to Meiken Capi (Nobody's Boy).

This short review of Japan shows that the artists of the Land of the Rising Sun have now found a form of art which well suits their temperament. With their recent research, they are also finding new directions in which that temperament creates wonders.

There is absolutely no doubt that in coming

One Thousand and One Nights (1969)
by Osamu Tezuka, Japan.

Cleopatra, Queen of Sex (1970) by
Osamu Tezuka and Eichi Yamamoto,
Japan.
Atakku Nanba Wan (1970) Japan.

years, the progress of the Japanese full-length animation will be one of the most important phenomena of the world film industry. Both by the diversity of styles and of subjects treated, their productions will be able to satisfy most tastes and most audiences.

AUSTRALIA AND NEW ZEALAND

Australia and New Zealand did not, until a few years ago, have a real animation industry. Now, however, the governments of these two countries have taken steps to encourage their respective cinemas, and production companies are organising themselves towards the regular production of stop motion films.

A notable example is a company in Sydney, sponsored by the toy manufacturers Kenner Toys Inc., called Astrasian Studio, which is producing a series of 30 minute episodes for television. Some films in the series have already been bought by American television stations, which has provoked some discontent among the American animators.

This studio was planning a series of four 60-minute animated films for television which presently are in production.

Nobody's Boy (1971) by S. Fukumoto, Japan.

Kyojin No Hoshi (1970) by Tadao Nagahama, Japan.

The Fantastic World of Ukiyoe (1969) by Leo Nishimura, Japan.

Treasure Island (1971) by Hiroshi Keda, Japan.

16

EASTERN EUROPE

The animation produced in Eastern Europe countries is of a very high standard and has an international reputation. The Czechs and Yugoslavs are regarded as among the best animators in the world; the Rumanian, Polish and Bulgarian stop-motion has been very successful and new horizons are emerging in Hungary for the co-production of films. Paradoxically, only a few full-length films have emerged from these countries—in only two or three has such a venture been undertaken and a total of approximately ten films have been produced between them.

RUSSIA

The Russian animation industry has a history dating back to the nineteen-twenties when the experimental studios were set up in Moscow. The Soyuzmultfilm Studio in Moscow is one of the largest in the world with a staff of more than 550. There are also studios in the provinces, at Kiev, Leningrad, Tbilisi and Tallin. But only Soyuzmultfilm planned to make full-length films in the years of its growing success—from 1955 to 1960—at a rate of one per year.

Led by several of the great names in Soviet animation, this studio seems to have been on the whole able to achieve its aims, but only up to 1964, for no full-length films produced since then are known of with certainty. Several medium-

length films have, however, been successful.

While a certain proportion of Russian short films are known abroad, full-length productions are rarely seen, and only the films mentioned below have escaped the obscurity which is the fate of so many, particularly the more interesting films. Unfortunately, the films do not always receive the approval of the critics, because they are marked by a rather conventional approach.

Between 1947 and 1964, eleven full-length films were produced by the Soyuzmultfilm studios, and all but two were animated cartoons in the classic style. The mainstay of the studios then was the still active Ivan Ivanov-Vano, who is widely known for his short films and has also directed five feature films. These are *Konjok-Gorbunok* (*The Hunch-backed Horse*), 1947, *Snegurotchka* (*The Little Snow Maiden*), 1952, *Dwenadzat Messkazew* (*The 12 months*), 1956, *Priklutschenija Buratino* (*The Adventures of Buratino*), 1959, and *Levsha* (*The Mechanical Flea*, or *Left Handed*), 1964.

This last film was the first in the world to sustain the animated cut-out system through a feature length film, but like most other Russian animated feature films, it still relies for its subject matter on a version of folk legend.

Lev Atamanov using a classic style of animation, has adapted Andersen's *The Snow Queen* (1957), and attempted to introduce a new look to his animation which, although traditional, is more

The Hunchbacked Horse (1957) by Ivan Ivanov-Vano, Russia.

Left, top. *The Adventures of Buratino* (1959) by Ivanov-Vano and D. Babitchenko, Russia.

Left, bottom. *The Mechanical Flea* (1964) by Ivan Ivanov-Vano, Russia.

The Bluebird (1972) by V. Livanov, Russia.

БАНЯ

The Spa (1962) by Sergei Yutkievitch, Anatoli Karanovitch, Russia.

The Snow Queen (1959) by Lev Atamanov, Russia.

The Little Golden Key (1939) by Alexander Ptuschko, Russia.

sensitive than Disney's. The impression of snow covered landscapes and the relative simplicity of the characters' features has made this an excellent representative of Russian full-length animation.

Two films—*I Drew the Man* by the sisters V. & Z. Brumberg and *The Spa* by Anatoli Karanovitch and Sergei Yutkievitch—are moral and political fables of little narrative interest, although the techniques used in *The Spa*, puppets and live action, as in *Novii Gulliver*—meant that it did attract some attention at the time of its release in 1962.

Since *Levsha*, there has been little news of any new productions. Ivan Ivanov-Vano announced in 1960 that a full-length satirical film was in production in Russia, which he was to direct, entitled *Comedy of the Dolls*—but no more has been heard of this. Another uncertain title was *The Golden Antelope*. On the other hand, a film of *Bluebird*, by V. Livanov from the story by the Belgian author Maeterlink, seems to be definitely in production, in fact was completed during 1972 but for the time being shelved.

Few Russian productions have found success in Europe. Those which have are *The Night Before Christmas*—which tells the story of the Empress's slippers; *The Spa*; *The Snow Girl* (by Ivanov-Vano) and *The Snow Queen* (by Lev Atamanov).

This certainly is very little, considering that before the war Russia presented such great promise with Ptuschko's two full-length films, *The New Gulliver* (1935) and *The Little Golden Key* (1939).

CZECHOSLOVAKIA

The Czech animation industry is the best known after America, particularly for its puppet films. The Czech animation cinema is 25 years old and in spite of its relative youth, can claim to have a well-founded tradition. A list of Czechoslovakian animated films which have won international distinction would take up several pages of this book.

An Invention of Destruction (1958) by Karel Zeman, Czechoslovakia.

Baron Munchhausen (1961) by Karel Zeman, Czechoslovakia.

The two most important studios in Czechoslovakia are the Gottwaldov and the more recent Barrandov. Among the many titles, about fifteen merit attention in the context of this study of feature length films.

First, there are the films which are more important in the application of techniques than in their actual content; namely the creations of one of the great masters of the Gottwaldov Studio, Karel Zeman. Then there is the masterly work of Jiri Trnka, and several other endeavours and co-productions.

Journey into Primeval Times (1954) by
Karel Zeman, Czechoslovakia.

KAREL ZEMAN

Born in 1910, Karel Zeman was a commercial artist before devoting himself to animated puppet films at the Zlin studio (which has since become Gottwaldov). This was set up at the time when the Bata shoe factories were growing in importance and commercials for this organization were made there. In fact, Gottwaldov was the first animation studio in Czechoslovakia, and its works have always been distinguished by their experimental character. It was in this adventurous atmosphere that Karel Zeman started his experimental short films and continued to make them regularly from about 1940. From the long list of his films the most memorable are *Dream of Christmas* (1946), five *Mr. Prokook* films (1947 and 1948), *Inspiration*, a unique film made by animating blown glass (1949) and *King Lavra* (1950).

Before embarking on full-length films containing a large proportion of animation, he directed *The Treasure of Birds' Island* (1952) 120 mins. This is a traditional feature with unusual animation sequences, where he mixes several types of film such as live action with actors, landscapes real and drawn, animated engravings and sophisticated special effects imitative of Persian miniatures.

For the sake of the purist, it must be emphasised that Karel Zeman's full-length films are not pure animation, but exhibit animation techniques to such an extent that they could not be omitted from this book.

He made his second full-length film in 1954, *Journey into Primeval Times*, which is a new conception of reality in the surrealism of the drawn image, using the graphic style of wood or lino cuts, or even in the etchings to be found in adventure stories of the nineteenth century—in particular the illustrations of the works of Jules Verne by Gustave Dore. Zeman shows great fidelity to Jules Verne in his subjects.

Without doubt, Zeman's two greatest international successes are *An Invention for Destruction* (1958) based on Jules Verne, which enjoyed a remarkable success at the Brussels Expo 1958, and *Baron Munchausen* (1961) which received great ovations at the Festivals in Locarno and Cannes. These two films and *Journey Into Primeval Times* are the only ones to qualify for a filmography of full-length animation as the following productions, apart from some very short sequences, contain hardly any stop motion scenes.

In 1964 Zeman made *Jester's Tale* (which also appeared under the title *The Two Musketeers*), a rather bizarre historical adventure which takes place in the Middle Ages, quite removed from his preoccupation with Jules Verne. Returning to his old leaning, in 1966 Zeman finished *The Stolen Airship* based on a novel by Jules Verne. This film was also called *Directing Flight*. He finished a full-length film entitled *Mr. Servadac's Ark* in 1971, based on Jules Verne's *Suar la Comète* which depicts the life of people on a piece of land which has become detached from the Earth.

A Midsummer Night's Dream (1959) by Jiri Trnka, Czechoslovakia.

JIRI TRNKA

Born in Pilsen on the 24th February 1912, Jiri Trnka died in December 1969. He was one of the great names of the world of animation, and also one of the most remarkable individualists. His work has been sufficiently studied for us to approach it succinctly in the context of this book, emphasising his importance and the irreversible influence which he has inspired in the art of animated puppetry.

He devoted his whole life to art—folk art in the noblest sense of the term. From his earliest youth he was influenced by the puppet theatre which, in Czechoslovakia, is a serious medium to which every artist has devoted at least a part of his life. Following the example of Josef Skupa, who in fact was Trnka's art teacher, he was initiated into the secrets of the marionette theatre and found expression for his creative genius in the manipulation of these artificial beings, to which he was almost able to impart life. The complete artist, Trnka began as an illustrator of children's books and his sensitivity was employed in this field with mastery.

He then decided to make animated cartoons and produced several from 1945 and 1947, before abandoning this form of animation in favour of puppet animation. This form allowed him more freedom and brought him closer to his art, avoiding the many sub-divisions of work necessitated by animated cartoons. Thus, he could retain close contact with his personal creation.

Through the succession of films he directed, he was able to establish a team of faithful partners allowing them when necessary to direct films for themselves, or working on their themes himself. Among Trnka's partners we must mention Jiri Brdecka, who claims a share in several scripts and five of his prestigious animators, Stanislav Latal, Bretislav Pojar, Brohuslav Sramek, Jan Karpas and Josef Kluge. These names regularly appear in the credits of Trnka's films, as does that of Trojan, his regular composer.

Ever since his first experiments with puppets, Trnka was the creator of carefully prepared films, and a quest for aesthetic perfection can be seen throughout his work; he exhibits a baroque lyricism with a rich, sumptuous decor.

The six full-length films he has directed are nearly all inspired by legends or folk tales from Bohemia, as are some of his short and medium length films. The distinctions won for the Czech film industry by Trnka's films amount to about a hundred, and his fame is emblazoned in gold letters at the Barrandov Studio.

After the war, Trnka directed his own puppet theatre before settling permanently in films where, after his few animated cartoons, he went straight on to full-length puppet animation with *The Czech Year* in 1947.

The Czech Year is a film made by a man in love with his country, and with his particular part of it. He shows us rural occupations during the different seasons. This folk tale (and this is true of all Trnka's full-length films) received, possibly the first "grand" treatment in animation. For Trnka knew how to create a grand stage set with his many and various subjects and characters, whereas for traditional animation it is more a question of putting things into flat pictures.

Trnka's second full-length film came immediately after *The Czech Year,* and it is better known internationally. This is *The Emperor's Nightingale* (1948) taken from a story by Andersen, a film enriched by the sensitivity of childhood. The beauty of the narration and enchanting characterisation in this film made Trnka's genius recognised throughout the world. In addition to his sensitive artistry, the film has the wonderful music of Vaclav Trojan. The clever back-lighting when the nightingale is singing is remarkable.

In 1950, Trnka made *Prince Bayaya,* which may be described as a lyrical romance in a wonderful medieval setting. Between *The Emperor's Nightingale* and *Prince Bayaya,* Trnka made three short films. In 1953 he brought out *Old Czech Legends* based on the mythology of Bohemia, and in 1955, the angry yet amusing adaptation of Jaroslav Hasek's story, *The Good Soldier Schweik.*

There followed a sterile period, during which Trnka was no longer directing with his usual vitality, and one might have thought he was going into a completely unproductive phase. In fact he spent several months simply thinking. Then with even greater perseverence, he dedicated himself once again to his art, and the products of the last ten years of his life, including his last full-length film, his medium-length and short films, have probably brought the greatest nobility to marionettes and have confirmed the universal talent of Trnka.

1959 saw the birth of Trnka's most ambitious work, a lyrical moving fresco, adapted from Shakespeare's *A Midsummer Night's Dream.* In this film he brought the workmanship of his puppets to an even higher degree of perfection, and his period backgrounds can never be equalled by any other puppet animator. As well as this, the improvement in photographic material and film have lent the work even greater brilliance among the works of this great creator, artist emeritus of Czechoslovakia.

The only full-length Czech animated cartoon made before 1970 was made as long ago as 1957. It was entitled *The Creation of the World* based on drawings by Jean Effel and directed by Eduard Hofman.

The Trojan War (1970) by Attila Dargay, Hungary/France.

Eduard Hofman is also one of the great characters of Prague animation. Born in 1914, he has worked in animated cartoons since 1943 at the Barrandov studio. He did not start there as an artist, but as an administrator and, by the experience of working with Trnka, he evolved a talent for animation, which he used in the sphere of educational films. He directed about ten short films, but only acquired national fame with *The Creation of the World*. The subject of the film, taken from the caricatures of the French illustrator, Jean Effel, did not seem to please the Vatican overmuch, when it came out. It is a very free treatment of the story of the Creation, with God and the Devil being involved in constant conflicts at the time of this great event. Hofman was visiting an exhibition of Jean Effel's in Prague, when he had the idea of animating these cartoons, surprisingly popular in Czechoslovakia, and the collaboration was very fruitful. In Eastern European countries the film enjoyed great success.

Currently, Jean Effel is preparing a new feature project, based on other books of his cartoons on the subject of Adam and Eve.

At the time of Expo '67 in Montreal, the Czech pavilion presented a multiple-projection animation show lasting 20 minutes, which required about 11,500 feet of film; this was Dr. Raduz Cincera's *Cineautomatic.* In view of its length and importance this unique piece of animation deserves a place in this study.

Since Hofman's experiments with animated cartoons, the Czech film industry has opened its studios to co-productions, and foreign directors may now go to Prague to work on their projects.

Several animated features of this type are discussed under the director's country of origin. Co-productions with the Italian director Pino Zac are *Gatto Filippo, Licenza di Incidere* and *Il Cavaliere Inesistente*, and with the French director Rene Laloux *La Planete Sauvage*. This film was finally completed during 1973 and was presented in both the Cannes and Annecy film festivals. It had a very successful season in Paris.

OTHER EASTERN EUROPEAN FILMS

Apart from the USSR and Czechoslovakia, other Eastern European countries are also beginning to make feature films. We shall return to two East German films, *Die Seltsame Historia von den Schiltburgern* and *Der Arme Mullerbursche und*

Hugo the Hippo (1974) by Bill Feigenbaum and Jozsef Gemes, Hungary/USA.

das Katzchen at Defa-Film, later, when dealing with German films.

Bulgaria, whose animation industry is now developing, thanks to work on animated cartoons over the past five years, has modestly collaborated in a full-length film, *Fablio Le Magicien.* This is actually a French production, in which Radka Batcharova directed one of the six episodes, *Le Chat et le Vieux Rat* at the Sofia Studio.

Under the influence of its leading director, Todor Dinov, the great vitality apparent in Bulgarian animation will certainly lead soon to the production of a complete full-length film, and from information available from the Bulgarian film industry this seems very likely.

Hungary probably best demonstrates the extent to which Eastern Europe is progressing towards making animated feature films, some by the intermediate step of the experience gained by making television series. The main director of the film produced by Georges de la Grandière, *Fablio le*

John the Hero (1973) by Marcell Jankovics, Hungary.

Magicien was Attila Dargay, who directed four of the six episodes, (*La Grenouille qui veut se Faire Grosse que le Boeuf; Le Loup et le Chien; Le Lion et le Moucheron; La Tortue et les deux Canards*) as well as the linking material.

In a recent study of Hungarian animation by Mari Kuttna, we learn that Pannonia Film, the

Budapest studio, is to start production of a full-length film around the character Gustavus, who has become famous through a series of shorts, and that Attila Dargay is creator of a feature film on the Trojan wars, an ambitious subject which has been close to his heart for a long time. In fact, the title of this film is *Trilogy*, and it was completed in 1971.

During the year 1973 Pannonia Film also produced the first Hungarian feature film based on Sandor Petofi's epic poem entitled *John the Hero.* Marcell Jankovics, the talented young Hungarian director, designed the storyboard and directed the film adapting the national Hungarian style to modern graphics. In the same year the studio also completed a 100 minute film *Hugo the Hippo* which was commissioned by Brut productions, New York. William Fergenbaum directed and Jozsef Gemes was the animation director.

The new wind which blew through the studios of Eastern Europe, setting in motion the production of full-length films, which is just reaching Poland. It is planning its first feature entitled "Round the World with Bolek and Lolek". However, Anima-film Studios in Rumania, influenced by the strong personality of Ion Popesco-Gopo, has not escaped the movement. A new *Homo Sapiens* was started in mid 1970. It is a collection of several of Gopo's shorts, with his little-known character, whose adventures were each conceived with the object of putting them together one day, with only linking material, which after so many years is now happening. Thus *Homo Sapiens* will represent the synthesis of 15 years of the animation of Ion Popescu-Gopo. Victor Antonescu is the director of one episode of the full-length film *Fablio le Magicien—La Cigale et la Fourmi.*

It was announced in 1965 that Boris Kolar of Yugoslavia was to direct *The Return to Oz,* but no more has been heard of this project other than that it was abandoned upon the death of the producer.

WESTERN EUROPE

The situation in the full-length animation cinema in Western Europe is governed by a series of factors which, for 20 years after the last war, prevented the development one might have expected.

In the three geographical blocks we have dealt with, distribution is almost guaranteed. In the United States this is due to the great number of large cinemas and the well-organised distribution network. The same is true of Japan, and in Eastern European countries, films get automatic distribution.

However, in Western Europe, there is no organised system of circulation between countries, although it now seems that a re-structuring is taking place in this ؛phere, particularly in the case of the Common Market countries.

In no single European country could a full-length animated film offer a full return on its production costs just by internal distribution. It is therefore imperative that a film of this type should be conceived as an exportable commodity, and its production should be carried through with this in mind.

It is not surprising that between 1945 and 1965, only 20 animated feature films were made in all of Western Europe, although there is greater production of animated shorts than elsewhere.

Also, apart from two or three cases there does not exist any large studio permanently occupying more than 100 people working solely on animation.

Certain other factors have a bearing on the general problem and we shall consider these later. The language factor is one. Another is that each production tends to be forgotten fairly soon after coming out, having travelled the circuit only once.

We must hope, however, that these films may be released again when distribution is improved and economics become better geared to the requirements of the industry.

When examining these productions, country by country, certain titles crop up fairly frequently in discussion.

GERMANY

Although *Prince Ahmed* and the other Lotte Reiniger films appeared at the outset of German animation, and this medium has a strong appeal to German artists, unfortunately one period escapes analysis, as this is the Nazi period. We know that animated films, mainly propaganda, were made during this time, but the whole range of German animation has not yet been brought to light.

The full-length animation cinema of the two Germanies, can be considered as a single entity. The Germanic form is perhaps less international than the Latin or Anglo-Saxon style, which could explain the fact that German animated films provoke less reaction on an international level than those of other countries. But for all that, it has a powerful tradition.

The formulae chosen for the films are also determined by the necessity of making them distributable within the country of origin—another reason which might explain why films from this region are so little known to us. We must hope that recent films will be more widely distributed outside Germany, especially since this country is one of the largest European producers of full-length films; it is actually fourth in rank, with eight films.

We have seen Lotte Reiniger's contribution to the history of the cinema with her *Prince Ahmed*, and it is noteworthy that this film is often quoted in the history, not only of animated films, but also of the cinema as a whole, as one of the most important products of German expressionism.

In 1960 the second German full-length animated film, *Tobias Knopp Abenteuer Eines Junggesellen,* directed by Gerhard Fieber, was released.

Born on 20th October 1916 in Berlin, Gerhard Fieber was for many years artistic director and head designer of the German animation studio

UFA. In 1948 he founded his own studio EOS, in Wiesbaden, where he made *Tobias Knopp*. The film is based on adventures from a cartoon strip by a German who was a pioneer in this field, Wilhelm Busch (1832–1908) and who is better known for his celebrated *Max and Moritz*. This film was intentionally made in black and white, to preserve the graphic effects which were found in Busch's cartoon strip. We have scraps of information about two other full-length films made during the post-war period, although it has not been possible to verify all the facts.

The Dean Studio (this must have been a studio of the Dean Brothers) which specialised in puppet films, produced a full-length film entitled *The Seven Ravens*, based on the famous novel. J. M. La Duca in his *History of the Animated Cartoons* (1945) said that a Berlin studio had started work on an animated cartoon entitled *The Awakening of Rubezalh*.

More recently, there is the Defa Film Studio in Dresden, which is the only East German studio. It employs several hundred people and has a long

Tobias Knopp—Adventures of a Bachelor (1950) by Gerhard Fieber, Germany.

The Conference of Animals (1969) by Kurt Linda, Germany.

Adam 2 (1969) by Jan Lenica, Germany.

history of activity in the sphere of short and medium-length films as well as puppets; (the *Filopat* and *Patafil* series), paper cut-outs, shadow and object-animation and animated cartoons.

Two full-length films have been made at the Defa Studio, one puppet film and one animated cartoon; others are being planned. The first was the responsibility of one of the best puppet specialists in Europe, Johannes Hempel, several of whose short films have won great distinction. He aimed his production mainly at young people, but even though the German puppet style is particularly slanted towards young audiences, it still bears comparison with the Czech and Polish puppets. Hempel's film, made in 1961, is called *Die Seltzame Historia von den Schiltburgern* (*The Strange Story of the Inhabitants of Schiltburg*), based on a script by the director.

There are even fewer full-length puppet films than animated cartoons but it seems that Defa-Film managed a good performance, especially since it was a first attempt in the genre, and the mastery which Hempel acquired via numerous short and medium-length films is obvious in this film too.

In 1970 an animated cartoon was produced at the Defa Studio, based on a free adaptation of a tale by Grimm, and made in a sober but pleasing style of drawing. Directed by Helmut Barkowsky and Lothar Barke, it is called *Der Arme Mullersbursche und das Kätzchen* (*The Poor Miller's Apprentice and the Little Cat*).

The surrealist film *Germany Dada*, by Helmut Herbst, and Jan Lenica's *Adam II* (produced at Munich), will be discussed in the chapter on new directions in the animated cinema.

BELGIUM

Although it has a slight overall film production, Belgium has a lively animation industry and possesses one of the biggest European studios, Belvision. Belgium also has a long tradition in the area of magazines and publications for young people, and Belgian strip cartoons have an excellent international reputation.

It is not surprising that animation should have taken roots in this favourable atmosphere, and that it should be prospering, as several of the productions of this country are based on the subjects of its strip cartoons. For the moment only the Belvision Studio has produced full-length animated cartoon films. They already have five to their credit, a large number from any one source, and these have been produced continuously, which is rare.

The only type of film which had any success before the creation of Belvision was puppet animation, and this had only local acclaim.

A dynamic woman, a writer, Claude Misonne founded a small puppet studio just after the war where many commercials and some short sponsored films with dolls were made.

These dolls were of definite interest, but this aspect of Belgian animation is little known. The 'stars' of two of these shorts were dolls representing heroes of well-known stories, and the films *Formule X24* and *Je Suis l'Empereur* were very well made.

But the full-length film produced by the Studio Claude Misonne, which was shown at the 1948 Venice Film Festival was unfortunately not distributed well enough, and must be considered a commercial failure for this reason. This puppet film, *The Crab with the Golden Pincers*, taken from a story by Herge, had a running time of 1 hour 45 minutes. After this, the studio produced only short films, among which was the first Belgian animated cartoon in colour.

In explaining this miscalculation the director alleged that they were asked to make the film by a sponsor whose financial position was not sound. The studio was to be reimbursed by the revenue from distribution. When the film was completed, the sponsor refused to entrust it to a specialist organisation and undertook to take care of the distribution himself. As a consequence, the film was shown in a theatre on Place Sainctelette where the Ice Shows were held. The screen was that normally used for commercials between acts. The reproduction of the sound was atrocious because of the resonance produced by the ice, and the image was poor because of the inferior quality of the screen. The sponsor quitted the country, leaving behind nothing but debts.

Several Belgian studios were formed within publishing houses specialising in books for young people, whereas in other countries they often originate from the advertising sector, or are developments from old film companies.

Belvision came into being in 1955 when Raymond Leblanc, editor of the Journal Tintin decided to set up an animated film studio in Brussels. The studio first made a series of partially animated films for the RTB and in 1957, the ORTF co-produced two series using the character of Tintin. Very simple animation was employed in all these productions, but in order to compete with foreign productions, the studio had to be organised to produce real animated cartoons. This implied three essential conditions:

1. Exceptional subjects
2. Specialist studios, and
3. A distribution organisation.

The subjects were already there, in the strip cartoons, and distribution could be found.

Although a few years behind the United States, Europe has understood the importance which the strip cartoon can have in popular culture. For the benefit of those not familiar with the subject, the *Asterix* strip cartoons appeared from 1959 in the

Asterix the Gaul (1967) by Goscinny and Uderzo for Belvision, Belgium.

Asterix and Cleopatra (1968) by Goscinny and Uderzo for Belvision, Belgium.

pages of the paper, *Pilots*. They were first published in album form in 1961, The creators, who have been responsible for this strip cartoon now for more than ten years, are Rene Goscinny for the text and Albert Uderzo for the drawing. About fifteen albums of the adventures of Asterix, Obelix his faithful companion and Ideefix the miniscule dog, with their infallible sense of justice, have appeared so far.

This film was the lucky stroke of fate (probably contrived) which assured the future of Belvision. Although marred by a few imperfections, it was the first European full-length animated cartoon to guarantee exposure large enough to satisfy the most optimistic hopes, as was proved by the audience figures.

Made with a large budget, an estimated $1,200,000 plus, (similar to the amount that smaller American companies would have spent on a film of this type) *Asterix le Gaulois* benefitted from well-organised distribution and promotion with a marketing system similar to that used in America.

Because of his invincible nature and in spite of his small size, there was sufficient audience in Europe, child and adult, to assure Asterix a great success. So the producers, Raymond Leblanc and Belvision, and the directors, Rene Goscinny and Albert Uderzo, decided to start work on a new adventure, *Asterix et Cleopatre*, which was released during the 1968 Christmas festivities.

This had an even more spectacular success than the first film, possibly due to the fact that the album with the adventures of Asterix and Cleopatra had been published about a year before, which gave the film greater topicality.

Also in the second Asterix a distinct improvement was noticeable in the quality of the drawing and in the creation of characters. Experts were surprised at this in a European production.

The great problem was to establish studios capable of producing animated cartoons with assured regularity, and to engage a large number of specialists, who are not easy to find in Belgium, or even in Europe. After a visit to the Hollywood

Pinocchio in Outer Space (1965) by Ray Goossens, Belgium.

Tintin and the Temple of the Sun (1969) by Belvision, Belgium.

started work on other series of shorts—*Gibusle Magicien*, *Fables et Legendes du Monde Entier*, etc.

The production of a full-length film seemed the logical progression from this activity. This film, *Pinocchio in Outer Space* (71 mins.) made in 1965, was a co-production with the well-known American producer, Norman Prescott (currently heading the Hollywood studio Filmation), and directed by the Belgian Ray Goossens. It is based on the famous story by Collodi, but with a completely original script. Of this film, 650 copies were made and it had great success in the United States and Japan, but did not have very wide European distribution.

Belvision's second full-length film, *Asterix le Gaulois*, had a great success in Europe, and it is this film which made the studio's name. *Asterix* is one of the great phenomena of European popular literature. Originating from France and the European French-speaking countries, Belgium, Luxembourg, Monaco, Switzerland, it has overcome language barriers to the extent that in spite of certain national and linguistic idiosyncracies in these books, Asterix has a truly European nature, for in Italy, Germany and Austria the Asterix albums are among the best sellers of all cartoon strips.

The reputation of Belvision is now well established, and it is fortunate to have Raymond Leblanc a man with many years' experience of what the public likes in the way of strip cartoon, and who is equally competent in the handling of his new instrument, the full-length animated cartoon.

During the winter of 1969 Leblanc's creation might easily have been a third Asterix adventure, but probably wary of being too repetitive, he gave his staff a completely new challenge, which resulted in yet another success.

Returning to his first love, Tintin, the strip cartoon which first brought fame to his publishing house, he notched up yet another European animated film of international standing.

In bringing Tintin back to the screen, Belvision was assured of a double audience, comprising both children who are always on the look-out for cartoon adventures, and adults for whom Tintin had been bedside reading during childhood.

The character of Tintin was another hero of the European strip cartoon. Herge, his creator (real name Georges Remi), born in Brussels on the 22nd May 1907, began in cartoons as early as 1923, and created Tintin in 1929 in a Brussels weekly paper. The first book was published in 1930, *Tintin au Pays des Soviets*, and up to 1968 there have been 22 books in addition to other cartoon strips and other books by the Belgian cartoonist.

Bringing their experience of nearly 40 years up to date, Leblanc and Herge started work on a full-length animated cartoon based on the adventures of Tintin. Using the contents of the two books as a base—*The Seven Crystal Balls* (1948) and *The Temple*

Studios and the making of a pilot film on the adventures of Tintin by an American Studio, Leblanc decided to take up continuous production. In the United States and in Japan, as in the socialist countries, this type of enterprise is much easier to undertake than in Western Europe, but it does seem that after 15 years of existence, the Belgian effort has been well rewarded.

In 1960, having increased its staff from ten to eighty members, the studio produced 104 five-minute films of the *Adventures of Tintin*. They then

Lucky Luke (1971) by Goscinny for Belvision, Belgium.

Right, top. *The Magi of Dreams* (1967) by Francisco Macian, Spain.

Right, bottom. *Cinderella* (1975) by the Studio Macian, Spain.

of the Sun (1949), Herge did a new storyboard, and this new animated cartoon was made to a good standard.

During the winter of 1969, therefore, *Tintin et le Temple du Soleil* appeared, a film of high quality, and comparable to American competitors. The good distribution of the film is another proof of its success. In view of former successes, Belvision is now able to look far into the future especially because of the success of their latest production *Lucky Luke* by R. Goscinny, based on the drawings of Morris. Thus Belvision appears to have demonstrated the need for the continuous production of feature-length animation films—for this is the first case of productions which are regular and not subject to the chances of funding availability. Having established this principle the studio will guarantee its continued existence.

It is pleasant to see an example being set by a country with a small output at a time when Europe is unifying and the heads of the film industry are beginning to cooperate with one another.

SPAIN

Spain has a surprisingly large output of full-length animated films, destined mainly for domestic consumption and the South American market. Something like six films have been made.

Spanish animation dates from about 1915 and there are several production houses for animated films with an international reputation. The first Spanish full-length film was made in 1947 and was entilted *Garbancito de la Mancha,* but is also known as *Garbancito Pelegrina* (*The Knight Garbencito*). This was 72 minutes long and was directed by

Arthur Moreno, an illustrator of children's books.

The film received some accolades and was also distributed in France. The story was of a child in a Spanish village who has a fight with a giant and is helped by a fairy. As its title implies, it bears a certain similarity to the classic Spanish romance of Don Quixote of La Mancha.

Following the success of this first film, Moreno undertook a second production in 1948 but, probably due to excessive haste, his second attempt at full-length animation (64 minutes) was rather less effective. The same characters were used but the second film, *Alegres Vacaciones* (*Happy Holidays*) was not distributed and Arthur Moreno had to wait a long time before returning to animation. However, the studio in which his two films were made, Balet y Blai, led by a lively team of animators, decided to carry on making full-length films, and a third was produced.

This was *Suenos de Tay Py*, also known as *Oh Mi Karay Kiki,* directed by Jose Maria Blay and F. Winterestein. It was an attempt to imitate Disney at a time when the musical revue was enjoying much popularity. In this film the songs were sung by animals dressed up as film stars.

But the most successful Spanish film in this field was, without doubt, *Erase una Vez.* It was originally made under the working title of *La Cenicienta* (*Cinderella*), which had to be changed for copyright reasons.

This time the director sought a different style from Disney. The film was full of movement, had a Mediterranean rhythm, and differed completely from the European approach.

The drawings were extremely delicate, resembling the classical type of fairy story illustrations in picture books. The production was directed by Jose Escobar, and made by the Estela-Film Company with the collaboration of five associate directors: Alexandre Cirici Pellicer, Ferrandiz, Fresquet, Tur and Ferran, all of whom had come from the just disbanded Chamartin Studio.

The three other films are also completely different from the Disney style. In Spanish full-length films there always has been an effort to create a Spanish style suitable for the South American market to avoid duplication in a territory invaded by American productions.

The first three films have as subjects strip cartoons by Arthur Moreno, published in many children's magazines, including *Micken* which began in 1935.

Although there is little talk of Spanish animation in Europe, it is widely known in the United States and the activities of artists such as Moreno, Escobar, Blay etc., have attracted the attention of several experts, Walt Disney among them, who delegated his brother Roy to try to set up a European branch of the studio in Spain some years ago.

In fact, several American studios, as well as other countries, have Spanish artists among their

M Tecnofantasy (1971) by Francisco Macian, Spain.

Right. *Mr. Wonderbird* (1953) by Paul Grimault, France.

designers, who left the country after the period of political uncertainty in 1955. But following the calmer period since 1965, interesting things are happening again in full-length films, thanks to the man whom the Spanish critics have designated their "new Disney". He is Francisco Macian, illustrator of various children's magazines, and a musician.

He founded his own studio in 1955 and rapidly earned distinction for his advertising and short films.

In 1963 he began a full-length film, finished in 1967, *El Mago de los Suenos*, which has won several national and international prizes. According to the 1969 figures in South America, this film has beaten all box-office records for animated films since Walt Disney. The film portrays Macian's characters, the Telerin family who were, and still are, the subject of popular cartoon strips in Spain, France and other Latin countries. For example, in Buenos Aires this film was seen by 25,000 people during a single week.

Francisco Macian has undertaken many new productions: *Candilita, Maravellosos Cuentos Espanoles*, two new full-length animated cartoons and, notably, a full-length film based on a science fiction story by Ray Bradbury, which utilises a new technique developed by Macian entitled M. Technofantasy, a system which he already used in some sequences of a film entitled *Bring a Little Lovin*.

This system produces an animation style very close to the aesthetic values of the modern strip cartoon. It allows the skilful and artistic combination of cinema, animation and cartoon, in the sphere of visual imagination.

FRANCE

Animation was born in France. It was born there twice in fact. The first time was before the invention of the cinema, by means of the Praxinoscope and Emile Raynaud's Praxinoscope Theatre. Then, in 1909 there were the cinematographic animated cartoons of Emile Cohl.

French animation has always shown great vitality, yet consists always of single phenomena with no co-ordinating factor. Although encouraging, varied and relatively prolific, critics wonder whether one day it will blossom out. Paradoxically, French animation has actively existed ever since Emile Cohl, and through the long years has made its contribution to world animation. What the critics are perhaps complaining about is a certain lack of internal organisation. It is true that there are few studios of long standing. Firms are set up and sometimes disbanded almost immediately. There is not one studio in France with more than 100 people which has functioned over a long period.

However, in spite of many defects, there have been and are particularly in Paris, several well-known names in the world of animation, half a dozen studios and about 50 directors who might be termed "independents".

The word "independent" is in fact a suitable qualification for the whole of French animation and, if in some ways a fault, it is more often a good quality, opening up new possibilities for the makers. The full-length films made in France, are of independent character and—often—of striking originality.

Besides, in the context of European production,

with ten films completed and two almost complete, French production is greater than that of most other Western European countries.

But things are not always that simple, and several of the films did not come up to the directors' aspirations. In certain cases the most memorable contradictions and improbable stories exist. As in other countries, undertaking a full-length animated film is not an easy task. It is difficult, if not impossible, to get together a large enough staff for a long enough period in premises which are not normally used for such work, and hope to end up with a product which can compete with foreign productions distributed on the local market.

Producers willing to take the risk are few and far between, and it is often the directors themselves who produce the films, sometimes undertaking great feats of financial and artistic acrobatics. But films are made and each time one is finished, it is regarded as something of a miracle.

In the chapter on the pioneers we have already discussed Ladislas Starewitch's puppet film *Le Roman de Renard*. It is Jean Image who takes the honours for having directed and produced the first French full-length animated cartoon in 1950.

Jean Image had been living in Paris for some

years, and had directed a number of commercial and sponsored films. Up to the present time he has finished three full-length films, and this puts him among the more prolific producer-directors, in this field. Adapting to local conditions, Jean Image managed to complete his first feature film in 18 months with a relatively small team, varying between 12 to 40 members, at a modest cost of £5,000.

During production in 1950 the only laboratory in Europe equipped to develop Technicolour negative was in London. By clever planning and strict attention to time limits Jean Image, supported so ably by his wife who wrote the script, managed to make the film *Jeannot l'Intrepie* without too much difficulty. Although using the same characters from Perrault's *Thom Thumb*, the style was deliberately different from Disney. At Venice in 1951, it won the Grand Prix for children's films. The film did well, and Jean Image undertook a second full-length film which he finished in 1953, but this film was less successful. It was based on a script by Fraine with dialogue by Claude Santelli. The film entitled *Bonjour Paris,* revolved round Paris and the Eiffel Tower, which one day decided to get up and walk. The words were spoken by François Perrier

Twenty Thousand Years of France (1967) by Jacques Forgeot, France.

and the music written by Jean Yatove, but in spite of all these trump cards, the film was a relative failure. This must be put down to the subject which was at the time considered unusual.

The film was recently shown again on French television and although it seemed a little out of date, it was nonetheless a charming programme for children.

In 1953 a film came out which was possibly one of the best animated cartoons ever made in Europe, a masterly film called *La Bergere et le Ramoneur* (*Mr. Wonderbird*) by Paul Grimault. The script was written by the director in collaboration with the well-known author Jacques Prévert, and based on a tale by Hans Christian Andersen. Although both the director and the script-writer have criticised the way the film was distributed, which they felt completely inadequate, nevertheless the means of distribution used by the producer was regarded as one of the great events of French animation. The film won the Jury Grand Prix at the Venice Biennial Festival.

The story of this film, poetic and surrealist, tells of the persecuted love affair in an imaginary kingdom, containing past and contemporary references.

Aladdin and his Magic Lamp (1969) by Jean Image, France.

The action is fast-moving, with humour and caricature as the essential elements. But the main reasons for its success were the great aesthetic value of the impressive surrealist backgrounds, with their feeling of perspective, and the perfection of the design and animation. Paul Grimault had been well-known in France for a long time for his commercial and short films; he was capable of making a good full-length film, and he did so.

The final result may not be exactly as intended but *La Bergere et le Ramoneur* is nevertheless one of the purest works of art in the field of animated cartoons.

According to critics and journalists, *La Bergere et le Ramaneur* demonstrated the existence of a French style in animated cartoon. But there was still some scepticism as to the likely outcome of such a venture, and similar experiments were not made again for another 15 years, when a new French full-length animated film appeared. This was *20,000 Ans a la Francaise*, which will be dealt with in the chapter "New Directions", along with *Le Theatre de M. et Mme. Kabal, Le Socrate*, and *Je, Tu, Elles*, three other important experimental films.

The traditional form of French animated cartoon is represented by the entry into this field by Georges de la Grandière, who has produced several long films, including *Monsieur Vincent*. Georges de la Grandière (Edic Films, Paris) collaborated with studios in Hungary, Rumania and Bulgaria, for a series of short films illustrating the fables of La Fontaine. Six of these films have been put together with a linking character called Fablio, forming one full-length film entitled *Fablio le Magicien*. With the coordinatory skills of George de la Grandière, the Hungarian Attila Dargay was the main director of the film and was responsible for four of the six episodes as well as the linking material. The Rumanian, Victor Antonescu and the Bulgarian, Radka Batcharova directed the other episodes. This film proves the great potential that lies in co-production. Although the film is aimed solely at a young audience, it is nevertheless a valid piece of work. It was, to a certain degree, produced in the American style with a well organised marketing campaign. Plastic models of characters from the film can be seen in toy shop windows, and books based on these characters have been translated into several languages. This brings to mind another France-Czech full-length animated film, *Le Creation du Monde*, mentioned in the Czechoslovakian section, with designs by Jean Effel, who is at the moment preparing a new long animated cartoon based on his own drawings entitled *L'Histoire d'Adam et Eve*.

In 1969 Jean Image returned to full-length films. He directed and produced *Aladin et la Lampe Merveilleuse* which took from 15th April to 15th November 1969 to complete. The film was an adaptation for children of the tale from *The Thousand and One Arabian Nights* with a script by Jean Image and his wife, France.

This work has no pretensions beyond being good entertainment for children, and it is extremely successful in its objective. The colour is of surprisingly high quality and the classical style and backgrounds are excellent for a work which was completed so quickly with the relatively small team of fifty people at the most.

Jean Image who definitely has specialised in children's films, and whose studio is one of the oldest in France, is very popular with children owing to his several television series, among them the famous *Kiri, the Clown*.

The characters of *Aladin et la Lampe Merveilleuse* are completely suited to a young public, simplified to the correct degree. The settings from the *Thousand and One Arabian Nights* are well

Dougal and the Blue Cat (1972) by Serge Danot, France.

The Savage Planet (1973) by Rene Laloux, France.

done and some of the backgrounds even have modern illustrations with a welcome touch of Psychedelia. This film is probably the best of all productions from the Jean Image studio.

A rare phenomenon in the full-length animated cinema is the film for very young children, from four to ten or twelve years old. Serge Danot, with his film *Pollux et la Chaton Bleu* (*Dougal and the Blue Cat*) finished in December 1970, made with a team of 30 people fills this gap. Dougal is a puppet, a shaggy dog, very familiar to the youngest televiewers since he, together with many of his other friends found in the full-length film, star in the *Manege Enchante* (*Magic Roundabout*) television programme.

The production time was 12 months. The dialogue for the film was by a young writer, 27 year old Jacques Josselin who won the First Prize for poetry in 1969. The subject of the film revolved around the slightly improbable adventures of Dougal, Florence, Zebedee and other characters, in a forest where strange happenings occur (highly reminiscent of Anglo-Saxon nonsense literature), putting the characters into delicate and humorous situations.

Another full-length film, financed equally by France and Czechoslovakia, has been completed in a studio in Prague with a French director and designer. Rene Laloux, famous for several animated shorts, together with the satirical cartoonist Roland Topor, directed two short films which were fairly successful, one of which was *Les Escargots*, again spotlighting surrealism in animation. These two artists have been working on the full-length film *La Planete Sauvage*, despite some production difficulties for four years. This film is a lyrical fresco of surrealism and science fiction, taking place on an imaginary planet.

After a considerable time gap a new studio, Idefix, has been formed in Paris under the artistic direction of Gruel & Watrin. The studio plans to complete by 1976 the third *Asterix* feature and by 1978 the second *Lucky Luke* film. Both projects are being produced by Rene Goscinny for Dargaud publishers based on Uderzo's comics.

Each of the current French full-length animated films, although different from one another, have one thing in common. All are a complete departure from the Disney style. This increased the likelihood of their acceptance, and also avoids obvious comparisons, both factors being evidence of a very individual approach which is so typical of the French character.

GREAT BRITAIN

British animation is really explosive. In London there is the "Soho Crowd", which includes most of the London animators, with an atmosphere of collaboration between directors, animators and producers which is probably unique in the world.

British animation is of long-standing, like the French, for the first animated shadows by Armstrong date back to 1910.

Currently there are several large studios in London, some of which have a world-wide reputation as a result of many years' activity.

With the exception of Halas and Batchelor however, the number of full-length films made in these studios is small in proportion to the number of shorts produced, and in view of the length of time these studios have been going. But the small quantity is certainly compensated for by the high quality.

At the present time only eight such films have been made, two of which are educational films. It appears, however, that new projects are on the point of commencement.

There is certainly a reason for the small quantity of full-length films, and this is probably the fact that British animation is most effective when it is caricature, or when it takes the form of a moral or satirical fable.

These elements make good short films, but are possibly not suited to feature-length work.

As well as this, there is an economic factor to take into consideration. The British studios are compelled to keep to commercials in order to stay in work, and the time left for unsponsored films is not sufficient for full-length productions, especially since distribution is not guaranteed.

HALAS AND BATCHELOR

This is the name of one of the largest studios in Western Europe and one of the earliest. It was founded in 1940 by the husband and wife team John Halas and Joy Batchelor. These two great creators of animated film, from a modest beginning some 30 years ago, have succeeded in building up a studio which now occupies two establishments, one in London and one in the West of England and employs a permanent staff of 100 people, a number which can be vastly increased for the production of series or of full-length films.

As well as traditional production and sponsored films, Halas and Batchelor has always attached great importance to experimental work as well as the educational application of the frame by frame method. The result is a range of activity which covers all possibilities and uses of animation.

Although educational films in full-length animation are rare on a world-wide scale and do not, in fact, total more than half a dozen, two of these were products of the Halas and Batchelor Studio. They are *Handling Ships* (1946), made for the Admiralty for training sailors, and *Water for Fire-Fighting* (1949) made for the Central Office of Information training firemen in the techniques of firefighting.

But the great fame of these two film makers is due above all to another full-length film, distributed on a world-wide scale, *Animal Farm* made in 1954, with the backing of Louis de Rochemont II.

Animal Farm (1954) by John Halas and Joy Batchelor, Gt. Britain.

Ruddigore by Joy Batchelor (1966)
Gt. Britain.

Animal Farm is traditional as far as the style of drawing is concerned. The subject, however, is a total departure and is not exclusively for children, which was the general tendency at that time. The film is based on the story by George Orwell, which tells of a conflict between the farm animals and the farmers and which exposes the reality of present day conflicts. It is a subtle satire on the totalitarian system, containing some poetic overtones.

The critics at the time this film came out were unanimous in praising the producers' courage in making a full-length film with a serious and adult subject and for dealing wtih a theme of the basic philosophy of democracy.

It requires some courage to undertake experiments in the field of short animated films, for one can never be sure what the result is going to be. In full-length films, the idea of doing something completely original is very tempting, but demands a measure of cheek and a certain liking for a gamble as well as courage.

Animal Farm demanded from John Halas and Joy Batchelor a high degree of all these, and it paid off.

It seems if originality is particularly sought after by the British film makers since two other, later, full-length films are yet again completely original creations.

Joy Batchelor directed, this time alone, the first cartoon opera in 1966, *Ruddigore* (produced with John Halas). This feat of originality had as its subject the comic opera by Gilbert and Sullivan, well-known in Anglo-Saxon countries.

During the last ten years there have been several important changes in film presentation. These included new formats such as Cinemascope, Cinerama, Todd-AO, Dimension 150, Panavision, Metroscope and many others. Most of these presentations use 65mm negatives, which are printed into a positive of 70mm and projected on to a curved screen, giving the audience an overall vision of 142° to 150°.

While these various presentations have substantially changed the experience of watching a film, they still depend on existing optical systems and the use of cinema screens. Little that is revolutionary in that way has taken place. The installations, the projectors and the screens, though all increased in size, still depend on the ideas introduced at the beginning of the century. Around the mid 1950s a multiple-projection technique was developed by Svoboda and Radok, artists and engineers in Prague. The new system was called 'Lanterna Magica' (Magic Lantern) and was soon followed by another 'Living Screen' developed by the stage designer Ralph Alswang in New York. The latter was simpler and more practicable. 'Living Screen' combines the techniques of screen and stage to create a new form. It is a combination of recent developments in film production, stage lighting and picture screens. This set up gives the illusion that a living actor on stage can walk through the cinema screen and become a film personality; or walk out of the screen and appear on the stage in the flesh in perfect visual continuity, or appear with his own screen caricature or his own double, and conduct a dialogue with himself.

The system was tried out for the first time in London in 1964 in a screen-stage play entitled *Is There Intelligent Life on Earth?* Later a shorter version of this production was presented at the New York World Fair using mainly the animation sections.

John Halas produced two hours of film, mostly animation, for Ralph Alswang for this system.

The technical problem of including animation with stage actors and live action film was a difficult task to solve. The main characters were three Martian senators arriving on Earth to determine and find out what the title implies. The play-film was a satire on contemporary society, and this framework gave John Halas an excellent opportunity for animation experiments, humour and special animation effects wherever space travel was involved.

The potential of this combined system has not been fully exploited, in spite of the fact that it does offer an experience which audiences have never had. Both the British and the American press were in agreement that the marriage of stage and screen had a rosy future, and it has opened new vistas in the world of entertainment.

'Review' 30th March 1964 said: "Well, we all know what happened to the talkies and those who forecast their early doom. Today a big breakthrough appeared which awaits the judgment of time. It is a process called 'The Living Screen'. It's here to stay".

However, since 1964 there have been no more experiments with 'The Living Screen', and other multiple projection techniques, such as 'Circlorama' have been relegated to occasional expositions and trade fairs.

Is There Intelligent Life on Earth? (1964) by John Halas, G.B./USA.

The Yellow Submarine (1968) by George Dunning, Gt. Britain.

OTHER BRITISH PRODUCTIONS

In 1967, the craziest full-length animation experiment ever produced came from another British studio, George Dunning's TV Cartoons.

The film was produced by the Beatles' firm Apple with a large financial contribution from the King Features Syndicate and produced by Al Brodax with several directors in collaboration, under the coordination of George Dunning.

This film, *Yellow Submarine*, is based on the fame of the Beatles and the songs of John Lennon and Paul McCartney—and is pop art fireworks. The animation was directed by Jack Stokes and the American Robert Balser.

It was a controversial film and was all the more successful for that. By making use of a selection of unconventional animation techniques George Dunning produced a completely original piece of work, in which every element is new—the graphic quality of the characters (the Beatles), drawn by German artist Heinz Edelman, and the whole subject, which is representative of some of the preoccupations of our times, and treated with a very British whimsicality. This production had the same explosive effect in the field of full-length animation that only *Hellzapoppin* had in the traditional cinema—getting far away from logical narrative structure. It is very close in atmosphere to the spirit of Lewis Carroll.

The film is a masterpiece, and it has opened up new and undreamed of horizons for animation. It bears seeing several times for its content to be fully appreciated, and it has given such an impetus to the full-length animation cinema that it is already a classic. Since the time of *Yellow Submarine*, the commercial and artistic possibilities of the full-length animated film have inspired the imagina-

The Glorious Musketeers (1974) by John Halas, Gt. Britain/Italy.

Deadeye Dick (1975) by Bill Melendez. Drawings by Ronald Searl. Gt. Britain/USA.

tion of many film-makers, and original pieces of work are now being produced on animation benches all over the world.

As is often the case, however, the commercial success of *Yellow Submarine* was not passed on to George Dunning, the film's director, and although he has two projects for feature films, one based on *Gulliver* and one on Malory's *Morte d'Arthur*,

neither have yet started production and TV Cartoons has to survive on short sponsored films.

The same applies to Richard Williams, another famous British animator, who has been working for some years on a feature entitled *Nasruddin*, based on an oriental tale by Mulla Nashrudin. He is, however, never able to concentrate all his effort on it because of uncertain finances. Similarly, little is known about a project by Charlie Jenkins, also in London, who has bought the rights of Gunter Grass's book *The Tin Drum*.

A newcomer to the British scene, the American Terry Gilliam, was responsible for 25 minutes of surrealist cut-out animation in a feature entitled *And Now for Something Completely Different*, taken from a successful BBC television series, *Monty Python's Flying Circus*.

During 1974 John Halas finished a 70 minute animated version of Alexandre Dumas *Three Musketeers*, which is released under the title of *The Glorious Musketeers* by the French producer Patrick Wachsberger. Halas established a world record of production spread of six months for the feature by coordinating the services of many nations. The music is by the French composer Michel Polnareiff.

Bill and Steve Melendez also completed *Dick Deadeye*, another feature in London during 1975, a Gilbert and Sullivan opera based on Ronald Searle's spirited drawings.

It looks as if, despite financial troubles, in Great Britain European full-length animation certainly holds a trump card.

ITALY

The four Italian films which concern us were made between 1945 and 1965.

Italy has always boasted some important personalities in the field of caricature and illustrations for children's books and magazines. Currently, this country is a paradise for the strip cartoonist.

After the end of the war, several studios and animation production teams were set up, and at the 1949 Venice Festival, Italy excelled itself by presenting two full-length animated films, *I Fratelli Dinamite*, directed by the brothers Nino and Toni Pagot, and *La Rosa di Bagdad*, by Antonio Gino Domeneghini. But unfortunately these good beginnings were not followed up until 1965.

Pino Zac (real name Pino Zaccaria), an Italian cartoonist who came to international notice through some of his short films, is a trenchant anti-establishment caricatural animator. In 1965 he made a film with a combination of techniques, entitled *Gatto Filippo, Licenza di Incidere*, in collaboration with another animator, Francesco Maria Gibba. This story of a cat alienated from all the inhabitants of the town, is a satire on modern life.

The character is from Zac's newspaper cartoon strip which dates from 1953, and it was the attractiveness of this character which prompted Zac to make the film. This is an Italo-Czech co-production.

Also, in 1965, came Bruno Bozzetto's masterpieces, *West and Soda*, whose subject is quite different from anything seen so far in full-length animation. It is a Western, similar to Morris's *Lucky Luke*.

Bruno Bozzetto is unique in animation. He started very young, and at the age of 18 had already acquired the rudiments of the animator's art and was able, in a very few years, during which he worked with John Halas in London, to set up the largest studio in Italy, in Milan.

His short films *Tapum* and *Rossi* had immediate success and he proceeded to risk making a full-length film with a relatively small team. The end product was as good as many American productions, yet there were never more than 90 people working on this film, which has the impressive record of 100,000 hours of work, 1,400 backgrounds 120,000 drawings. The film is 1½ hours long.

West and Soda marks the turning point for both Italian and European animation. It also was promising for the development of the full-length animated film in Europe for, in 1965, this future development was not obvious, American supremacy being fairly marked at that time. The cinema In Europe had never thought of itself as having a style which might be specifically "European".

But again, one must wait and see. Since 1969, Italian production has begun to take another direction, with three new films: *Il Cavaliere Inesistente* by Pino Zac, whom we have already discussed, *Vip Mio Fratello Superuomo* by Bruno Bozzetto, and *Putiferio va Alla Guerra* by Roberto Gavioli.

Bruno Bozzetto made his second full-length animated cartoon, *Vip, Mio Fratello Superuomo*,

West and Soda (1965) by Bruno Bozzetto, Italy.

The Non-existent Knight (1969) by Pino Zac, Italy.

Putiferio Goes to War (1968) by Roberto Gavioli, Italy.

The Super V.I.P.'s (1968) by Bruno Bozzetto, Italy.

The Adventures of Pinocchio (1963) by Raoul Verdini, Italy.

over a period of three years, with his usual team. Breaking away from the accustomed subject-matter, Bozzetto created a modern fable, a satire on the world of today. It is an adventure of the strip cartoon type with grotesque or touching characters. There is invincible Super Vip, complex-ridden Mini Vip, there is the grossly fat vamp Happy Betty, Innocent Lisa and Wicked Schultz. The backgrounds are those to be found in the best science fiction, war or horror cartoon strips.

In this film the critique of modern life is achieved by up-to-date means. The cartoon heroes represent real people of the past or character "types".

Once again a critique of today's world and the stupidity of war is the basis of the other film started in 1969, Roberto Gavioli's animated cartoon, *Putiferio va Alla Guerra.*

The graphic values of the film are a return to the classical school. The drawing is very delicate and the characters, all forest-dwellers, ants, owls and others, are skilfully executed and conceived. The backgrounds in the style of engravings with vivid colours are just as original as the treatment of the film. It gives a good idea of the dimension in which the action takes place—on one tiny piece of ground which represents Earth. The subject is a war between two tribes of ants. There are the classical heroes, a girl and a young general in the opposing tribes who eventually get married. The film is based on a well-known story by Mario Piereghin. The music track by Beppo Morasch adds considerable value to this film.

The newest full-length animated film to emerge from Italy will be, at last, a strong rival to the Disney treatment of *Pinocchio.* The Cenci Brothers (Guiliano and Renzo) in Florence are at present putting the final touches to their version of the story based on Collodi's tale.

The Cenci Brothers began with adverting television films before setting up their own studio, Cartoons Cinematografica Italiana Srl.

The traditional style of drawing tries to retain the atmosphere of the original *Pinocchio.* The film was completed in 1974. Also that year, after $2\frac{1}{2}$ years of work, Peynets *Round the World with Lovers* has been finished. A co-production between Italy and France, it was directed by Cesare Perfetto based on Raymond Peynet's story and drawings.

Unfortunately, Italian animation is not well distributed in Europe for, apart from anything else, there are language problems. Nevertheless, Italy is a very useful partner for co-production.

DENMARK

The Danish full-length animation cinema started early, with *Fyrtojet* (1945), an adaptation by *T.* Johnsen and Svend Methling of one of Andersen's stories. However, the design was more like pre-war caricature than polished animation, and it was not until 1972 that the second Danish feature-length cartoon was produced.

This was *Benny's Bathtub*, a film in a variety of styles, made by Yannick Mastrup and Flemming Quist. It enters into the world of children and treats the adults as interesting but strange phenomena. It is a success both as a satire and as a graphic work.

Among a number of new directors who have entered the field is Ib Steinaa. He is currently working on a full-length animated cartoon which is to be another free adaptation of a Hans Christian Andersen story.

Magic Tinderbox (1945) by Svend Methling, Denmark.

SWEDEN

The erotic film *I Huvet Pa en Gammal Gubbe* (*Out of an Old Man's Head*), the first full-length Swedish animation is described in the chapter "New Directions". The same team Per Åhlin and Gunnar Karlsson, have also just completed a new film for a more junior public. The title is *Dunderklumpen* (*Thundering Fatty*) and it draws heavily on Swedish folk lore. It is a mixture of animated cartoon and live actors. It has taken three years to produce. The film was first presented in the winter of 1974 in Stockholm.

SWITZERLAND

Swiss animation, although going back to the early days of Julius Pinschewer in Berne in 1912, has had not worthy successors known internationally, apart from a few prize-winning advertising and educational films.

However, since 1969, a renaissance has been under way and unsponsored animated films can now achieve an international reputation; also a number of very young directors have entered the field.

One full-length film has been in production for several years, *Der Gestiefelte Kater* (*Puss'n Boots*) and should run for 90 mins. The film is progressing slowly, as the director, F. G. Rindlisbacher of Berne is working on it spasmodically. He has to be sure his studio keeps functioning and this can only be achieved by sponsored work.

FUTURE PRODUCTIONS IN WESTERN EUROPE

Several European film-makers have to wrestle with the process of full-length production in much the same way. They start work on full-length films, with no certainty of ever finishing them, and they can only work on them when they have time to spare. But for these directors, completing the film is an ideal to work towards—the creation of a full-length film is, to artists in the frame by frame cinema, the greatest possible achievement.

If there could be a system of coordination between the film-making countries (and it is hopeful that such a system could come into being within the next few years, together with various customs and trade agreements), Western Europe would be able to set about co-productions with a much greater chance of commercial success. As a unit, Western Europe has already produced almost as many films as Japan and the USA, but it is the fragmentation of European production which has held back better distribution. Apart from a few exceptions, European full-length films have a language problem. The lack of distribution agreements with neighbouring countries is also a drawback. Although the opening up of frontiers may help to solve this problem.

NEW DIRECTIONS

A NEW GOLDEN AGE

In 1966 it might have been thought that animation was a dying art, and that after Disney, no one would be able to entertain the public as he had.

The attitude shown in the film industry at the time gave no grounds for hope that animation could contribute anything—for it was thought out-of-date. Certain material difficulties were experienced by producers of full-length animated films, which seemed to condemn the medium to an early demise.

The death of Walt Disney in December 1966, only accentuated the general public's feeling that an era had come to an end.

This was partly true, but the capacity of animators for inventing and adapting has since then brought about the complete rehabilitation of the full-length animated film. Today, it can offer original works which suggest that a new "Golden Age" is on its way.

Animators are exploring new paths and producing works of a richness which would never have been thought possible from the traditional Disney style animation.

Since there is a compulsion to lower the costs of these films, certain ingenious techniques have been evolved for the sake of economy, and these too, hold the promise that animation still has much to offer. As for traditional animation, it is certain that this will remain, and that studios which are well equipped will always be able to enjoy commercial success through this type of film.

Following the different stages of development of the animated cartoon and of the animation cinema, 1966 marks the beginning of a new chapter which may be called the Renaissance, or the Post-Disney period.

And this is currently taking place in most of the countries whose productions have been quoted.

In the pioneering days from 1916 to 1945, the full-length animated film was establishing itself and entering a period in which the accepted traditions were created. These traditions are still strong, but in various parts of the world since 1966, many film makers have been searching for other ways and formulae. It needs courage to leave set traditions in any branch of art, but in animation and particularly full-length animation, it requires a great deal of talent to convince the public and a great deal of bravery to face the inevitable criticism. The film-makers mentioned here had these attributes.

STYLISTIC POTENTIAL

Animation is now being tried with every possible technique and process—dolls, paper cut-outs, drawings, real people superimposed. A number stress the stylistic originality and aesthetic composition of great painters. There are passing glimpses of Kandinsky, Chagall, Matisse, Picasso, the blurred landscapes of the impressionists, the shapes of the cubists, and the symbols of pop-art. As a work of reference for graphic styles, this film medium is unequalled in its capacity for condensing and passing on to a wide audience the artistic talent of a place and a period, but up until *Yellow Submarine* it had not fulfilled its promise in this direction.

During the period 1937–1957, which can be regarded as 'classical', one particular 'cartoon' style of cel-animated drawing was the visual method, with puppets used only occasionally. This was mainly for an aesthetic reason; the puppet is not very flexible because the gestures made by a solid figure are necessarily slower in development than the animated drawing in which rapid action and swift scene changes are quite acceptable.

The same is true in the present period—the beginning of the 'second generation' of the full-length animated film. None of the new film-makers make much use of puppets, and it remains to be seen what will happen to this particular branch of the medium. In so-called 'cartoon' animation, on the other hand, there has been an explosion of talent though, except in the case of 'one man' films, there are certain conventions which still apply in the treatment of characters which are to have wide appeal.

However revolutionary the graphic treatment of backgrounds, fantasy inserts, etc., it is still necessary for the animated actors to be economical of line, specific in expression and gesture. Where, as in most films, they are taken from literary models, this can lead to some exaggerations in the original characters; although the critics may regard it as in bad taste, the creative artist would not necessarily agree. Some type characterisations are necessary for easy identification. Anyone who has tried a little elementary drawing knows that a circle containing two horizontal lines at the top, a vertical line in the centre, and another horizontal line below can represent a face, and the lines only need be drawn curved downwards to have a sad expression, and upwards to have a gay expression. So it follows that characters in a full-length animated film are quite often tied to such conventions. This is true of any film with dramatic content, but especially in the case of 'one-man' films, to be discussed later, it is now being shown that with sufficient talent and courage, even the most limiting conventions can be overcome by the use of original content and inventive design.

THE CHANGING MARKET

Traditionally the full-length animated film has always been considered as a medium for children and for family audiences. For fifty years frame by frame films with a running-time of more than 50

mins. have concentrated on this exclusive category. Distributors have brought them out for showing at Christmas, Easter and Summer holidays. Producers and directors who seek to make their films profitable are right to restrict themselves to making films for children and for the family, for other types even now do not appeal to very wide audiences. But since a wide variety of forms is becoming more familiar to the public, specialists in the animation cinema have sought new directions for the animated feature, and from 1966 we have witnessed a blossoming of experiments which it would have been hard to imagine a few years previously. Of the twenty-seven films made in the whole world during the last two years, twelve are "not for children and family". So there are currently two definitions of the full-length animated film, that which may be called "traditional" and that belonging to the "new direction" of things. Since the death of Walt Disney (this is not a cause and effect situation), activity in this sphere has blossomed on a far greater scale than before and on a world-wide basis.

RENAISSANCE: FIRST PHASE

When it was peacefully approaching its fiftieth birthday, the animated feature film was dramatically expanded with three experimental films. These were George Dunning's *The Yellow Submarine* (already mentioned), which was well distributed and made a great impact on the public, and two French films, Jacques Forgeot's *20,000 Ans a la Francaise* and Walerian Borowczyk's *Le Theatre de Monsieur et Madame Kabal*. These French films have hardly been shown, and deserve a full description here.

In 1953 Jacques Forgeot (born in 1923), founded one of the best animation studios in France, with branches in Great Britain, Germany and Italy. This studio brought a great reputation to such artists as Walerian Borowczyk, Jacques Vausseur, Andre Heinrich, Dick Roberts, Frank Smith, Jim Fabian, Bruno and Guido Betiol and many others.

In 1968 the studio underwent an unfortunate setback in the premature death of its founder, Jacques Forgeot. He had animation in his blood, and his film *20,000 Ans a la Francaise*, a mixture of live photography and animation of documents and engravings, was intended to represent a great fresco of the history of France, going back to the frescoes in the Lascaux Caves. *20,000 Ans a la Francaise* was a new departure, probably ahead of its time, and indicated the future possibilities and potential for frame by frame films. This is one of the outstanding films whose importance will only come to be recognised through some chance happening in distribution procedure. When recognised, its importance will probably appear all the greater since it will be considered posthumously.

The film is conceived as a history lesson covering 20,000 years of activity on French soil, but seen through the eyes of the film-maker and amended by him. It comprises several episodes, right up to the most recent events in France. This film took two years of preparation, four years in production, 12,000 miles of reconnoitring, 8,000 photographs etc. In short, the film is the museum of its creator's mind.

Jacques Forgeot had achieved a coup in setting up a studio of undeniable importance, covering all sectors of animation with specialist directors, scriptwriters and musicians, as well as qualified animators. A favourable climate was developed little by little, and from 1963 to 1967 the studio's output was prolific. Apart from the main shorts (commercials being the bread and butter of the organisation), two full-length films were produced.

This studio, known as the "Cineastes Associes" had several years of success, and it is impossible to count the number of distinctions they have earned.

It is a great pity that this talented unit broke up after the premature death of Jacques Forgeot.

Le Theatre de Monsieur et Madame Kabal was of a completely different nature—a one-man film by Walerian Borowczyk.

Walerian Borowczyk was born in 1923 in Kwilcz (Poland), where he practised all branches of graphic art, and won several distinctions including the Polish National prize for his lithographic work in 1953. He made half a dozen animated shorts, some in Poland but mostly in Paris. In 1960 he joined the "Cineases Associes", where he made further shorts of great merit, among them *L'Encyclopedie de Grand'maman*, *Renaissance*, *Le Jeu des Anges* and *Le Concert de Madame Kabal*, a short film in which there are two protagonists, a good man and an awesome and domineering woman, both of whom we meet again later in the full-length film *Le Theatre de Monsieur et Madame Kabal*.

This film was considered quite revolutionary, in being aimed solely at adult audiences. It was made by a small team, so the director was closely involved at every stage, making the film all the more personal.

The graphic style is very hard and, though it is a colour film, there is little colour in it. A green butterfly flits here and there, or a kind of two-legged pink rhinoceros passes. By this means, the characters' state of mind is expressed, via fleegtin glimpses of various colours. The principal characters, as in the short, are Madame Kabal, enormous and nasty, but occasionally touching with her ineffectual coquettish gestures, and Monsieur Kabal, a small man, a slave, fearing but nevertheless loving her. The faults and the qualities of this couple are exaggerated, thus constituting a modern fable, a moral tale about the couples of today. Without dialogue, the film is a model of universal and immortal animation, even though so far it has been sparsely distributed apart from around specialised circuits and in cinema clubs.

Yellow Submarine, 20,000 Ans a la Francaise, and *Le Theatre de Monsueir et Madame Kabal* had a revolutionary influence on the full-length animation cinema.

In the older context of the Disney era there would be other titles one could quote, but they did not succeed, as did these three, in provoking both directors and producers into a realisation of the new possibilities and the new paths to be explored.

THE RENAISSANCE: SECOND PHASE

Among the important films made since 1967, three categories may be defined; firstly there is the film whose sole object is an artistic achievement (the one-man film). Secondly there is the film that seeks artistic innovations but is made with old conceptions, incorporating relatively large teams, while avoiding the financial burden of a "big production"; and lastly the film which expressly aims for an adult audience, the erotic film, which today is beginning to be good box-office material.

ONE-MAN FILMS (CREATORS' FILMS)

There are a surprisingly high number of films which have been made by very small teams, often in the shortest imaginable production period. A Spaniard, a painter, who employs the techniques of spontaneous painting, presented in 1970 what is perhaps the most surprising of all full-length animated films, silent, in Cinemascope, and lasting 75 mins.—*Ere Erera Baleibu Icik Subua Arvaren* (Scope, Colour, Muda 75). This abstract film was made in 17 months, from October 1968 to February 1970, by the painter from San Sebastian (born in 1932), Jose Antonio Sistiaga, painted directly on to film, by himself alone. With Sistiaga's film, new horizons are reached in animation, for this is the first feature painted directly on to film. Made in the painter's studio at Fuenterrabia it involved no photos, no sketches, no preparatory drawings. The only part of the film to be photographed was the credits, which appear over thousands of coloured leavres with variations of colours between them, conveying a first impression of visual rhythm.

In the year 1963, with very considerable painting activity behind him (exhibitions, either of his work alone, or shared with other artists, in Paris, London, Madrid, Ibiza, Bilbao, San Sebastian, etc.), Sistiaga turned his attention to artistic expression among children, and active teaching methods, following the methods of the Frenchman, C. Freinet. Together with other famous painters he established bases for these methods in Spain, formed schools and trained teachers. In 1966 he took part in the creation of the Grupo Gaur—a new artistic movement of the Basque School. But in 1968 he went back to his own research work in painting by the medium of the film. The distribution of his film, in the context of present systems, will probably never be very wide. But, because of its unusual nature it will leave neither the public nor the specialists indifferent. This film, a painter's film, however, is not unique. Other painters or illustrators have recently directed original pieces of work, and there are at present four other "one-man" films to be seen in which animation plays a more or less important role.

Helmut Herbst of Hamburg, the German animator, famous for founding the Cinegraphic Studio, made a documentary on the Dada movement in which several sequences are animated. Entitled *Germany Dada*, it was made for an American organisation—Universal Education and Visual Arts—and shown on American television. This film contains work done on a titling-bench, yet it does not comprise very much animation. Even so, in the context of the possible evolution of the full-length film, it is notable for its use of animated cut-outs as an aid to a documentary on an artistic subject; but because there is little actual animation it does not appear in the catalogue of this study.

Le Socrate (1968), directed by Robert Lapoujade, does on the other hand, give a new direction to the mixed film with live-action, special effects and animation. Although this is a live film, the animation sequences in it are significant and could not be replaced by live-action; this second film by a painter, half surrealist, half pop, may serve as a foundation for a new form of cinematographic expression.

In this same category of painters' films with live-action and animation mixed is Peter Foldes' film *Je, Tu, Elles* (1971) in which the animation is used to give initial impetus to live-action sequences. But the experimental nature of these three films forbids us to consider them entirely as full-length animated films; also they reveal that their directors are still searching for a new formula in animation. It is, however, necessary to mention them, all the more so because Robert Lapoujade is at the moment preparing a new full-length film—*Le Sourire Vertical*—of which a large proportion will be made in stop motion under the rostrum camera.

A film made entirely in animation, by one artist almost single-handed, is *Adam 2* by Jan Lenica (Grand Prix for German films, 1969). Jan Lenica, like Walerian Borowczyk, is of Polish origin, and the work of these men certainly has points of similarity, both in subject matter and in graphic style. Alf Brustellin, a journalist who specialises in Lenica, has given his work a name (which would fit Borowczyk's films too)—"Pessimistic Parables". Lenica and Borowczyk worked together on some of their early films—*Once Upon a Time, Love Rewarded* in 1957 and *Dom* in 1958. But the film which really brought Lenica's name to fame was made in

1958–1959, *Monsieur Tete.* Others were *Labyrinthe* (1962), *Rhinoceros* (1963), *A* (1964) and *La Femme Fleur* (1965)—all shorts, and together illustrating a real evolution of the director towards a mastery of graphic design, which is probably the most perfect in the whole of contemporary animation.

But Jan Lenica (born in 1928 in Posnan) is also well-known for his cinema and theatre posters, and possesses a wealth of artistic experience, having studied music and architecture before embarking on graphics. Lenica is one of the great globe-trotters of animation. In Germany he found a producer for his latest creations, particularly for *Adam 2.*—Boris von Borresholm (Lux-Film). *Adam 2* was drawn entirely by Lenica himself, and in its production, apart from the producer, he was assisted only by the musician and the cameraman. Production of this film was, even so, relatively rapid, for it took three years. *Adam 2* contains no dialogue, and the role of the music becomes correspondingly more important. The beauty of the drawing and the relationship between sound and picture reinforces the value of Lenica's work. It is probably also the animated film which has so far best illustrated the possibilities offered by the feature length film which is not in the traditional style, that is, the "creator's film"—entirely representing his own conception. It contains a complete vision, and a very severe one, of the world today, of man in his universe, questioning man. And, with suffocating pessimism, Lenica manages to slip in a few elements of humour as relief. Unfortunately, the film is one of those whose importance will not be obvious to us for several years. It is without doubt ahead of its time.

A comparative newcomer in feature film production is the Hungarian studio *Pannonia* Films in Budapest. Two films, as already mentioned, have been completed by 1974, a task that few studios could tackle considering all the other assignments which a studio normally handles simultaneously. The features *Hugo the Hippo* and *John the Hero* are each approximately 80 and 100 minutes long.

CHEAPER FILMS

It has been normal, hitherto, to quote impressive production costing figures when talking about animated features, particularly the "giant" budgets of Disney productions. The high cost of cartoon films has implied the absolute necessity of very wide distribution. The American producer, for example, has reckoned on earning at least 33 to 40 per cent of his revenue outside North America. Consequently, his films had to be suitable for all countries and available with versions in several languages. In Europe, producers are even more compelled to fulfil this demand, and Belvision in Brussels, for example, with high budget features, has to cater for a wide market and provide films of international appeal. But the classical techniques of productions have been greatly simplified for television and it is now possible to make "cheaper" feature films by means of simpler but no less effective techniques.

In Italy, Pino Zac for example, in his new feature film *Il Cavaliere Inesistente*, a mixed film with live-action and animated puppets and cartoons, has tried to create a medieval legend, an approach which seems to suit him well. This film, although Italian, was partly made in the Barrandov Studios, Czechoslovakia, on a relatively small budget.

In the United States, two films made in 1969, showed a decided tendency towards a more economical mode of production. These are *Shinbone Alley* and *A Boy Called Charlie Brown.* *A Boy Called Charlie Brown* is one of the great success stories of recent American animation. *Peanuts* (the world famous characters from the daily cartoon strip published in more than 300 daily papers and a large number of weeklies all over the world, and created by Charles M. Schulz), had already earned enviable honours. Charlie Brown, Lucy, Linus, Snoopy and their friends already had, as well as their highly philosophical strip cartoon, a show on Broadway, the honour of featuring on the covers of *Life, Time* and *Newsweek*, and a series of animated cartoons on television.

These well-known characters were directed by Bill Melendez in their new feature-length animated cartoon studio. From its first showing in the Radio City Music Hall in New York at the end of 1969, it aroused great enthusiasm in the United States. Made in simplified animation without elaborate backgrounds, the adventures of Charlie Brown and his friends, thanks to their rather disconcerting philosophy, are the prototype of a new school of animation in America. the animated strip cartoon. Schulz's characters were perfectly suited to animation and the relatively small team of Bill Melendez benefitted, in the production of this first full-length film, from the experience of half a dozen episodes of 30 mins. made for television. There is, however, one shadow on this picture of success—since most of the gags are based on the American idiom, it is certain that translations will make the film lose a lot of its initial impact.

This fact, however, does not seem to have unduly worried the producers, Lee Mendelson and Bill Melendez, since they have already completed a second full-length animated cartoon called *Snoopy, Come Home*, using the same characters, and are working on a third one. Graphically, the strip cartoon style is greatly respected. It allows the use of a very simplified animation technique in which cost and production time are very much lower than for traditional animation. So the risks are obviously reduced and the public's enjoyment of strip cartoons (American first, then European—at the moment for the sake of snobbery but soon as a matter of taste) should give this formula a really rosy future.

The copyrights of popular strip cartoons are very expensive in the United States and this may handicap expansion of the production of animated cartoons. Despite this, another famous strip cartoon—*Pogo* (by Walt Kelly who was, incidentally, a designer at the Disney Studios)—is also at the moment being animated, and it is contemplated as another full-length film.

FILMS FOR ADULTS

A type of show which enjoys a great deal of success in the United States is the musical. Disney embarked on productions in this field, but new possibilities are now appearing with John Wilson's latest film, *Shinbone Alley*. John Wilson, a British artist, acquired his animation experience working at the Disney Studios and at U.P.A. Later he set up his own studio, Fine Art Films, where he made some animated cartoons which were popular in the United States and obtained various prizes and distinctions; e.g., *Tora the Stone Cutter* (1954), *Petrouchka* (1956), *Journey to the Stars* (1961) —a film in cinorama for the Seattle Exhibition, and many TV series. In Europe, it was primarily the animated credits for Billy Wilder's film *Irma La Douce* which brought to people's attention the quality of John Wilson's work. The hero of *Shinbone Alley* is Archy, a famous cockchafer from the poems of Don Marquis, which were published in American newspapers from 1915 to 1930.

Several of these poems were illustrated by the great designer George Herriman during the twenties, in an album entitled *Archy and Mehitabel*. From 1956 onwards, Wilson dreamed of making a feature film on this subject, and started to make some attempts. This film is one of the first full-length animated cartoons for adults made in the United States, and presents the relationship betweeh Archy and the loose-living cat Mehitabel in a form which follows the Marquis poems via a Broadway musical interpretation, also called *Shinbone Alley*. As a general rule the simplified nature of modern animation is not entirely suited to films of more than ten minutes running time. Used in a full-length film, it rapidly tires its audience. Wilson proves the contrary, for the power of the drawings, of certain movements, of the "kinetic" quality of the subject he has chosen, render quite bearable 125 minutes of drawings sometimes reduced to simple sketches, often without even a background. The experiment was conducted by a relatively small team of 60 people. By using the Xerox technique, the original drawings from the character's creators preserve their spontaneity.

Several types of animation are used, integrated so closely that they form one complete new style. Side by side with drawings showing a respect for those of Herriman, are seen collage, op, pop, psychedelic, and underground techniques, and accompanied by a style of music which is itself new and could be called "Jazz-Opera". Its production cost was only $800,000 which is very small compared with the Disney films *The Aristocats* and *Robin Hood*, both $4 million.

Although the idea of a full-length animated film designed for adults is, in the United States, a recent development, in Japan and in Europe this type of film has a slightly longer history. We are now seeing films being made in which the aim is new—orientated towards eroticism, and sometimes flavoured with a hint of pornography. In this respect, Sweden and Japan brought out two remarkable animated cartoons in 1968 and 1969.

I Huvet Pa En Gammal Gubbe (*Out of an Old Man's Head*) was a completely new experiment for the Swedish cinema, for this is the first full-length film ever made in that country, and its sponsor instead of being satisfied with making a film in the classic traditions, sought to do something original. Under producer Gunnar Karlsson (G. K. Films) in a period of only one and a half years, eight people made 55 mins. of animated cartoon to which live-action sequences were added as introductory material to the actual subject. An old man is put into an old people's home (shot in live-action), where he starts thinking about his life, and soliloquising about his actual or desired past; these sequences are in different styles of animation according to the mood of his soul— simple and childlike when he thinks of his childhood, bright colours and full movement for his first amorous experiences or his visits to brothels, melancholy when he looks back on his marriage, and sombre and tragic when his ideas become libidinous towards the end of his life. The very small preproduction team on the animation side consisted of two writers, Tage Danielsson and Hans Alfredson (humorists and cabaret artistes, well known to the Swedish public, who wrote the script for the whole film), Per Åhlin (designer and key animator), four other animators and a cameraman. His second feature *Dunderklumpen* also with producer Gunnar Karlsson, combining live and animated techniques, as in the first film, have been completed at the end of 1974.

In Sweden, incidentally, in spite of the fact that the first film included several erotic scenes, it is nevertheless considered to be a film suitable for a family audience. Everywhere else it may only be seen by an adult audience who would really appreciate its main charm and appeal.

In Japan to commemorate the 10th anniversary of the Nippon Herald Motion Picture Company Ltd., representatives of this firm commissioned Mushi Productions Inc. to make the first erotic version of a classic of the screen and, indeed of animation, *A Thousand and One Nights*. This film is a very free adaptation of the original story, directed by Osamu Tezuka. Tezuka is one of the most remarkable personalities of the Japanese animation cinema, and the owner of one of the largest studios, Mushi Films, founded in 1961. He is a director of the Japan Cartoonist Association, member of the S. F. Writers Club and one of the directors of the Japan Animated Film Producers Union. He has also worked on the 1970 Osaka Expo. He won the Ofuji Grand Prix and is famous for a number of full-length films of which several have won prizes and distinctions at festivals. Mushi Film cartoons are among those which suits all audiences and are consequently very popular. But with *A Thousand and One Nights*, made in a classic style and with a large team, Japan's treatment of eroticism in animation became more daring than any other country. The very delicate thread-like drawing of the figures, and particularly the women, is very successful. It is suitable for the wide screen and affords new possibilities to the animated cartoon, especially since the adaptation lends itself to a richness of sexual and fantastic interpretations which is possible in a free treatment of the subject. Several of the most popular episodes in the legend were used in this story, well integrated in ancient Arab folklore, while bringing out a modern meaning. The action—comedy, satire and spectacle—includes several sensual scenes which were treated in a way which would be impossible in live-action. The designer of the film, Eichi Yamamoto, began in animation with Otogi Productions, and then designed the Mushi film *A Story on a Street Corner*, which earned him the Ofuji Prize, a high distinction for Japanese animators. *A Thousand and One Nights* was made by a traditional technique of classical animation, but used a multiplane camera to give a three-dimensional effect, and real photographs as backgrounds. The film was a triumphant success in Japan and it is certain that an audience now exists for full-length erotic animated cartoons, just as audiences exist for westerns, science-fiction and war films.

Osamu Tezuka and his firm have now completed a new erotic full-length animated cartoon—*Cleopatra, Queen of Sex*. This had even more erotic sequences.

Another major animation studio in Japan is the Toei Company, which up to 1972, specialised in children's films, with more than 19 full-length animated films in this category. A film made recently by this unit is worthy of note, since it is completely different from the company's previous production. This film was *Maruhi Gekiga, Ukiyoe Senichiya* (*The Fantastic World of Ukiyoe*), directed by Leo Nishimura. In this film we find characters from Japanese mythology (Geishas, Samurai) without an exclusively Japanese background. The treatment is erotic, brutal and sadistic, with violent images. This film is also aimed at an adult audience.

The Toho company is now aiming to push Toei and Mushi out of the market for erotic animation, and has produced no fewer than four full-length films, all starring the same characters, a baseball team under the name *Kyojin No Hoshi*. But these films, unlike *Ikiyoe*, are more akin to crude pornography than the subtle treatment of *A Thousand and One Nights*.

The most recently completed feature animated films at the time of writing are the American production *Fritz the Cat, Heavy Traffic* and *Nine Lives of Fritz*. Released first on February 1st 1972, then consecutively during 1973, 1974, the first two directed by Ralph Bakshi and produced by Steve Krantz, the third directed by Robert Taylor, from three comicstrips by the underground artist Robert Crumb, it shows the full-length animated film returning to its original form of 1917—political satire. They are also highly erotic films and promote the half-mocking idea that all the revolution, drug culture and drop-out existence of modern American youth stems from the desire for—easy sex. Crumb's style, which is reminiscent of Herriman, has been adhered to faithfully, but it is to be feared that these films like *One Thousand and One Nights* are likely to spawn a number of crude imitations.

Nevertheless, all over the world interesting experiments are either in production or completed, and it is obvious that the birth of the "adult" or "progressive" full-length animated film is now going to be taken very seriously by the specialists, and the public will certainly not complain.

The feature-length animated film has a history of half a century. Yet only in the past five years has it begun to exist for adults and to adopt an adult attitude (though there were occasional adult subjects produced before this period, such as *Fantasia* and *Animal Farm*.)

Following the worldwide attention of the Peanuts series *The Boy Called Charlie Brown* and *Snoopy Come Home* and *Fritz the Cat,* all financially successful productions, it is natural that there should be an upsurge of new projects. Al Brodax, the producer of *Yellow Submarine* plans to produce Dante's *Divine Comedies* with the collaboration of Salvador Dali in Barcelona. The same subject was attempted in Italy in 1964 by Nelo Risi and some experimental sequences have been produced but the film is still incomplete. It was to be designed by Antonino Pagliato. In Australia, Eric Porter is working on *Marco Polo Returns*. Screenplay has been completed by Sheldon Motoff and the head animator is Cam Ford who formerly worked as one of John Halas's assistants in England. In London, Ray Jackson is planning a new version of *Alice* called provisionally *Alice Through the Looking Glass*. The Rumanian studio Animafilm in Bucharest is also working on a new version of *Robinson Crusoe*. The director is Victor Antonescu. The energetic Swiss animation group has, finally, joined the long list of feature film makers with Santiago Arolas's new version of *Puss in Boots*. In France, the Hungarian born Jean Image is working on the *Tales of Scheherazade* and hopes to follow it with a new version of *Baron Munchausen.* Apart from the lively London scene with Richard William's *Nashrudin* still in production as well as John Halas' and Joy Batchelor's new computer-made film on the *History of Physic,* ten new subjects have been announced by Kinney's Warner Bros. Unit and Filmation. These include the following familiar classics, *Oliver Twist, Cyrano de Bergerac, Swiss Family Robinson, Don Quixote, From the Earth to the Moon, Robin Hood, Noah's Ark, Knights of the Round Table, Arabian Nights, Call of the Wild.*

With such a sudden rise in activity in the production of full-length animated feature films, currently around thirty productions, there will inevitably be a shortage of skilled animators throughout the world. This is a great challenge for the new generation of animators and directors.

These new approaches to full-length animation have, for directors, opened up new possibilities in the cinema medium. The production of a feature film is a real adventure, and the director must put all his physical and intellectual force into it. But at the end of this adventure there is the near-certainty of success. There is also the great satisfaction due to any builders of a colossal monument. But quite often there is criticism and disappointment. And in this revolutionary period, many critics await tomorrow's full-length animated films. A tomorrow has already started with the end of the Disney era. The King is dead—but we cannot yet cry "Long live the King".

INTRODUCTION TO THE CATALOGUE

The first attempt to establish some record of animated feature film was made back in 1957. Naturally several versions have been drawn up during some twenty years but it will be quite an impossibility to detect how many animated feature films have commenced which have been left unfinished and never heard about afterwards.

Another problem lies in the ambitious announcements of producers. Press releases stating an intention to produce an animated feature film may not be an absolute assurance that it will ever be started. Many others may be in production for years waiting for financial assistance from somewhere or other. It is not unusual for a producer to attempt to earn money from the production of television commercials to pay for a longer film during slack periods. It is sometimes difficult to define therefore when such films will be completed.

The lists in the catalogue fall into four sections:

a) Films produced and completed in the past.
b) Productions expected to be finished in the near future.
c) Films which have been started but never completed.
d) Films with insufficient information.
e) Projects which have been announced but physical production not started yet.
f) Combined features, predominantly live action, with animation inserts.

English title:	THE APOSTLE
Original title:	EL APOSTOL
Year:	1917
Country:	Argentina
Running time:	60 mins.
Medium:	Animated cartoon/black and white—the animation based on human figures
Production:	Frederico Valle
Distribution co-ordination:	Frederico Valle Juan Vergez
Assistant Directors and Key animators:	Diogenes Tabora, Quirino Cristiani
Animation team:	Vincente Caceres, Manuel Costa, Carlos Espejo
Script and models:	Andrés Ducaud
Photography and cameraman:	Andrés Ducaud

Subject:

A political satire on President Irigoyen, taken from the book by Alfredo de Laferrere. Irigoyen is asleep at his home, dreaming. His other self leaves his body and goes to Olympus, where he asks for and obtains Jupiter's thunderbolts which, among other things, he uses to destroy the corruption and vice of the lords of the city. The film contains humorous touches alluding to presidential policy and the ministers and there are other references to current events.

English title:	PELUDOPOLIS
Original title:	PELUDOPOLIS
Year:	1931
Country:	Argentina
Running time:	60 mins.
Medium:	Animated cartoon/black and white
Director, writer, producer:	Quirino Cristiani
Synchronised sound:	Vitaphone system (with records)

Subject:

Another satire on president Irigoyen.

English title:	UPA IN APUROS
Original title:	UPA EN APUROS
Year:	1942
Country:	Argentina
Running time:	16,000 ft was made, out of which 2,000 ft was used
Medium:	Animated cartoon/colour—chromatic bipack system

	developed by Carlos Conio Santini and Rosiano in Alex-colour
Director:	Dante Quinterno
Producer:	Dante Quinterno
Co-ordinator and Adviser:	Julio Lobato
Animation:	Dante Quinterno, Oscar Blotta, Eduardo Ferro, José Gallo and others
Music:	Melle Weersma
Supervision/backgrounds:	Gustavo Goldschmidt

English title:	THE CRAB WITH THE GOLDEN PINCERS
Original title:	LE CRABE AUX PINCES D'OR
Year:	1948
Country:	Belgium
Running time:	1 hr. 45 mins.
Medium:	Puppets/black and white
Directors:	Wildred Bouchery, C. Beerbergen
Production:	Studio Misonne

Subject:

Based on a story drawn by Hergé, the creator of Tin-Tin comics.

English title:	PINOCCHIO IN OUTER SPACE
Original title:	PINOCCHIO DANS L'ESPACE
Year:	1965
Country:	Belgium/U.S.A.
Running time:	71 mins.
Medium:	Animated cartoon/colour
Director:	Ray Goossens
Producer:	Norm Prescott, Fred Ladd, Raymond Leblanc
Assistants:	J. Dutillieu, L. J. Aronson
Screenplay:	Fred Laderman, based on an idea by Norm Prescott taken from the original story by Collodi
Character drawings:	Ray Goossens, Willy Lateste Bert Freund, John Bean
Animation directors:	Willy Lateste, Vivian Miessen
Animators:	Bob Zicot, Eddy Lateste, Nic Broca, Luc Maezelle
Backgrounds:	Claude Lambert, Eddy Ploegaerts, Carl Seldeslachts

Special material:	Aircraft Co. Inc., North-American Aviation Inc.
Technical supervision:	Martin Caidin
Photography:	Francois Leonard, Roger Dobbelaere, Etienne Schurmann
Special effects:	Jos Marissen, Danny Provo, The L.J. Dassonville Laboratory
Editors:	Pablo Zavala, A. Pellet
Filmed:	By Belvision
Musical direction:	Dan Hart
Musical arrangements:	Billy Mure
Songs, lyrics etc.:	Rober Sharp, Arthur Korb
Musical supervision:	Mortimer Palitz

Subject:

Pinocchio, a walking wooden puppet, on the way back to school, meets his old enemies the fox and the cat, who sell him a book about hypnotism. Pinocchio, convinced that he can hypnotise anyone, sees coming towards him Nurtle, a tortoise-like creature, just arrived from outer space. Nurtle thinks he has arrived on Mars. Pinocchio explains to him his mistake and sympathises with him rapidly. They go off together in search of a strange planet which they assume to be habitable.

After a perilous flight, the two friends arrive on Mars (faithfully portrayed as seen through a telescope), where they are put to flight by monstrous animals whose existence had been unknown to the scientists.

They narrowly escape and soon discover strange rays emanating from a laboratory deep underground, which have the power to change creatures into giant monsters.

Who creates these horrible beings and why? Do the Martians want to conquer the universe?

A terrible and sudden storm forces our friends to abandon Mars, but they are travelling towards another danger. Half-way to the Earth they are firstly swallowed by Astro, the space whale, but they escape from him and try, in vain, to hypnotise him.

Finally Astro is pulled down towards earth by the action of the rocket. When they land, Pinocchio and Nurtle have a heroes' welcome. Nurtle leaves for his own planet and Pinocchio is rewarded for his bravery and changed into a little boy.

English title:	ASTERIX THE GAUL
Original title:	ASTERIX LE GAULOIS
Year:	1967
Country:	Belgium/France
Running time:	80 mins.
Direction:	Belvision
Script:	Goscinny, Uderzo
Co-production:	Dargaud-Belvision
Music:	Gerard Calvi

Subject: (Source: Image et son)

In the year 50 B.C. the Gauls of one village are still resisting the Romans, and the patrols of Roman legionaries are returning from their incursions into this area in a pitiful condition. The secret of the extraordinary strength of the Gauls is a magic potion, prepared by the Druid Getafix, which they drink every day. A Roman spy, the legionary Minus, discovers this secret. The Romans capture the Druid, but Asterix goes to find him in the fortified encampment. Both of them are captured and ordered to make the miraculous drug. They pretend to do so, and the Romans drink the potion, which makes their hair and beards grow at an incredible rate . . . This joke could have had dire consequences for the Gauls, had not Mulius Caesar arrived leading reinforcements, and discovered from them that Caius Bonus wanted to acquire this fantastic strength, not for the service of Rome, but in order to usurp Julius Caesar. So it finishes up with a meal in Gaulish style.

English title:	ASTERIX AND CLEOPATRA
Original title:	ASTERIX ET CLEOPATRE
Year:	1968
Country:	France/Belgium
Running time:	72 mins.
Medium:	Animated cartoon/colour
Direction:	Belvision
Script:	Goscinny, Uderzo
Original music:	Gérard Calvi
Lyrics:	Pierre Tchernia
Film adaptation:	J. Marissen, E. Lateste
Co-production:	Dargaud-Belvision
Sound effects:	Henri Gruel
Director (voices):	Claude Dupont
Animation: in between execution:	Vivian Niessen, Nic Broca, Marcel Colbrant, Eddy Lateste, Christiane Segers, Claude Monfort, Michele Cnop, Nicole Gautier, Henri Verbeeck, Christiane Michel, Claude Viseur, Jean-Pol Chapelle, Norbert Ketels, Emmy Borremans, Michel Carpentier, Claudine Vande-Winckel, Andre Paape, Danielle Hoebreck, Christiane Gobeau, Freddy Brugheans, Phillippe Van Steensel, Jean Marie Borbouse

Subject:

"Your people are decadent; they are incapable of great achievements!" declares Julius Caesar. Cleopatra's anger is aroused and the shouts of the Queen of Queens spread panic among the palace and servants.

She decides to prove that Caesar is wrong and wagers that in three months she will build him a splendid palace at Alexandria.

Edifis, an Alexandrian architect is instructed to carry out the work. If he fails he will be thrown to the crocodiles.

Being a somewhat mediocre architect, Edifis feels incapable of winning the bet on his own. He needs the help of a wise man.

And, most unhappily for the crocodiles, Edifis does know a wise man. This is a Druid from Gaul by the name of Getafix, who lives in a little village of invincible warriors whose principal activity is to make life difficult for the poor Romans who occupy their country.

Edifis visits Getafix, who agrees to help him. Better still Asterix, Obelix and their mascot, Dogmatix, (French name Idéefix) agree to set off and give assistance if necessary.

And it is necessary, time and time again. Savage pirates, Artifis (a rival architect to Edifis), exasperated Romans—all try to prevent Cleopatra from winning her bet.

Asterix, Obelix, Getafix and Dogmatix make light work of the difficulties and with great good humour succeed in overcoming all the many obstacles that are put in their way.

Our Gauls are unperturbed by the dangers and take advantage of the trip to do some sightseeing. They visit Alexandria, the Sphynx and the pyramids, go up the Nile, briefly stay in Cleopatra's prisons and intersperse their wandering with a few glorious punch-ups which gave them great satisfaction.

Finally, thanks to their help, Caesar's palace is built in the alloted time, Cleopatra wins her bet and nothing more remains for our friends to do but to go back to Gaul where a great feast awaits them to celebrate yet another victory.

English title:	TINTIN AND THE TEMPLE OF THE SUN
Original title:	TINTIN ET LE TEMPLE DU SOLEIL
Year:	1969
Country:	Belgium/France
Running time:	85 mins.
Medium:	Animated cartoon/colour
Direction:	Belvision, Brussels
Animation:	Nic Brocé, Marcel Colbrant, Vivian Miessen, Claude Montfort, Lawrence Moorcroft

Co-production:	Raymond Leblanc, Brussels & Dargaud, Paris
Executive producer:	Raymond Leblanc
Screenplay:	Based on Hergé's cartoon album of the same title; Eddie Lateste, Joe Marissen, Laszlo Molnar, Hergé.
Music:	Francois Rauber
Original songs:	Jacques Brel
Dialogue:	Greg
Backgrounds:	Claude Lambert, Bob de Moor, Jean Torton, Michou Wiggers, Robert Flament
Chief sound recordist:	Francois Leonard
Editing:	Laszlo Molnar, Roger Cacheux

Subject:

This film is based on the two Tintin albums *The Seven Crystal Balls* and *The Temple of the Sun*, and was made for the fortieth anniversary of Hergé's character (Hergé whose real name is Georges Remi.) Tintin first appeared on the 10th January 1929 in a story entitled *Tintin au Pays des Soviets* in *Le Petit Vingtieme*, the weekly supplement of the Brussels daily paper, *Le Siecle*.

Story:

A sports car is travelling towards Moulinsart. A powerful saloon car appears from trees at the roadside and sets off in pursuit of the first car. The pursuers, two men with pronounced Latin features, catch up with their victim. A crystal ball, ejected from a pea-shooter, shatters at the feet of the driver of the convertible . . . he is enveloped in a cloud of smoke . . . he immediately loses control of the vehicle, which crashes into a ditch. Charlet, a member of the Sanders-Hardmouth expedition, will not reach Tintin! He is the sixth victim of the mysterious crystal balls.

One man remains safe, Professor Bergamotte, a friend of Tryphon Tournesol and consequently of Tintin.

Professor Bergamotte has hidden at Moulinsart castle, where the prize in this game is to be found. It is the mummy of the Inca Prince Rascar-Capac, which was brought from Peru by the expedition which included Bergamotte and Charlet.

But alas no protection, even from Tintin, can prevent the avengers of the mummy from punishing the last of the desecrators. During a violent storm, Bergamotte too, falls into the lethargy caused by the crystal balls. The mummy is broken into fragments by a flash of lightning. All is destroyed except a piece of jewellery—the "sacred bracelet" which Tournesol unwisely puts on himself.

Thus, in the eyes of the fanatical Indians, he becomes the eighth desecrator, and he is therefore kidnapped—for this act has earned him a special punishment.

Tintin, his inseparable friend Haddock and the Dupont-Duponds do not see it this way. With the help of the brave Milov, they start off in pursuit of the kidnappers, which is to lead them through a host of dangers, into the South American jungle to the foot of the Andes and finally into the fantastic Temple of the Sun, the retreat of the last of the Incas. A dreadful fate awaits them there. They are captured and condemned by the sun-worshippers and led to the stake. Tintin overcomes this danger, as he does all the others, via a spectacular series of adventures.

English title:	LUCKY LUKE
Original title:	LUCKY LUKE
Year:	1971
Country:	Belgium/France
Running time:	75 mins.
Medium:	Animated cartoon/colour
Director:	René Goscinny
Production:	Belvision with Dargaud-Films, Paris, and Les Artistes Associes
Design:	Morris
Screenplay:	Adaptation and dialogue by René Goscinny, Morris and Pierre Tchernia
Music:	Claude Bolling
Sound effects:	Henri Gruel

Subject:

The solitary daisy out on the prairie gave the town its name. But as fast as the frontier town grew, in came the outlaws, bank-robbers and card sharps, drunkards and brawlers. Then, into town rode Lucky Luke on his horse Jolly Jumper.

Luke was slow of speech, a man of few words. But he could draw quicker than his own shadow. Single-handed he stopped the saloon brawl and, when the outlaws ganged up on him, he flushed them all out, ready for tar and feathering. A grateful town appointed him Sheriff. But the celebration Barn Dance is interrupted by the news that the stage-coach has been held up.

The horses from the stage-coach carry the notorious Dalton Brothers to Daisy Town, where they run into Lucky Luke who tells them to clear out. Instead they make their mark in a series of robberies and plan to take over the town, renaming it Dalton Town. The townspeople, living in fear, refuse to support Luke and he resigns as Sheriff. Now the Daltons stand for public office—as Sheriff, Judge and Mayor. But dumb Averill Dalton, who is left out, starts his own election campaign and in the fight that follows no one wins.

The Daltons, re-united, plan a final shoot-out in the main street—four to one against Lucky Luke. Folks tremble with fear—except for the gleeful undertaker.

But Lucky Luke is unconcerned and, in the showdown he and Jolly Jumper turn the tables on the Daltons who are tarred and feathered and driven out of town.

Captured by Indians the Daltons warn the Indian Chief that the presence of towns like Daisy Town will change the face of the West. He predicts a horrifying future for the Indians who immediately don war-paint and set off for Daisy Town, but first they turn in the Daltons to the State Prison and claim their reward.

The celebration barn dance is interrupted by the news that the Indians are on their way to Daisy Town. The townsfolk want Luke to protect them. But desperate messages sent to the cavalry are intercepted by the Indians. All seems lost so Lucky Luke leads a wagon train out of town. The wagons form a circle as the Indians arrive, the crazed warlike braves getting closer and closer to the helpless settlers.

English title:	SYMPHONY OF THE AMAZON
Original title:	SINFONIA AMAZONICA
Year:	1953
Country:	Brazil
Running time:	70 mins.
Medium:	Animated cartoon/colour
Direction, Script Design, Animation, Photography, Production:	Anelio Latini Filho
Music:	Latini Filho and a selection of popular and classical melodies.
Distribution:	Unida-Filmes (Brazil)

Subject:

A collection of legends from the Amazon featuring animals and characters from Indian folklore—the treatment is in the Disney style.

English title:	CHRISTMAS PRESENT
Original title:	PRESENTE DE NATAL
Year:	1971
Country:	Brazil
Medium:	Animated cartoon/colour
Director/Producer:	Alvaro Henriques Goncalves

Subject:

A seasonal tale about Christmas. A first film by Goncalves, a lawyer by profession, who worked eighteen years to complete his film singlehanded.

English title: THE LIFE OF SOIL
Original title: A VIDA DO SOLO
Year: 1968
Country: Brazil
Running time: Part 1—47 min.
    Part 2—27 mins.
Medium: Animated cartoon/colour
Director/Animation: Orion Silva Mello
Screenplay: Dr. Anna M. Primavesi, Dr. Arthur Primavesi
Drawings: Glycia Doeller, Orion Silva Mello
Commentary: Luiz Fernando Vinade
Production: Universidade Federal de Santa Maria

Subject:

A humorous presentation of the biological phenomena, physical and chemical, taking place in the soil.

The film aims to illustrate the interrelationship between the life of the soil and the dependence on it of agricultural methods.

The first part of the film shows the deterioration of the soil brought about by the use of the wrong agricultural methods, and the second part illustrates how to regenerate the soil.

Title: THE ENCHANTED VILLAGE
Year: 1955
Country: Canada
Running time: 62 mins.
Medium: Animated cartoon
Directors: Marcel and Real Racicot
Production: Marcel Racicot.
Animation: Laura Ledoux, Pierre Lanaud, Charles Hebert, Guy Parent
Music: Emilien Allard
Narration: Pierre Dagenais

Subject:

In this first full length animated film the main character Jean le Meunier decides to clear a section of a thick forest. He dreams that by this act he will transform it to a prosperous village with a church, schools and houses. But his dream goes wrong, by some evil forces until at the end he does succeed.

Title: TIKI TIKI
Year: 1970
Country: Canada
Medium: Animated cartoon and live action
Director: Gerald Potterton
Co-director: Peter Sanders
Production: Potterton Productions, S.D. I.C.C. and Commonweath United

Subject:

A parody of a Disney musical comedy, *Tiki Tiki* is the story of a gorilla, who is a Hollywood producer, and a monkey, a fashionable young director, who make a big budget musical involving children, pirates, clowns and an old professor.

English title: A CHUANG TAPESTRY
Year: 1959
Country: China
Running time: 52 mins
Medium: Animated cartoon/colour
Director: Chien Chiao-Chun
Screenplay: Hsiao Kan-niu
Music: Wu Yin Chu and Miao Shu-yun
Production: Shanghai Animation Studio

Subject:

This is based on a beautiful old legend of the Chuang people in South West China.

A poor Chuang woman, Dabu, lives with her three sons in a remote mountain district, Dabu weaves silk tapestries and her sons collect firewood for a living.

One day Dabu goes to market to sell her tapestry, and buys a beautiful landscape painting. Enchanted by the happy scene in this picture, she decides to reproduce it in a tapestry. Day and night she weaves without rest, and after three years she finishes her work.

She and her sons are gazing at it, when a whirlwind sweeps it away and it soars out of sight.

Overwhelmed with grief, Dabu begs her sons to recover the tapestry for her; but her first and second son turn back half way, discouraged by the difficulties.

The third son, Loro, is a brave, industrious lad. He determines to recover his mother's tapestry. The way is revealed to him by an immortal, and a stone tiger comes to life to carry him across the hills and mountains, and past icy cliffs and seas of flame.

But throughout all danger he never wavers. Overcoming all difficulties at last he reaches Fairyland and finds the tapestry in the Palace of the Sun.

Loro and his mother are gazing happily at the tapestry when the rich beautiful countryside shown on it suddenly becomes real. So their dream comes true.

And the Seventh Fairy in the Palace of the Sun descends to share their joy and happiness.

English title:	TROUBLES IN THE KINGDOM OF HEAVEN
Year:	1962 + 1965 (Part 1 and 2)
Country:	China
Running time:	120 mins. (in two 60-min. parts.)
Medium:	Animated cartoon/colour
Director:	Wan Lai-Ming
Screenplay:	Li Ke-jouo, Wan Lai-ming.
Collaborator:	Tang Tcheng
Models:	Tchang Kouang-yu

Subject:

Taken from the 16th century fantasy *Journey to the West*, it depicts the combat between the intelligent intrepid king of the monkeys, Souen Wou-Kong and the authorities at the celestial court, whom he has defied.

English title:	THE PEACOCK PRINCESS
Year:	1964
Country:	China
Medium:	Animated puppets/colour
Director:	Tchin Hsi
Screenplay:	Tchin Hsi, Yin Keou-yang.
Music:	Wou Ying-kiu
Backgrounds and models:	Tcheng Che-fa
Production:	Shanghai Animation Studio

Subject:

Based on a legend from the Tai region in southwest China. The king of Mengpankia has a valiant and loyal son, Prince Tchaochoutoun, who is remarkably strong. The King has given his son a very special weapon, the magic bow, which may only be strung by someone of such strength.

One day Tchaochoutoun meets the old hunter Kehhakan, and together they arrive at a magic lake, the Golden Lake.

On every seventh day, seven princesses from the Peacock Kingdom come to amuse themselves at the Golden Lake and this sight delights Tchaochoutoun. A giant bird chases the youngest, Princess Nanmanonna and the prince saves her life.

They fall in love with each other. At their wedding, the daughter of the prime minister shows her sadness as she is in love with the prince, and her father thinks up a wicked plan to break the love of Tchaochoutoun for Nanmanonna.

The plan to kill Nanmanonna is put into action, but Kehhakan foils this. She returns to the Peacock Kingdom where her prince joins her on his victorious return from a series of battles.

English title:	THE GIRL WITH LONG HAIR
Year:	1964
Country:	China
Medium:	Animated puppets/colour
Director:	Yue Lou
Screenplay:	Yen Li
Music:	Tchang Tong
Production:	Shanghai Animation Studios

Subject:

An adaptation of a folk tale of the Tong people. In the Tong region there was a mountain known as Teoukaochan (high and steep mountain) which pierced the clouds and where the countryside was beautiful with joyous, limpid streams.

One day the springs dried up for no apparent reason and there was a drought. In a poor village at the foot of the mountain there lived a brave girl with long hair who, while pulling up a red turnip on the mountain, discovered a spring. But it immediately closed up again, carrying off the girl to the cave of the monster of the mountain.

The monster made her swear not to reveal its secret or she would die. But the villagers went to the mountain, pulled up the red turnip, and the water sprang out again. The young girl was saved and the monster was killed.

English title:	THE CZECH YEAR
Year:	1947
Country:	Czechoslovakia
Running time:	74 mins.
Medium:	Animated puppets/colour
Director:	Jiri Trnka

Subject:

A full-length film composed of six parts, showing the customs of the country people during the different seasons of the year.

Story:

1 *Carnival*. This is a parade of masked figures on a snow-covered village green, complete with a performing bear and rustic manners.

2 *Spring*. Children play games, dance, and sing songs—at first nostalgic for winter then full of the excitement of a hunt.

3 *The Legend of St. Procopius*. A devil attempts to interfere with the saint's ploughing, but is made to wield the plough himself.

4 *Pilgrimage*. Led by the choirmaster and the village band, villagers make their way to Church. They all pray for their various desires to come true.

5 *Harvest Festival*. The village green is crowded with stalls and entertainments, magicians, soothsayers and actors. A puppet theatre performs the tragic tale of the Turk and the Squire's daughter.

6 *Bethlehem*. Christmas food is prepared, a carol

is sung, and first the shepherds, then all the village people make their way towards Christ's manger.

English title:	THE EMPEROR'S NIGHT-INGALE
Year:	1948
Country:	Czechoslovakia
Running time:	73 mins.
Medium:	Animated puppets/colour
Direction and Screenplay:	Jiri Trnka, Jiri Brdecka
Music:	Vaclar Trojan

Subject:

A sick child imagines that the objects around him come to life. They play out the famous tale by Andersen, *The Emperor's Nightingale*. The Emperor is a child, all-powerful, but a slave to etiquette. His whole life is regulated, his leisure time included, by a mechanical cymbals player. A stranger, a sailor, comes to upset this beautiful routine. He leaves a present for the Monarch, a book in which there is a picture of a bird which he had not encountered—a nightingale. A little girl, who knows this singing bird, discovers its name and brings it to the Emperor with great ceremony. But soon the Monarch comes to prefer the music of a mechanical nightingale. The real nightingale takes flight and the Emperor falls into inertia, is on the brink of death and about to be usurped. The little girl makes the nightingale return. Death retreats, and the Emperor comes back to life, but from now on he will not allow his life to be run by the Head of Protocol.

To the charm of a children's story, this film adds a remarkable musical background, the rich imagination of an amazing team of artists and the naive depth of a superb fable, incorporating many lessons. This is without doubt one of the masterpieces of the animated cinema.

English title:	PRINCE BAYAYA
Year:	1950
Country:	Czechoslovakia
Running time:	81 mins.
Medium:	Animated puppets/colour (Eastmancolor)
Director:	Jiri Trnka
Assistant director:	Vladimir Janovsky
Scenography:	Karel Sobotka
Screenplay:	Jiri Trnka, based on a fable by Bozena Nenkova
Photography:	Ludvik Hajer, Emanuel Franek.
Music:	Vaclav Trojan, played by the Prague Cinema Symphony Orchestra

Editing:	Helena Lebduscova
Dialogue:	Vitezlav Nezval
Sound:	Josef Zavadl
Animation:	Bretislav Pojar, Jan Karpas, Bohuscav Sramer, Zbendek Harabe, Stanislav Latal
Producer:	Bohumir Burlanek for Loutkov Film, Prague

Subject:

This film, taken from two Czech folk tales, *Prince Bayaya* and *The Magic Apples*, is Trnka's attempt at an epic treatment. The mixture of fantasy and social satire is well achieved, but the battles with the dragons are repetitive and the film has little solidity.

Story:

A poor boy called Bayaya is lying awake one night when a white horse appears at the window of his father's cottage. The horse tells Bayaya that it is his mother and he must ride on its back to free her from Purgatory. Bayaya goes on the horse to a distant castle, and enlists in the service of its king. The king has three daughters who are doomed to be eaten by three dragons, but Bayaya kills the dragons and rescues the princesses, keeping his identity secret. When the king wants suitors for his daughters, all the noblemen who apply are stupid or degenerate, but Bayaya's suit is spurned by all the princesses although the magic apples which are to choose their husbands all roll to his feet. Then there is a tournament which Bayaya wins, and eventually he gets to marry one of the princesses.

He takes her back to his cottage, and his mother's spirit is set free.

English title:	THE TREASURE OF BIRD'S ISLAND
Year:	1952
Country:	Czechoslovakia
Running time:	77 mins.
Medium:	Live with animation/colour
Director:	Karel Zeman
Screenplay, models, sketches:	Karel Zeman

Subject:

The film is taken from a story about some miniature people, and is the tale of an island on which there is some treasure which causes more trouble than happiness.

English title:	OLD CZECH LEGENDS
Year:	1953
Country:	Czechoslovakia
Running time:	84 mins.

Medium:	Animated puppets/colour (Agfacolor)
Director:	Jiri Trnka
Production:	Prague puppet animation studio
Story:	M. Jirasek
Adaption:	Jiri Trnka, M. Karatochvil, Jiri Brdecka
Photography:	L. Hajek, E. Franek
Music:	Vaclav Trojan
Production managers:	J. Janovsky, J. Mozis
Editing:	H. Lebduskova
Sound:	J. Zadavil, Poledni, E. Formatek
Animation:	Bretislav Pojar, Jan Karpas, Stanek Labal, Brohuslav Sramek.

Subject:

The story of the creation of the Czech nation. Fourth full-length work of the undisputed master of puppet animation. In the poetic style which gives such charm to his works, he tells of the birth of his country.

Story:

A slave nation, led by the noble Tchek, is searching for a country in which to settle. After lengthy wanderings they finally find it and instal themselves. At the death of Tchek, his son Krik reigns and dies without leaving any male children.

One of his three daughters, Libuse, the youngest, is chosen as princess. A fearsome boar spreads terror among the inhabitants of the land. The young Bivoj tracks it down and brings it back alive to the castle. The Princess realises that the people need a man to govern them. She sends out messengers, ordering them to go wherever their noses take them. In this manner they arrive at the home of a poor peasant and it is he whom Libuse takes for a husband. This action does not appeal to certain women, and they revolt. Then war breaks out between the Men and the Women. But just as the battle is imminent peace comes. Under the rule of Kresomysl, trouble was provoked by a passion for gold, which made everyone forget his work on the land. The Czechs were then invaded. And their Duke, Neklane, was a coward. Luckily a Pope then led the troops and vanquished the invading savages.

The personality of each little figure and the quality of the animation show that, within this sphere we are not far from perfection. It is a shame that the film is spread over six little stories, of which three at least have no plot, and are not enlivened by any note of humour. On the other hand, the action scenes, for example the struggle against the boars, the woman's war and the invasion of the barbarians with their fearsome wolves and their birds of prey, are excellent, and stimulate interest which might sometimes have lapsed.

English title:	JOURNEY INTO PRIMAEVAL TIMES
Original title:	CESTA DO PRAVEKU
Year:	1954
Country:	Czechoslovakia
Running time:	92 mins.
Medium:	Live with animated/colour
Director:	Karel Zeman
Screenplay:	Karel Zeman, J. A. Novotny
Photography:	Vaclav Pazdernik, Antonin Horak
Music:	E. F. Burian
Scientific adviser:	Professor of Augusta
Voices:	Vladimir Bejar, Peter Herrman, Zdenek Hustak, Joseph Lukas

Subject:

A children's story, presented in such a way as to teach them the history of the world, especially in primaeval times. This is seen through the eyes of four children who take part in this adventure.

English title:	THE GOOD SOLDIER SCHWEIK
Year:	1954/5
Country:	Czechoslovakia
Running time:	3 episodes (1) 23 mins. (2) 22 mins. (3) 33 mins.
Medium:	Animated puppets/colour
Director:	Jiri Trnka
Animation:	Jan Karpas, Staneck Latal.

Subject:

A full-length film of animated puppets, retelling the three episodes of the world famous novel by Jarslev Hasek. At the 1954 Karlovy Vary Festival it won first prize for the best puppet film and in 1956 at Montevideo it won the Grand Prix in the category of animated cartoons and puppets.

The first two episodes of *The Good Soldier Schweik* are disjointed. Trnka's attempt to convey the main plot of Hasek's novel with puppets and the sub-plot with black and white cut-outs made the story hard to follow and the style very mixed. However, the third episode makes only very sparing use of cut-outs, and there is an exquisitely natural development of story. There is very little commentary, and the use of dialogue is ultra-realistic. The third episode deals with Schweik's arrest, interrogation, journey under escort to Pisek, and return to his regiment.

English title:	THE CREATION OF THE WORLD
Original title:	STVORENI SVETA

Year:	1956/7
Country:	Czechoslovakia
Running time:	82 mins.
Medium:	Animated cartoon/colour
Director:	Eduard Hofman
Screenplay:	Eduard Hofman and Adolf Hoffmeister, based on Jean Effel
	Drawings, commentary and Couplets: Jean Effel
Animation:	Barrandov Studio based on drawings by Jean Effel
Production:	Czechoslovak State Film, Prague
Music:	Jean Weiner and Jan Rychlik
Voices, French version:	Francois Perrier, Martine Sarcey, Georges Aminel, André Vessieres.

Subject:

Colour cartoon about God, the Father, busy and kind, in the satirical drawings by Jean Effel.

Story:

Awakening one day in a little cloud where he lived, God, the Father, realised that he was looking into nothingness. That nothing had been done. And the creative diligence, which is innate in the human, I beg your pardon, divine race would not let him rest. It was all very boring—And from that moment on he and his angels are involved in one great adventure. Everything is done in order. He strikes a match to create light so that they should be able to see properly while working and after the Universe he creates first of all the Earth, the seat of all work.

And we follow these delightful doings in the slightly ironical but above all intimately human cartoons of the French painter Jean Effel about the creation of the world and the good-natured busy figure of God, the Father, as this heavenly creator mixes a bewitching drink, one part oxygen, two parts hydrogen—water. Or, if he finds the surface of a river too uninteresting and flat the angels give it a permanent wave.

And naturally, the picture of the world would not be complete if the eternal counterpart of good, the Devil, were not there to disturb this creative activity with his satanic tricks. If God creates a mountain, the Devil must needs turn it into a volcano. If God makes a star the Devil must spoil it and make it a comet.

English title:	AN INVENTION FOR DESTRUCTION
Year:	1958
Country:	Czechoslovakia
Running time:	75 mins.
Medium:	Live with various types of animation/colour
Director:	Karel Zeman
Screenplay:	Karel Zeman and Frantisek H. Rubin, from Jules Verne's book 'Face ou Drapeau'
Adaptation:	Karel Zeman

Subject:

Professor Roch (A. Navratil) is on the point of being able to liberate the enemy contained in a matter. He considers this a great service to humanity. Count 'Artigas (M. Holbub), an adventurer, desirous of getting hold of Roch's process to gain power for himself, captures the professor and his assistant, Hart, (L. Tokos).

The two men are taken on to a pirate boat and then a submarine and arrive on an unknown island where 'Artigas has his workshop. The professor is invited to carry on with his work and, with the facilities put at his disposal, he unintentionally produces the instrument of dreadful destruction, the atomic bomb. Hart has discovered 'Artigas's plans, and with the help of a girl (J. Zatloukalova) who has miraculously escaped a shipwreck, he manages to warn the world of the danger.

The international fleet of ships arrives at the den of this shady adventurer, who plans to get rid of them by firing a shell with the professor's invention. Hart and the girl manage to escape by balloon and the professor makes the shell go off early, thus putting paid to the plans of D'Artigas.

English title:	A MIDSUMMER NIGHT'S DREAM
Year:	1959
Country:	Czechoslovakia
Running time:	76 mins.
Medium:	Animated puppets/colour
Director:	Jiri Trnka
Screenplay:	Jiri Trnka, Jiri Brdecka
Editor:	Hana Walashova
Music:	Vaclar Trojan
Explanatory commentary:	Jiri Brdecka
Animation:	Bohuslav Sramek, Stanislav Latal, Bretislav Pojar, Jan Karpas, Vlasta Juraj-Dova, Jan Adam
Photography:	Jiri Vojta

Subject:

This spectacular wide-screen re-enactment of Shakespeare's play is widely held to be Trnka's masterpiece. There is no dialogue, and only occasional commentary. All the conversations are conveyed by gesture, and Trojan's music is dominant. Trnka called it "a ballet of mime and fairies," and this description shows the lightness, intricacy and magical quality of the film. There is a wide range of individual characterisation, despite the lack of dialogue, and in his creation of the grotesquely comic but sometimes poignantly sad Bottom, Trnka makes Shakespeare's Bottom seem crude by comparison.

Story:

Egeus complains to Theseus, Duke of Athens, (who is shortly to marry Hippolyta) that his daughter Hermia refuses to marry Demetrius, the husband Egeus has chosen, but pines after Lysander instead. Theseus orders her to marry Demetrius, but that night she and Lysander escape to the woods. Helena, who loves Demetrius, tells him about the elopement and he gives chase. Helena follows Demetrius, in an attempt to persuade him to love her instead. Oberon, King of the fairies, who is having an argument with his wife Titania, overhears Helena wishing for Demetrius to love her and tells his servant Puck to arrange it. Puck unfortunately mistakes Lysander for Demetrius, and makes Lysander fall in love with Helena. Meanwhile a company of tradesmen are in the woods rehearsing a play for Theseus' wedding. To spite Titania, Oberon arranges that Bottom, one of the tradesmen, is given an ass's head. Titania, who has been charmed in her sleep to fall in love with the first creature she sees, wakes up to see Bottom, and she and her fairies treat him regally. By this time Lysander and Demetrius are fighting over Helena, but Oberon undoes all his enchantments, Titania comes back to him, and Demetrius and Helena agree to marry. All the Athenians go back home. Bottom and company perform their play at Theseus' wedding, and all the characters are reconciled.

English title:	BARON MUNCHHAUSEN
Original title:	BARON PRASIL
Year:	1962
Country:	Czechoslovakia
Running time:	84 mins.
Medium:	Object and special effect animation and live action/colour
Screenplay, direction, sketches, models:	Karel Zeman
Music:	Znenek Liska
Voices:	Milos Kopechy (Baron Munchhausen) Rudolf Jellnek (Tonik), Jana Brejchova (Bianca), Jan Werich (Captain of the Dutch Boat), Karl Hoger (Cyrano), Bohus Zahorsky (The Admiral)

Subject:

A young astronaut, Tonik, a figment of the contemporary author's imagination, meets on the Moon his predecessors from the age of the Romantics—Cyrano de Bergerac, Barbican and Captain 'Nicol from Verne's novels and Baron Munchhausen.

They all think that Tonik is an inhabitant of the Moon and invite him to visit the Earth. He is the Baron's guest and shares his remarkable adventures. They begin at the Sultan's Court where they liberate the beautiful Venetian, Bianca. Their adventurous voyage over the sea continues: they are shipwrecked in the entrails of a whale, they are carried off by a fabulous bird, they ride seahorses and are shot into the air by a cannon. The relationship between the Baron and Tonik is complicated by the fact that they both fall in love with Bianca and secretly compete for her favour. The romantic hero throws into the field his courage, wit and fantasy. The young astronaut has only his youth—but in the end he wins. The film is original in all its aspects, beginning with the dramatic conception—the idea of giving the romantic hero a modern partner. The presence of Blanca creates dramatic tension.

Compared with Zeman's previous films, *Journey to Primaeval Times* and *An Invention for Destruction*, *Baron Munchhausen* uses even more combinations of trick techniques and makes an entirely original use of colour, that is, to emphasise the dramatic significance of close shots. Music and sound effects are also used in an original way.

Title:	CINEAUTOMATIC (Montreal Expo. 1967)
Year:	1967
Country:	Czechoslovakia
Total length:	3,500 metres
Medium:	Animation of various figurative and abstract elements, with three and five projectors simultaneously
Director:	Dr. Raduz Cincera

This full-length animated film, 3,500 metres long, was shown in the children's programme at the Montreal Expo. It was invented by the director, Dr. Raduz Cincera. The programme was projected on to three screens, with five projectors.

The whole performance was intended to be more of an 'attraction' than a full-length international film.

English title:	THE MAGIC TINDERBOX
Original title:	FYRTOJET
Year:	1945

Country:	Denmark
Running time:	73 mins.
Directing and planning:	Svend Methling
Medium:	Animated cartoon/colour
Producer:	Allan Johnsen
Production company:	A/S Dansk Farve-Og Tegne-film. From the story by Hans Christian Andersen
Screenplay:	Peter Toubro-Henning Pade,
Design:	Borge Hamberg, Bjorn Frank Jensen, Preben Dorst, Frede Henning Dixner, Kjeld Simonsen, Finn Rosenberg Ammitsted
Music:	Eric Christiansen, Vilfred Kjaer
Songs:	Victor Skaarup
Photography:	Marius Holdt, N. O. Jensen.
Sound recordist:	Eric Rasmussen-As Palla-dium, Hellerup
Editing:	Edith Schlussel, Henning Ornbak
Copies:	Eclair Laboratory, Paris
Voices:	Paul Reichardt (soldier), Kristen Hermansen (prin-cess), Knud Heglund (king), Karen Poulsen (witch), Edith Foss (astrologer)

Subject:

This film opens with a few words about Hans Christian Andersen and his tales. We see the night-watchman calling the hours. It is ten o'clock, bedtime.

But not everyone is asleep, and we see an astrologer who has, on this particular night, seen in the stars that the princess will marry a simple soldier.

The astrologer runs to see the king, wakes him and tells him what she has read in the stars.

The king gets up and orders that the princess, still asleep, should be taken and kept in a tower, to avoid such a calamitous marriage.

A soldier is marching towards the town of Copenhagen. By an ancient tree he finds an old witch, who instructs him to climb into the hollow tree to look for a tinderbox which had been left there long ago by her grandmother. She gives him her apron and tells him that he will find money there and that he may take away as much of it as he can carry.

Beneath the tree the soldier finds three caves. The first is guarded by a dog with eyes as big as saucers, the second by a dog with eyes as big as millstones, and the third by a dog with eyes as big as a tower.

He avoids the dogs and fills his pockets and his bag with golden coins.

When he returns to the surface, the soldier asks the old witch why she prefers the old tinderbox to the wonderful golden coins. She refuses to tell him, so he becomes very angry and cuts off her head with a sabre.

The soldier arrives in town and finds lodgings in an inn. Here he buys drinks for all the customers and carries on for several days spending his money completely freely. He learns about the beautiful princess who is locked up in the tower—nobody knows why.

Soon all the money has been frittered away, and the soldier has to be satisfied with living in an attic room. We see him trying to repair his old boots. He drops the needle on the ground and it is too dark to see where it has fallen. He wants to light the candle but he has no matches, but then remembers the tinderbox and strikes it to light the candle. Immediately the first dog appears. 'What does my master desire' he says. The dog tells him that each time the soldier strikes the tinderbox once he will appear. If he strikes it twice the second dog will appear, and if he strikes it three times all three dogs will come. All he has to do is ask, and the dog will get him whatever he wants.

Now the soldier is rich again. He dresses smartly and does not allow people to rob him.

He is troubled by the thought of the princess who is locked up. If only he could see whether or not she was as pretty as they say. He strikes the tinderbox and asks the dog if it is possible to show him the princess, even though it is the middle of the night.

The dog goes off and returns immediately with the sleeping princess on his back. The soldier falls in love with the princess.

The next morning the princess tells the king and the queen of the extraordinary dream she has had. The king is worried, thinking that this may well not be a dream. He orders a lady of the court to keep watch over the princess during the night.

The soldier sends the dog off to find the prin-cess, and the lady of the court runs after it. They discover where the soldier lives and he is arrested. He is tried and condemned to hanging. On the scaffold he asks the king for leave to smoke his last pipe and the king consents.

The soldier strikes the tinderbox three times and the three dogs arrive and quickly chase everyone away.

The king promises that the princess will marry the soldier and will as is fitting, receive half her kingdom.

The wedding is followed by a great feast to which all the population and the three dogs are invited.

English title:	BENNY'S BATHTUB
Original title:	
Year:	1970
Country:	Denmark

Medium:	Animated cartoon/colour
Directors:	Jannik Hastrup and Flemming Quist Muller
Production:	Fiasco-Film
Script and design:	Flemming Quist Muller
Layout:	Per Tunnes Nielsen
Photography:	Poul Dupont
Editing:	Henrik Carlsen
Sound:	Siegfried Nilsen and Axel Pless
Music:	Hans Henrik Ley
Lyrics:	Jan Bredsdorff

Subject:

Benny's Bathtub is the most ambitious work to come from this little production company to date. Just as in Jannik Hastrup's and Flemming Quist Moller's short cartoons, there is an abundance of grotesque humour and disrespectful satire in *Benny's Bathtub*. In its whole approach the film is entirely on the side of the children, and time and again the child's dream-world triumphs over the unimaginative world of the grown-ups.

The boy, Benny, has a number of strange adventures on the bottom of the sea, portrayed in a series of dynamically drawn episodes, and now and again the artists make bitter attacks on adult environments that have no regard for children The pictures are often overburdened with a mosaic of colours and the style is far removed from the rounded, harmonious figures of Disney's naturalism—in fact it is more in keeping with John Hubley's short cartoons. (from Danish Film News 1971).

English title:	THE STORY OF THE FOX
Original title:	LE ROMAN DE RENARD
Year:	1925–1936
Released:	1940
Country:	France
Running time:	70 mins.
Medium:	Animated puppets/black and white
Director:	Ladislas Starewitch
Screenplay:	Irene Starewitch
Music:	Vincent Scotto
Adaptation:	Roger Richebe

Subject:

Under the orders of King Lion, Master Fox holds in check all the animals of the earth who have set off to war against the king. Eventually the king makes Master Fox the prime minister.

This film is a work of great patience, having taken ten years to make. The puppets are very expressive and amusing and there are some charming ideas. The backgrounds are witty and varied. The music is good, the dialogue witty. The photography is first class.

English title:	THE INTREPID JEANNOT
Original title:	JEANNOT L'INTREPIDE
Year:	1950
Country:	France
Running time:	80 mins.
Medium:	Animated cartoon/colour (Technicolor)
Director:	Jean Image
Dialogue:	Paul Colline
Production:	Films Jean Image
Versions in foreign languages:	French, English, German, Italian, Spanish
Music:	Rene Cloerec, songs by P. Colline
Animation Direction:	A. Champeaux
Animators:	D. Boutin, M. Breuil, O. Klein.

Subject:

Seven little boys are taking a walk in the forest and Jeannot the smallest of them, decides to fight the ogre, so that he can no longer go around eating little children. They find the ogre's castle, and Jeannot is taken prisoner in a cage, having been reduced to the size of an insect. A thieving Magpie snatches away the cage. How is he to get out? He is taken to Insectville and then, against his will, is dragged off on an extraordinary journey by a lizard, angry because Jeannot had wanted to tame him. He falls into an ambush of spiders' webs, but is saved by the intervention of the bees. There is great rejoicing in his honour, but the wasps, taking advantage of the general sense of euphoria, attack the hive. Jeannot comes out of the fight victorious, but he does not forget his friends, still prisoners of the ogre.

The bees help him to take his revenge. They sting the ogre's body and he is soon overwhelmed. Jeannot falls into the ogre's jar and while the ogre becomes minute, our friend returns to his normal size, and it is the ogre's turn to be shut up in a cage. There will no longer be an ogre to frighten the children.

English title:	MISTER WONDERBIRD
Original title:	LA BERGERE ET LE RAMONEUR
Year:	1953
Country:	France
Running time:	63 mins.
Medium:	Animated cartoon/colour
Director:	Paul Grimault
Production:	Les Gemaux

Producer :	André Sarrut	Photography :	Kosita Tchikins
Screenplay :	Jacques Prévert, Paul Grim-ault	Music :	Jean Yatove
		Backgrounds :	Pierre Baudin
Dialogue :	Jacques Prévert	Head animators :	Therese David
Director of animation :	Henri Lacam	Animators :	D. Boutin, M. Breuil, P. Watrin
Animation :	Pierre Watrin, Jacques Vausseur		
		Creative advisors :	M & P Sachs
Music :	Joseph Losma, played by the Royal Philharmonic Orchestra, directed by Muir Matheson	Production :	Les Films Jean Image

Subject:

Two pigeons love each other tenderly. As we follow their love story, we can admire the most beautiful views of Paris, from Notre-Dame with its Chimaeras, jealous of the pigeons' love, to the very famous Eiffel Tower, which plays truant and brings about a diplomatic incident, for the cry is raised 'They have stolen the Eiffel Tower!'.

Songs sung by :	Jacques Leanse, Eric Amato with Leo Noel and his Barbary organ
Voices :	Pierre Brasseur, Serge Reggiani, Anouk Aimée
English version :	Peter Ustinov, Claire Bloom, Alex Clunes

A great fishing expedition, an apache dance one starry night, a fairy-tale ballet performed by the snails of Paris, form a real music-hall show. A motion is passed for the reconstruction of the tower, but our two pigeons go off to look for it, and bring it back to the cheers of the crows, happy to regain what they have lost.

Subject:

Once upon a time in the kingdom of Takicardie there was a tyrannical king who amused himself by hunting birds which his huntsmen had already shut up in a cage in order to make their massacre easier.

The very Parisian songs complete the atmosphere of this film, for which Jean Cocteau wrote the preface.

One day the king is preparing to hunt down a little bird when the bird's father comes to save his child, and screams out all his hatred of the king. The latter is furious, and returns to his castle. Later, he falls asleep. Meanwhile, two pictures on the wall of his bedroom come to life—a portrait of a charming shepherdess and that of a chimney-sweep, nearby. The two declare their love for each other. But the portrait of the king also leaves its frame and starts to pursue them, for he too, is in love with the shepherdess. The two lovers meet the father of the little bird, who promises to help them at all times. The lovers are then chased into the town, the shepherdess is captured and the chimney-sweep sent to the lions. But the bird manages to save them both, and to bring about the death of the king, thus restoring happiness to the inhabitants of Takicardie.

English title :	20,000 YEARS OF FRANCE
Original title :	20,000 ANS A LA FRANCAIS
Year :	1965–67
Country :	France
Running time :	80 mins.
Medium :	Various types of animation/ colour (Technicolor)
Screenplay and direction :	Jacques Forgeot
Animation of drawings :	Michel Altermatt
Animation of engravings :	Walerian Borowczyk
Director of photography :	Guy Durban
Production manager :	Daniel Fauquet
Production :	Cinéastes Associés-Paris
Music :	Avenir de Monfred
Editing :	Collete Cueille
Photography of ancient documents :	Wilburn Rich
Research and presentation of ancient graphic styles :	Jacqueline de Monfred, Bruno Tavernier
Commentary by :	Jacques Forgeot, spoken by Jacques Thiebaud, Nicole Favard, Monique Laurie

Title :	BONJOUR PARIS
Year :	1953
Country :	France
Running time :	70 mins.
Medium :	Animated cartoon/colour (Technicolor)
Director :	Jean Image
Authors :	Screenplay by Eraine, Dialogue by Cl. Santelli
Commentary spoken by :	Francois Perrier
Songs sung by :	Les Quatre Barbus, Tohama, Lucien Jeunesse, Claire Genet

Gay Purr-ee by Abe Levitow (1962) USA.

Fables from Hans Christian Anderson (1968) by Kimio Yabuki, Japan.

Je Tu Elles (1969) by Peter Foldes, France.

Don Quixote (1975/6) by Fred Calvert, USA.

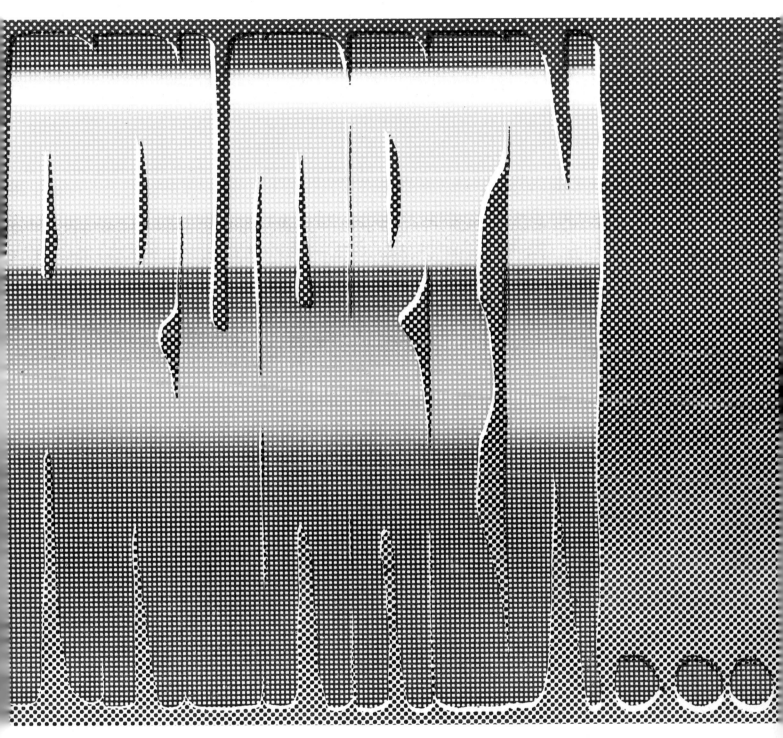

Scope, Colour, Muda 75 (1969) by Jose
Antonio Sistiaga, Spain.

A Thousand and One Nights by Osamu
Tezuka, Japan, for the Main Title.

Santa Claus Returns (1970) by Rankin and Bass, USA (Made in Japan).

The Theatre of Monsieur and Madame Kabal (1967) by Walerian Borowczyk, France.

Shinbone Alley (1970) by John Wilson, USA.

Out of an Old Man's Head (1968) by Per Åhlin, Sweden.

Opposite, top. *Fablio le Magicien* (1969) by Attila Dargay of Hungary/France.

Thundering Fatty (1974) by Per Åhlin Sweden.

Sound engineer:	Louis Perrin
Jazz and symphony orchestras under the direction of:	Paul Lemel

Subject:

From the Lascaux cave paintings to the geometrical forms of today's industrial world . . . This is indeed a portrait of France. But it is Jacques Forgeot's portrait, a real mixture of glory and smiles, of moving and amusing moments. The France of the middle ages, with its monks, its cathedrals, the France of Versailles, another France whose landscapes are less familiar to us now. A sort of mobile mirror, carried along a Roman road, a mirror which reflects only the memories and the tastes of the person who carries it.

It is a strange and enthralling film, enthralling not only because of what it shows us of France, but also for what it reveals of the author, his tastes, his fantasies and his dilettantism. It took four years of patient work, considerable funds and many ingenious and frequently poetic devices to produce this *20,000 Ans a la Francaise*, which, even so, will not satisfy everyone.

Strangely enough, this film takes a long time to appreciate, for it is a film made with love—a waking dream. This is not Disney, in spite of the realistic animated characters, in spite of the wonderful sequence of the corpses, or the fascinating fashion show in the Hall of Mirrors.

This is no classic, in spite of Forgeot's skill in passing from the frosty Versailles of the present time to the Versailles in the style of Epinal, without any visual shock. It is rather the work of an adult poet and child film-maker, both happy to make their double dream burst into pictures. For the film abounds in images of a sumptuous beauty, and it is hard to resist its subtle charm. It shows us something different: for though the tower of this old place is beautiful, the camera has to prowl for some time, awaiting the hundredth of a second when everything is perfect, even to the game with a bust of Caesar, which, facing an empty arena, holds forth in a style we often see on our television screens. Different from anything we have seen before, *20,000 Ans la la Francaise* is a very strange film.

Title:	LE THEATRE DE MON-SIEUR ET MADAME KABAL
Year:	1967
Country:	France
Running time:	80 mins.
Medium:	Animated cartoon/colour (Eastmancolor), wide screen
Director:	Walerian Borowczyk
Production:	Le Cineastes Associés
Producer:	Jacques Forgeot

Screenplay:	Walerian Borowczyk
Design:	Gerard Cox
Music:	Avenir de Monfred
Editing:	Callude Blondel
Associate producer:	Serge Vincent-Vidal
Production manager:	Daniel Pauquet

Subject:

The director creates his characters. Madame Kabal is argumentative and domineering.

The show begins, *The Theatre of Mr and Mrs Kabal.* This is a theatrical production of the banal or surprising aspects in the everyday life of this couple, at the seaside, at home where Mrs Kabal is ill and is being cared for or is cooking, or when they are manufacturing weapons of war. Mrs Kabal rules, served by her husband, who from time to time escapes in his dreams towards the paradise of the postcard and the pin-up.

An animated cartoon for adults or a cinema fable, this work is striking, though the graphic values of the character drawings may be rough and unpolished. The storytelling, done against the most remarkable backgrounds, is brilliant, and the sound effects and musical arrangement form a whole which is perfectly expressive yet can at times melt into the picture and at others form a counterpoint to it.

The rhythm, or rhythms, of the animation, (there are relationships between the movements of the characters and the progression of the plot) are varied, and perfectly adapted to the capacity of the spectator. He has time to see everything, and even to dream a little, and to question himself. And the Leitmotif, which could appear as useless repetition does, in fact, contribute to this process of allowing sufficient time while also marking the tempo of the action. *Le Theatre de Monsieur et Madame Kabal* is an 'open' film. The author's symbolism, while a little esoteric, is perceptible. But the spectator himself can think up a whole range of meanings and interpretations, both of the essence of the work as well as of the details, which often suggest this or allude to them—the faithful animals, for example. Are they dogs, little pigs, sometimes even cocks? Are they birds or butterflies that accompany the couple? In this work, there is certainly a sort of interchange between it and the spectator, which one would hesitate to qualify as 'guided', but which is nevertheless pivotted on the will of the director.

Original title:	LE SOCRATE
Year:	1968
Country:	France
Running time:	90 mins.
Medium:	Live action with animation and various special effects/colour (Eastmancolor)

Director:	Robert Lapoujade
Production:	C.E.R.T.—Pierre Domec-Jacques Pollet-Paris
Co-production:	Bayerischer Rundfunk—Telepool-Munich Research Department O.R.T.F.
Distribution:	France: C.F.D.C. Paris World: C.E.C.R.T. Paris
Writer:	Robert Lapoujade
Dialogue:	Colette Audry, Jean Patrik Manchette
Associate producer:	Fanny Berchaux
Backgrounds:	Michel Barbissan
Design:	Jean Jacques Renon
Editing:	Jean Ravel
Music:	Bernard Permegiani
Actors:	Pierre Luzan, R. H. Chauffard, Martine Brochard, Stefane Fay, J. P. Sentier
Animation:	Robert Lapoujade

Subject:

Le Socrate, adopting the philosophy of his Greek ancestor of the same name but in the modern world, abandons everything and goes wandering in the town in a quest for the truth. He is immediately followed by Lemmy, a policeman, who asks himself questions, and becomes obsessed by the man he has been ordered to follow, so that he gradually becomes a disciple of this tramp-philosopher.

These two creatures follow the path of life with one accord, observing love, despair, terror, nature and thought. The Socrates live one moment of celebrity and their ways diverge. The policeman is left alone. Did either understand the other?

English title:	FABLIO THE MAGICIAN
Original title:	FABLIO LE MAGICIEN
Year:	1969
Country:	France
Running time:	85 mins.
Medium:	Animated cartoon/colour (Eastmancolor)
Directors:	Georges de la Grandiere (France) Attila Dargay (Hungary) Radka Badcharova (Bulgaria) Victor Antonescu (Rumania)
Screenplay adaption:	Georges de la Grandiere
Dialogue:	Fables of Jean de la Fontaine, read by Jacques Degor
Animation studios:	Budapest (Pannonia-film), Bucharest (Animafilm) and Sofia Animation Studio (Bulgaria)
Production:	Edic Films Paris

Subject:

Six La Fontaine fables transposed, complete with radar, television, cinema, Olympic Games, refrigerators and washing machines—into our own times, in fact, with all our occupations and pre-occupations.

The six sketches are linked together by a little magician who removes anything that might seem too cruel and adds poetry to the fantasy and warmth to the visual beauty.

These are the fables which make up the film:

The Cat and the Old Rat—This film, made in Bulgaria, shows through the lives of some little mice and the old rat who is their teacher that it is worth listening to those who have more experience than oneself, and that it is better to be safe than sorry.

The Frog who Wanted to be as Big as the Ox—Satire about an Olympic champion who is drunk with his own success. Instead of sticking to what he knows he can do, he tries to create an even bigger sensation and hasn't the sense to give up when he realises that he has bitten off more than he can chew.

The Wolf and the Dog—Made in Hungary, this film shows that freedom is the most precious possession.

At the same time it is a parody of the detective film.

The Lion and the Gnat—A musical parody. David defeats Goliath, but the tables are turned in the end when he is punished for being in too much of a hurry to claim victory.

The Tortoise and the Ducks—All sorts of things can happen to people with more curiosity than sense and more pride than intelligence. And it is sometimes better for a chatterbox to keep his mouth shut.

The Grasshopper and the Ant.—This classic story made in Rumania, is a gentle satire on the hippies. Regimented ants move about in poetically beautiful surroundings, apparently suffering all the evils of collective life, but they end up happier than the hippies, who are not able to claim Social Security Benefits.

English title:	ALADDIN AND HIS MAGIC LAMP
Original title:	ALADIN ET LA LAMPE MERVEILLEUSE
Year:	1969
Country:	France
Running time:	60 mins.
Medium:	Animated cartoon/colour (Eastmancolor)
Director:	Jean Image
Screenplay:	France and Jean Image based on a tale from the Thousand and One Nights

Dialogue:	France Image
Design and photography:	Olaf Csongovai
Production:	Les Films Jean Image—Paris
Backgrounds:	Denis Wuarnier, Enrique Gonzales
Assistant cutter:	Olaf Csongovai
Music:	Fred Freed
Animation:	Denis Boutin, Marcel Breuil, Guy Lehiduex, José Xavier

Subject:

A magician whose vast fortune was not enough to satisfy his ambitions, dreamed of absolute power, which he would enjoy if he could become the owner of a certain wonderful lamp which was in the possession of some fabulous genies.

The magician lived in Africa and his only companions were the owl Hou-Hou and a magic ball through which he was able to question the genies.

He eventually found out that the wonderful lamp was hidden in Asia, deep in the earth, and could only be taken by an innocent hand, the hand of a child.

The magician set out. After many adventures he reached the borders of China and a town with three hills about which the genie of the Dark had told him.

There, among the minarets and gardens, he discovered the boy Aladdin, who lived in poverty with his mother and who seemed likely to be able to serve his purpose. The magician introduced himself as a long lost uncle, brought him fine clothes and set off with him in search of the lamp. The genie of a ring which the magician possessed guided them successfully to the Palace of Scheharezade, where they found the secret passage which was to lead Aladdin to the wonderful lamp—for from this moment on, the boy must act alone. So the magician gave him the ring which had the power to open all doors. And so Aladdin was able to lay hands on the lamp, and its power began working at once. Overcoming every obstacle, passing like a whirlwind under the very nose of the magician, Aladdin returned home to his mother and was given untold wealth and everything he could want.

Yet Aladdin was not happy. He had fallen in love with the Sultan's daughter, Badroulboudeur, and he persuaded his mother to go and ask for her hand. The Sultan agreed, on condition that the suitor should present himself at the Palace within three days with a procession of forty white elephants led by forty black servants and bearing forty crocks of gold.

The wonderful lamp performed the miracle, and the magnificent procession was seen heading towards the Palace.

But the magician had sworn to have his revenge. By disguising himself as a beggar he tricked Aladdin's mother into offering him hospitality, stole the lamp and hurried to the Princess's home, which he spirited off to Africa with the girl and all her servants.

The furious Sultan accused Aladdin of having the Princess carried off, but the young man managed to obtain five days grace in which to find the magician's hiding place and snatch the girl and the lamp from the kidnapper's hands.

The magician was shut up in his own magic ball with his owl.

Aladdin and the Princess were married and lived happily ever after, protected by the wonderful lamp.

English title:	DOUGAL AND THE BLUE CAT
Original title:	POLLUX ET LE CHATON BLEU
Year:	1970
Country:	France
Running time:	60 mins.
Medium:	Animated puppets/colour/characters from the 'Manege enchante' (Magic Roundabout) programme
Director:	Serge Danot
Distribution:	Valoria-Films
Production:	D.A.N.O.T.—Caguad
Dialogue:	Jacques Josselin
Voices:	Christion Rhiel (Pollux)

Subject:

It is morning, and a cuckoo wakes all the inhabitants of the Bois-joli, and Pollux too. Pollux has to go and warn Zebulon (the genie, ruler of the Bois-Joli) that an unknown danger threatens them all.

On his way he meets Azalée the cow, then Ambrose the snail, then Flapy the guitar-playing rabbit, then Goodman Jouvence the alert centenarian, finally arriving at Zebulon's house, to whom he relates his tragic night—when he saw the Swift Factory.

Zebulon accuses Pollux of having dreamed it, and he must silence his fears as Margote is coming. A blue kitten then appears, who gets acquainted with Margote.

Flapy, Azalée and Ambrose all take a fancy to the mysterious blue kitten, who has to enter seven blue doors to be made king.

A series of fantastic adventures gathers together all the inhabitants of Bois-Joli under the command of the Swifts.

They even send someone to the moon to paint it blue.

English title:	JOE THE LITTLE BOUM BOUM
Original title:	JOE PETIT BOUM BOUM
Year:	1972
Country:	France
Running time:	60 mins.
Medium:	Animated cartoon/colour
Director:	Jean Image
Production:	Les Films Jean Image
Dialogue:	Michel Emer and France Image
Pictures:	Olaf Csongovai

Subject:

An adapted "Western" played in a beehive with the character Joe and the Queen Bee. Joe emerges as the hero conquering Wou the terrible enemy, who tries to kidnap the Queen Bee.

English title:	THE SAVAGE PLANET
Original title:	LA PLANETE SAUVAGE
Year:	1973
Country:	France/Czechoslovakia
Running time:	72 mins.
Medium:	Animated cartoon
Director:	Rene Laloux
Screenplay:	Roland Topor and Rene Laloux
Producers:	Armorial Films and Czechoslovakia Film Export with ORTF
Original design:	Roland Topor
Graphics:	Joseph Kabrt and Joseph Vania
Music:	Alain Goraguer

Subject:

The film is based on Stefan Wul's fantastic science fiction novel.

Story:

The inhabitants of Planet Ygam are androids 39 feet tall with red eyes, blue skin and ears shaped like conch shells. They have reached the highest levels of scientific knowledge. Their lives are devoted mainly to thinking and leisure activities. Their favourite occupation is "meditation".

They own tiny pets, the Oms, which they treat kindly; several couples of Oms were brought from a distant planet that was destroyed. They have some degree of intelligence and are affectionate with their masters; their life cycle is faster and shorter than that of the Draags.

It all begins when Tiwa, the high magistrate's little daughter, adopts a baby Om which she calls Terr. At first little Terr is docile and submits to his young mistress's whims. But he soon takes advantage of the learning which is being directly infused into Tiwa's brain through "instruction earphones".

At the age of fifteen, Terr is tired of his confined life of luxury as a household pet; fearing his masters may discover his knowledge and prevent him from continuing to instruct himself, he runs away with the precious earphones. He goes to join the hordes of rebellious Oms who live like savages. After many mishaps, he becomes a member of one of the bands that are hiding in an abandoned park and shares in their adventurous life. But the Draags are worried about the increasing numbers of wild Oms and decide to "de-om" the park. Many are slaughtered. The survivors manage to kill a Draag and get to a place where abandoned rockets are stored. Gradually, thousands of rebellious Oms come to join them. They build a huge underground city where they busily study Draag technology and undertake to repair the abandoned spaceships. It takes them many long years which, for the Draags, are only a few weeks.

All over Planet Ygam, a major De-om-isation has begun. Just as the warning to the Draag ships sounds in the city of the Oms, one group under Terr's leadership succeeds in taking off in two rockets and getting to the Wild Planet.

There they discover the great secret of the Draag "meditation", necessary for their survival, and spread confusion in their sacred rites. Since the Draags are threatened in the most vital aspect of their lives and are at last convinced that the Oms are intelligent, they begin showing them respect and wish to collaborate with them.

From then on, Terr and his people live on the Wild Planet in peace, respected by the giant androids who become their friends again.

English title:	PLUK IN COSMOS
Original title:	PLUK NAUFRAGE DE L'ESPACE
Year:	1974
Country:	France
Running time:	74 minutes
Medium:	Animated cartoon/colour
Director:	Jean Image
Production:	Les Films Jean Image
Screenplay:	France et Jean Image
Pictures:	Olaf Csongovai
Music:	Fred Freed

Subject:

Somewhere in our galaxy, spaceship "Cosmos" is hurtling through the interstellar void with other mysterious flying objects in hot pursuit. After being surrounded and battered, the spaceship falls into enemy hands. Only one strange creature, a robot, manages to survive from this hellish encounter. Floating about through the galaxy, "Pluk", the lost shipwreck victim of outer space, heads for the nearest planet . . . Earth.

On this planet lives Niki, a clever boy with a passion for science fiction and space travel. That day, he enthusiastically explains to his girlfriend "Babette" and his trained dog "Jupiter" that he has built a spaceship to travel out in search of new planets.

At that very moment, the space-wreck victim, Pluk, turns up unexpectedly at Niki's house. Pluk, the robot from outer space, is gifted with extraordinary powers; the efficient assistance he gives his new friends enables Niki's spaceship, "Arago X 001", to travel out into space. In exchange, he asks Niki to help him find his spaceship "Cosmos".

The thrilling adventure begins. Our friends are pursued by a mysterious craft, "The Vulture", and are forced to land on the red planet. An uncanny force lures them into the phantom spaceship and they are caught inside. To save them from this diabolical trap, Jupiter risks his life, destroying once and for all the brain that controls the Vulture and it explodes.

Niki, Babette, Pluk and Jupiter barely have time to congratulate themselves on their success. No sooner have they taken off again than their spaceship engine begins to fail. The controls have stopped working and the ship is being irresistibly drawn toward an unknown sphere, the green planet.

The crew of Arago X 001 would certainly crash into it, if Niki did not bravely go out into space to adjust parachutes in order to slow their descent.

Thanks to Niki, their spaceship lands gently on the inhospitable planet. But Niki has been carried off by the wind and separated from his friends. Pluk, Babette and Jupiter start looking for him.

Meanwhile, Niki has been taken prisoner by the planet's voracious, bloodthirsty inhabitants, the "Strions". In a cave equipped as a laboratory, Niki is found and saved in the nick of time. Thanks to their cunning, they manage to escape in their spaceship. A bitter battle takes place in space, but the Arago succeeds in throwing the Strions off the scent.

The Cosmos is finally located. After contacting its crew, our friends agree to follow the Cosmos and land on "Druantearth". Suspecting a trap, Pluk orders them to turn back. Unfortunately, it is too late!

The Arago X 001 is sucked down, captured and its crew thrown into a dungeon.

All seems lost. They are tried before the Great Manitou, condemned and sentenced to undergo the laughing torture. They are freed just in time to help the "Goodruants" get rid of the "Badruants", enabling them to recover the Cosmos. Mission accomplished. The two spaceships travel together to Plukstar, Pluk's home, where they are acclaimed with fame and honour.

English title:	THE ADVENTURES OF PRINCE AHMED
Original title:	DIE ABENTEUER DES PRINZES ACHMED
Year:	1926
Country:	Germany
Running time:	65 mins.
Medium:	Animated silhouettes/black and white
Director:	Lotte Reiniger
Producer:	Comenius—Berlin (UFA)
Team:	Walter Ruttmann, Alexander Karadan, Berthold Bartosch
Music:	Wolfgang Zeller (musical score)
New hand-coloured version:	Produced by Primrose Productions, London 1954 with music by Freddie Phillips

Subject:

The story is taken from the Arabian Nights. It tells of the love of a poor tailor for a beautiful princess, and the battle between the White Spirits of the Magic Lamp and the mythical and monstrous Djinns and Afreets.

The film retains the original silent titles, but has a specially composed musical score.

English title:	TOBIAS KNOPP, ADVENTURE OF A BACHELOR
Original title:	TOBIAS KNOPP, ABENTEUER EINES JUNGGESELLEN
Year:	1950
Country:	West Germany
Running time:	100 mins.
Medium:	Animated cartoon/black and white
Director:	Gerhard Fieber
Subject:	From the cartoon strips of Wilhelm Busch
Production:	E.O.S. Filmproduktion-Wiesbaden (Berlin-Gottinger)
Screenplay:	Walter Peutzlin
Photography:	Tatjana Langus and Kurt Drews
Music:	Hans Martin Majewski
Voices:	Wolfgang Liebeneiner, René Deltgen, Harald Pailsen, Hannelore Schroth, Otto Gebuhr, Gerd Martinsen, Albert Florath, Grete Weiser, Gunter Luders

Subject:

The bachelor, Tobias Knopp, decides that it is high time his bachelorhood should finish. He goes off to visit old friends and above all his old flame.

He has a series of adventures: *A Shady Colleague; The Rustic Celebration; The Games Field; Bebbelmann; Friend Fly;* and *Happy Went*, in which he meets his wife.

This black and white film contains many graphic effects from the drawings of Wilhelm Busch.

Original title:	ADAM 2
Year:	1969
Country:	West Germany
Running time:	80 mins.
Medium:	Animated cartoon and cut-outs/colour
Director, design and animation:	Jan Lenica
Collaboration, producer:	Boris von Borresholm
Production:	Lux-Films, Munich
Photography:	Renate Ruhr
Music:	Josef Anton Riedl

Subject: (described by Jan Lenica himself)

If I were asked to summarise the subject of the work, I could say that *Adam 2* is a film about curiosity. Adam is curious. He takes it upon himself to discover the world, be it voluntarily or not.

I feel that curiosity is one of the most interesting phenomena of human nature, an instinct which might be considered absurd, since it leads to no practical result.

I could say, too, that *Adam 2* is a film about solitude. My Adam is more solitary than the first, his homonym. He does not even have a companion. Eve only appears indirectly in the film, and then just as a thing and not as a person. This reply would be just as correct as the first—and many other explanations would be possible.

But my intention was not to treat a problem. I was trying to compose a biography or, better, to draw a portrait. We must not attach too much importance to the name Adam; in my short films he was called Monsieur Tete, Janko the Musician or, as in *Labyrinthe*, remained anonymous. I lighted on this name because it is the same in all languages. This portrait is not without autobiographic elements.

Every artist who paints a portrait puts something of himself into the picture, yet it still does not become a self-portrait.

My Adam is a man like others, an "Everyman". My aim was to make the interested spectator the real hero of the film. I would like the spectator to identify himself with my protagonist, put himself in the place of my Adam and interpret his adventures in his own way. Perhaps Adam's actions and reactions are not always comprehensible at first sight, but it is only thus that they permit the necessary margin to allow for individual interpretation. I have been asked about the meaning of specific scenes, that for example, in the Land of Quadratonia, where the Square Heads have a deep repulsion towards all other head shapes. I have to emphasis my aversion for symbolism. Symbols claim always to have a meaning. I prefer ambiguity, a certain degree of inexactitude. The Land of Quadratonia is not any specific state, it could be any country.

The dictatorships here are in no way linked with a political system.

Thus my films are not apolitical but, in contrast to the living, direct manner in which Godard considers politics, have no obvious target.

English title:	THE CONFERENCE OF THE ANIMALS
Original title:	DIE KONFERENZ DER TIERE
Year:	1969
Country:	West Germany
Running time:	84 mins.
Medium:	Animated cartoon/colour
Producer:	Kurt Linda
Subject:	Taken from a children's book by Erich Kaestner
Screenplay:	Kurt Linds
Music:	Erich Fersti
Art director:	Borislav Sajtinac
Animation:	Paul Fierlinger, Vlado Kosanovic, Armin Becker, Heinrich Barta, Eva Marino, Nora Korti, Halina Weiss, Sonja Rutova
Photography:	Wolfgang Dietrich, Ivan Masnik, Barbara Linda

Subject:

Newspapers announce the breakdown of the 365th World Congress. The animals have had enough of man's warlike nature and decide to help the children by forcing man to stay at peace. The World Conference of Animals takes place in a mysterious animal tower.

The military learn of the plan and give the alarm. Mankind unites against the peace imposed by the animals. General Zornmuller appeals for a general mobilisation and surrounds the tower to cause the conference to break up. Some of the animals are disheartened, but the owl gets the insects to eat all the soldiers' uniforms and they are no longer able to fight.

All the statesmen of the world insist on all ou

war against the animals, but the animals side with the children, and overnight every child disappears from his home, to be hidden by the animals. The people are so upset by this juncture that they agree to the animals' terms and peace is established.

English title:	THE POOR MILLER'S AP-PRENTICE AND THE LITTLE CAT
Original title:	DER ARME MULLER-BURSCHE UND DAS KATZCHEN
Year:	1970
Country:	East Germany
Running time:	60 mins.
Medium:	Animated cartoon/colour (Orwo-Color)
Directors:	Helmut Barkowsky, Lothar Barke
Production:	Defa-Film, Dresden
Producer:	Bernhard Gelbe
Screenplay:	Lothar Barke, Helmut Barkowsky, based on the story by the brothers Grimm. A free adaptation
Dramatist:	Rudolf Thomas
Backgrounds:	Heinz Munster
Animation:	Lothar Barke, Sieglinde Hamacher, Will Hamacher, Manfred Lau, Herbert Kneschke, Helmut Barkowsky, Gabi Otto, Christian Biermann, Heinz Günther, Eberhard Platz, Irmgard Henker, Erika Engelmann
Photography:	Helmut Krahnert
Cut-outs:	Heidrun Sünderhauf
Music:	Gard Schlotter
Sound recordist:	Horst Philipp

Subject:

An old miller had three sons. The two older boys were lazy and quarrelsome, whilst the youngest was smiling, industrious and pleasant. While the youngest worked, the two older boys would squabble over a piece of bread and even for who would take over the mill. The old miller grew tired of this and sent his sons out into the world with the promise that the son who brought back the most beautiful horse would get the mill.

On the first night the two older sons abandoned the youngest. He was alone, apart from the company of a glow-worm. A little cat came along and promised him the most beautiful horse in the whole world if he would help the cat to accomplish three tasks. These were—to chop a great mountain of wood, to cut the grass in a very large meadow and to build a shelter for the grass and the wood. A

wicked tom-cat tried to foil the boy in his attempt, but was not able to do so.

When the three boys met again at the mill, the two older ones had only found an old hack, while the youngest rode a proud horse. His father wanted to give him the mill, but he refused, for the little cat had turned into a pretty girl and this was the best possible reward for his having kept his word.

English title:	THE STRANGE STORY OF THE INHABITANTS OF SCHILTBURG
Original title:	DIE SELTSAME HISTORIA VON DEN SCHILTBUR-GERN
Year:	1961
Country:	East Germany
Running time:	68 mins.
Medium:	Puppets/colour
Director:	Johannes Hempel
Production:	Defa-Film, Dresden
Dialogue:	Martin Remané
Music:	Wolfgang Hohensee, played by the Dresden Philharmonic Orchestra, sung by the choir of the Dresden State Opera
Cameraman:	Wolfgang Schiebel, Werner Kohlert
Puppets made by:	Gabi Otto, Heinz Ulrich Krause, Liselotte Voretazh-Linne, Beate Lose
Backgrounds:	Johannes Hempel, Walter Wallbaum
Puppet animation:	Ina Rarisch, Werner Krausse, Käte Wolf, Margitta Jänsch
Cut-outs:	Anita Mauksch
Sound recordists:	Horst Kunze, Horst Phillipp, Rolf Rölke

Subject:

The inhabitants of Schiltburg were considered by statesmen, kings and emperors the world over to be very good advisers.

But because of this they were never at home and all the work there had to be done by their wives. The wives, dissatisfied, asked their husbands to come back home.

They came back, and decided that the only way they could remain at home was to appear as foolish as possible.

They built a triangular town hall with no windows. They elected the most deranged amongst them as Burgomaster and other town officials. These officials lost control of the town. They declared that a cat was in fact a tiger, and could eat people as well as mice. In order to destroy this cat, they set fire to the town, which was destroyed. They themselves escaped to different parts of the world, very few staying in the area of Schiltburg to remind them of their foolishness.

Title:	*HANDLING SHIPS*
Year:	1946
Country:	Great Britain
Running time:	71 mins.
Medium:	Animated cartoon and puppets. (Technicolor)
Director:	John Halas
Screenplay:	Alan Crick
Photography:	John Halas and Alan Crick
Production:	Halas and Batchelor Cartoon Films Ltd. for the British Admiralty
Animation team:	John Halas, Bob Privett, Alan Crick

Subject:

The first animated instructional film to be made in Britain, this film teaches sailors various aspects of seamanship. Although produced as long ago as 1946 the film is still in use in many countries.

Title:	*WATER FOR FIREFIGHTING*
Year:	1949
Country:	Great Britain
Running time:	65 mins.
Medium:	Animated cartoon and puppets/colour
Directors:	John Halas and Bob Privett
Screenplay:	John Halas, Bob Privett and Alan Crick
Production:	Halas and Batchelor Cartoon Films Ltd. for Central Office of Information and the Home Office

Subject:

Another Halas and Batchelor instructional film, fully animated, to instruct firemen about the properties of water, its behaviour in various conditions and the techniques of fire-fighting. The film ends with a five-minute puppet section which is a resumé of the previous instruction. The final section invites questions from trainee firemen, and establishes a personal link between the film and the viewer. It is the first of many instructional films to use this technique.

Title:	*ANIMAL FARM*
Year:	1954
Country:	Great Britain
Running time:	75 mins.
Medium:	Animated cartoon/colour
Direction:	John Halas and Joy Batchelor
Production:	John Halas and Joy Batchelor for Louis de Rochemont
Music:	Matyas Seiber
Story development:	Lothar Wolff, Borden Mace, Philip Stapp, John Halas, Joy Batchelor
Voices:	Maurice Denham
Narration:	Gordon Heath
Animation direction:	John Reed
Animation:	E. Radage, A. Humberstone, R. Ayres, H. Whitaker F. Moysey
Layout:	Geoffrey Martin
Backgrounds:	Digby Turpin, Matvyn Wright, Bernard Carey
Photography:	S. G. Griffiths, J. Gurr, W. Traylor, R. Turk
Sound and effects:	Jack King
Recording:	W. Bland, G. Newberry

Subject:

The problem of transposing a literary satire to the cartoon medium was approached first of all by leaving out the minor animals and many of the subsidiary events, but giving the main protagonists of the story a high degree of individual human characterisation. The narration and dialogue had to be fairly limited to have maximum effect, so the animal noises and the music had a very important role in building on the difference and similarity between human and animal sounds in varying moods and situations, and sometimes in conveying Orwell's political asides. There is therefore in the film both a dramatic story evolving from the conflict of the characters and an element of continual comment on its meaning. Yet, because of its basically serious theme—which can be summarised in the phrase 'power corrupts'—the subtle presentation nevertheless gives the effect of severe simplicity. The result is a unique film which draws its strength from the tension between the lifelike, sometimes comic, interplay of the animals and the simple but tragic idea behind it.

Story:

Disgusted by the cruelty and drunken inefficiency of Farmer Jones, the owner of Animal Farm, the animals decide to revolt and drive him out. The revolution is carried out by Napoleon and Snowball, two highly intelligent pigs. The new regime is established and Snowball writes on the wall the five rules for animal behaviour, the greatest of which is "all animals are equal". Thwarting the

attempt of Farmer Jones and his cronies to re-
·capture the farm, the animals take charge, re-
christen it "Animal Farm", and set to work to get
in the harvest. Under their management the farm
prospers, and Snowball begins to organise the
farm's education. With the coming of winter, he
plans a windmill to generate electricity. Napoleon,
however, is against the whole idea, and finally he
summons nine enormous dogs, whom he has
secretly brought and trained, to drive out Snowball and deal with him.

Napoleon, helped by pig Squealer, and flanked by
the dogs, is now the head of Animal Farm—and
sets everyone to work on the windmill. The pigs
supervise everything, sleep in the Farmhouse, and
finally begin to trade with outsiders, swiftly sup-
pressing, with the aid of the dogs, any protest
from the other animals. The village men try again
unsuccessfully, to drive out the animals, but
Jones, bent on destruction, blows up the windmill,
so Napoleon sets the other animals to work re-
building it.

Under the pigs, the animals' lot is worse than
ever, and when they go to the barn wall to read
the commandments, only one remains: "All
Animals are Equal—but some are more equal than
others".

The pigs have by now become so like humans
that the animals realise something must be done.
Assembling quietly, they advance on the farmhouse, united, relentless—and on the wall Napoleon's portrait shatters under the impact of yet
another revolution.

Title:	IS THERE INTELLIGENT LIFE ON EARTH?
Year:	1964
Running time:	2 hours (60 mins. animation)
Country:	Great Britain
Medium:	Stage play with film, both live and cartoon in *Living Screen* format/colour
Director:	Ralph Alswang
Film director:	John Halas
Animation:	Vic Bevis
Backgrounds:	Tom Bailley
Special animation effects:	Brian Bothwick
Process:	Living Screen projected on stage

Subject:

A satire on the human condition as seen from a
Martian point of view. Three Martians (actors on
stage) arrive from the Red Planet in a flying saucer
to discover what deterioration has taken place on
Earth since they last came. After probing the
situation and asking searching questions of the
mortals whose behaviour they are witnessing,
they decide to return home as fast as possible.

An integrated mixture of special effects, animation and live action on film and stage, the presentation is basically a play with a cinerama screen for
a backdrop. The film is integrated closely with
the action of the live figures. The play and the
system were both originated and developed by
Alswang.

Title:	RUDDIGORE
Year:	1967
Running time:	55 mins.
Country:	Great Britain
Medium:	Animated cartoon (East-man color
Director:	Joy Batchelor
Production:	John Halas and Joy Batch-elor in association with the D'Oyly Carte Opera Com-pany
Animation:	Harold Whitaker, Tony Guy, Tony Whitehouse
Backgrounds:	Ted Pettingell
Design:	John Cooper
Voices:	John Reed, Ann Hood, David Palmer, Peggy Ann Jones, Kenneth Sandford, Donald Adams, Gillian Knight, George Cook, Jen-nifer Toye and the chorus of the D'Oyly Carte Opera Company
Music:	The Royal Philharmonic Orchestra directed by James Walker
Sound:	Jack King
Distribution:	Halas and Batchelor Dis-tribution

Subject:

Adapted from the opera by Gilbert and Sullivan.

Story:

The hobby of a bold Baronet of Ruddigore, the
first of his line, was to persecute witches. But one
of his victims, while being burnt at the stake, lays
a terrible curse on him: that he and all his line
must commit at least one deadly crime every day or
perish in agony.

In dread of this curse, young Ruthven Murga-
troyd flies from his ancestral home to live the
simple life of a young farmer in the village of
Rederring under the name of Robin Oakapple. His
younger brother Despard, believing him to be
dead, succeeds to the title and the curse. Robin
is too modest to declare his love for Rose Maybud,
and enlists the services of his foster brother,
Richard Dauntless, who promises to plead his
cause with Rose. But Richard falls in love with

Rose himself, proposes on his own account, and is accepted.

When Rose learns of the true state of affairs she tranfers her affections to the shy Robin. Richard thereupon reveals the true identity of Robin who now has to assume his family's title with the attendant curse. Sir Despard, now free, returns to Mad Margaret whose brain has been turned by his previous heartless conduct. Rose, in horror at the curse, bestows her affections once again on Richard.

With little interest in his title, Robin fails to observe the curse to the satisfaction of his ancestors, who come to life by stepping out of their picture frames. Dissatisfied with his crime sheet, they bid him carry off a lady or die in inconceivable agony. Old Adam, the family servant, is entrusted with the task and returns with a maiden who proves to be Old Hannah, the one-time love of the defunct Sir Roderick, who steps down from his picture frame once more to denounce Robin. But Robin is struck with a brilliant idea, and proves that a Baronet can only die by refusing to commit a crime, so consequently such a refusal is tantamount to suicide. Since suicide is itself a crime his ancestors ought never to have died, so they are all alive.

Title:	YELLOW SUBMARINE
Year:	1967
Country:	Great Britain
Running time:	88 mins.
Medium:	Animated cartoon/colour
Director:	George Dunning
Production:	Al Brodax
Production co-ordinator:	Abe Goodman
Designed by:	Heinz Edelmann
Musical director:	George Martin
Unit directors:	Bob Balser, Jack Stokes
Associate producer:	Mary Ellen Stewart
Special effects:	Charles Jenkins
Original story by:	Lee Minoff, based on the song by John Lennon and Paul McCartney
Screenplay:	Lee Minoff, Al Brodax, Jack Mendelsohn, Erich Segal

Subject:

"Once upon a time . . . or maybe twice . . . there was a place called Pepperland". On a peaceful day in this happy kingdom, a concert by Sergeant Pepper's Lonely Hearts Club Band is interrupted by an antimusic missile attack from the Blue Meanies. The chief Blue Meanie, his assistant Max, and their 99 numbered henchmen turn their splotch guns on the docile Pepperland populace, determined to rid the world of music, happiness and love. ("A World without music is a Blue World!").

Old Fred, the conductor of the Band, flees to the old Lord Mayor, who puts him into the Yellow Submarine for a last minute escape. The sub surfaces in Liverpool where Ringo wanders aimlessly in boredom. The sub, radar-like, follows Ringo to his house. Fred enters Ringo's house, explains the situation and enlists his aid. They proceed to round up the others. John materialises out of a Frankenstein-like figure, Paul, playing classical type music and George who appears out of a haze of transcendental meditation.

Armed with a battery of puns and four new songs, the Beatles board the Yellow Sub and head for Pepperland. They are detoured through the Seas of Time, Science, Monsters, Consumer Products, Nowhere, Phrenology, Green and Holes.

They undergo time warps, chase Lucy through her "sky with diamonds"; climb rocks and soup cans; become ancient and infantile, molecularised, actually "disappear up their existences", and almost drown in an avalanche of apples, among other adventures.

Characters they encounter on their mad *Trip* include the U.S. Cavalry, Father McKenzie, assorted monsters, including a Vacuum Flask monster, cowboys, Indians, King Kong and several unidentifiable things. Ringo takes a liking to the super-intellectual Boob, ("a poetic personification of nowhere man, Man") and takes him along on the trip. In the sea of green he is captured by a giant blue hand.

A pepper-powered sneeze propels the Beatles through the sea of Holes into occupied Pepperland which has almost completely been drained of colour. The Lord Mayor is astonished at the resemblance between the Beatles and the original Sergeant Pepper Band. Disguised as an Apple Bonker, they infiltrate the musical instrument compound. Then it's Beatles versus Meanies with guitars against splotch guns; the Ferocious Flying Glove, the Butterfly stompers; the Hidden Persuaders with guns in their shoes; the Snapping Turtle Turks with their mouths in their bellies; and the Countdown Clown with his nose-cone nose. A battle is waged to the tune of *All You Need Is Love* and love becomes the overwhelming power. A surprise ending carries the fantastic fracas right into the theatre.

Title:	THE GLORIOUS MUSKETEERS (THE THREE MUSKETEERS)
Year:	1974
Country:	Great Britain/Italy
Running time:	70 mins.
Medium:	Animated cartoon/colour
Director:	John Halas

Associate Director:	Franco Cristofani
Producers:	Patrick Wachsberger, Stephen Pallos
Production:	Pendennis Films, London, Michelangelo Studios, Rome
Animation:	Brian Larkin, Ian Emes, Bob Balser, Niso Ramponi, M. Michelini'
Music:	Michel Polnareff
Storyboard:	Paulo di Girolama
Screenplay:	Howard Clewes
Editing:	Mike Crouch
Voices:	John Fortune, Maurice Denham, Peter Bull, Roy Kinnear, Peter Hawkins, Adrienne Corri, Madeline Smith, Joyce Windsor

Subject:

Based on Alexander Dumas' story "The Three Musketeers" the film follows the well-known adventures of d'Artagnan, a young man from the country, until he becomes the fourth member of the King's guard. The story is told with a sense of adventure, pace and humour.

Title:	DICK DEADEYE
Year:	1975
Country:	Great Britain/U.S.A.
Running time:	75 mins. (approx)
Medium:	Animated cartoon/colour
Director:	Steve and Bill Melendez
Producer:	Bill Melendez
Animation team:	Dick Horn, Mike Hibbert, Doug Jensen, Ron Coulter, Peter Sacks, Annie O'Dell, Don MacKinnon.
Music:	Based on Gilbert and Sullivan by Jimmy Horowitz
Screenplay:	Leo Rost and Robin Miller
Voices:	John Baldry, Barry Cryer, George A. Cooper, Francis Ghent, Miriam Karlin, Linda Lewis, Peter Reeves, Liza Strike, Victor Spinetti
Design:	Ronald Searle

Subject:

A musical feature "Dick Deadeye" based on many of the characters and songs from Gilbert and Sullivan operas. Ronald Searle has designed the characters and backgrounds giving an individual and up-to-date style to this subject.

English title:	TRILOGY
Original title:	TRILOGIA
Year:	1969/1971
Country:	Hungary
Running time:	70 mins.
Medium:	Animated cut-outs and cartoon
Director:	Felix Bodrossy
Photography:	Felix Bodrossy
Production:	Mafilm Studios, Budapest
Distribution:	Hungarofilm, Budapest

Subject:

This film consists of three parts, which are each introduced by Hungarian experts on Ancient Greece, and revive the Homeric epics through animated classical vase decorations. The three parts are entitled: The Gods of Hellas, The Trojan War, Odysseus.

English title:	HUGO THE HIPPO
Hungarian title:	HUGO THE HIPPO
Year:	1973
Country:	Hungary/USA
Running time:	95 mins.
Medium:	Animated cartoon/colour
Director:	Bill Feigenbaum
Designer:	Graham Percy
Animation director:	Gémes József
Photography:	Istvan Harsögi
Production:	Pannonia Filmstudio—Budapest for Brut Production U.S.A.
Distribution:	Brut Productions, U.S.A.

Subject:

The film is a two-part adventure story for children based on a legend which surrounds a hippopotamus named Hugo actually living in East Africa today.

The first portion of the story is set on the Island of Zanzibar, and tells how a group of hippos, including the baby Hugo, were brought to the Island from the mainland to rid the coastal waters of a dangerous group of sharks, and tells how these hippos, with the exception of Hugo, were unmercifully slaughtered when they were no longer useful.

The latter part of the film portrays Hugo's miraculous escape back to the mainland of Africa, his friendship with the children of Dar-es-Salaam, his discovery by the farmers and authorities when he must forage for food in order to survive, and his ultimate trial and victory.

English title:	JOHN THE HERO	Direction, Photography,	
Original title:	JÁNOS VITÉZ	Animation:	Alina and Yoram Gross
Year:	1973	Screenplay:	Natan Gross
Country:	Hungary	Music:	Eddi Halpern
Running time:	80 mins.	Puppets:	John Byle
Medium:	Animated cartoon/colour	Puppets and	Leslia Amit, John Burning-
Director:	Marcell Jankovics	costumes:	ham, Roda Reilinger, Veron-
Animation:	Marcell Jankovics, Josef Nepp, Bella Ternovszky		ica Gross
		French narrator:	Marc Hillel
Production:	Pannonia Studio, Budapest	Dialogue read by:	A. Guevitz, S. Bar Shavit, A.
Design and			Gurlitzki, S. Atzmon, S.
backgrounds:	Zsolt Richly		Friedman, S. Ravid, I. Rud-
Screenplay:	Based on Sándor Petöfi original: Tamas Szabo-Sipos, Péter Szoboszlay and Zsolt Richly		nicki, A. Ronai, O. Teomi
		Editing:	Helga Cranston
		Sound recording:	D. Bein, A. Roberman
		Production company:	Yorma Gross Films Ltd.
Music:	Janos Gyulai-Gaál		

Subject:

The film version of "Childe John" by Sándor Petöfi was prepared for the 150th anniversary of Petöfi's birth. The Pannonia Film Studio in Budapest undertook the assignment to revive this classic epic as a full length animated film, which is the first in Hungary.

The story utilizes the international figures and occurrences of folk tales, but everything originates in the Hungarian reality and extends to "Fairy land". The story starts with the pastoral scene of Jancsi the orphan shepherd boy, and Iluska—who suffers from her vicious foster mother, then with their farewell, and the escape of Jancsi. The young man starts out to try his luck and returns as Childe John. He carried out heroic deeds, he lived through fantastic adventures, mainly as one of the Hungarian hussars who went to help the French King. The French king named him Childe John. He saves the kidnapped princess, and he only needs to extend his hand—the princess would be his together with the throne, but Childe John is faithful to his Iluska, and starts home with a sack of gold. At home, the news about his sweetheart's death awaits him: the vile foster mother drove the helpless orphan into her grave. Childe John leaves again—in search of death. He reaches the land of the giants, then he takes revenge on the foster mother of Iluska in the Night Empire of the witches. A giant crosses the ocean and takes him to the Isle of the Fairies where he defeats the gate-keeping dragon, and finds his Iluska—the Queen of the Fairies.

English title:	JOSEPH SOLD BY HIS BROTHERS
Year:	1961
Country:	Israel
Running time:	80 mins.
Medium:	Puppets/colour

Subject:

Adapted from the biblical story. Joseph goes to see how his brothers are faring while grazing their flocks, and is attacked by them. He is sold and taken to Egypt.

Joseph becomes the slave of Potiphar, captain of Pharaoh's guard. He finds favour with him and becomes Potiphar's overseer. But when Joseph resists the advances of Potiphar's wife she accuses him of trying to seduce her and he is thrown into prison.

Pharaoh's butler and baker are also in prison, and Joseph interprets their dreams to mean that the butler will be restored to favour but that the baker will be hanged.

So it turns out, and two years later, when Pharaoh has a dream that nobody can interpret, the butler sends for Joseph.

Joseph interprets the dream to mean that there will be seven years of plenty followed by seven lean years.

When the lean time arrives, Joseph's brothers come to Egypt to buy corn, all except the youngest brother, Benjamin, who is their father Jacob's favourite. Joseph accuses his brothers of being spies, and keeping one brother as hostage demands that Benjamin be brought to him. His brothers do not recognise Joseph, and when Benjamin comes to Egypt he fails to recognise him.

Joseph plants a silver cup in Benjamin's sack, then has him imprisoned as a thief. Jacob is heartbroken, and Judah, Joseph's elder brother, pleads to be made Joseph's bondslave so that Benjamin can be released and his father will not die of sorrow.

At this point Joseph reveals his identity, and Jacob and all the brothers come to Egypt to live in luxury.

English title:	THE WAR AND THE DREAM OF MOMI	Screenplay:	Ernesto d'Angelo, L. de Carlo
Original title:	LA GUERRA E IL SOGNO DI MOMI	Original story:	A. & G. Domeneghini
Year:	1916	Photography:	Cesare Pellizzari
Country:	Italy	Technical direction:	Guilio Bologna
Running time:	70 mins.	Artistic adviser:	Libico Karaja
Medium:	Puppets and live action/ black and white	Characters:	Boletti
Director:	Giovanni Pastrone	Music:	Pick Mangiagalli
Screenplay:	Giovanni Pastrone, Segundo de Chomon	Editing:	Lucio de Carlo
Photography:	Segundo de Chomon	Director of animation:	Gildo Gusmaroli
Production:	Itala-Film	Animation:	Angello Bioletto, Italo Orsi, Giorgio Sudellari, Gustavo Petronio, Omer Valenti, Nino Ferencic, Guido Zamperoni, Nando Corbella, Gigi Togliatto, Francesco Ferrari, Carla Ruffinelli, Nino Palazzo, Gian Franco Barenghi

English title:	THE ADVENTURES OF PINOCCHIO
Original title:	LES ADVENTURE DI PINOCCHIO
Year:	1936
Country:	Italy
Running time:	60 mins.
Medium:	Animated cartoon/black and white
Director:	Raoul Verdini
Screenplay:	Adapted by Carlo Lorenzini from the story by Carlo Collodi
Design:	Raoul Verdini
Photography:	Carlo Bachini
Backgrounds:	Gioachino Colizzi (Attalo)
Animation:	Ennio Zedda, Amerigo Tot, Milani, Cipolloni, Bellata
Production:	Gartoni Animati Italiani Roma (CAIR)
Note:	Some sources quote Umberto Spano as the director. The colour version planned for 1940 was never completed

Subject:

The wicked Caliph Giaffar, helped by his counsellor the magician, Buck, wants to take Bagdad, after having by a trick married the pretty Princess Zella, niece of the Caliph Oman. The young flute player, Amin, has a secret love for Zeila. Giaffar's plan is on the point of success when Amin, with the help of Aladdin's lamp, manages to save Zeila. Giaffar and Buck, defeated, throw themselves into the river, and in the midst of general celebration, Amin marries Zeila, and will one day be ruler of Bagdad.

Subject:

The original story of Pinocchio faithfully adapted from Carlo Collodi's children's tale.

English title:	THE ROSE OF BAGDAD
Original title:	LA ROSA DI BAGDAD
Year:	1948
Country:	Italy
Running time:	72 mins.
Medium:	Animated cartoon/colour (Agfacolor)
Director:	Antonio Gino Domeneghini
Production:	Ima-Film

English title:	THE DYNAMITE BROTHERS
Original title:	I FRATELLI DINAMITE
Year:	1948
Country:	Italy
Running time:	75 mins.
Medium:	Animated cartoon/colour (Technicolor)
Directors:	Toni and Nino Pagot
Designer:	Ferdinando Palermo
Backgrounds:	Franco Cagnoli
Animation:	Gualtiero Boffini, Ugo Heinze
Technical direction:	Paolo Gaudenzi
Production:	Pagot

Subject:

The Dynamite brothers, Din, Don and Dan are the sons of a captain engaged in the smuggling of spirits. Whilst they navigate with their father, near the Pasqualino islands, they are caught by a big storm and thrown onto an island inhabited by animals which have never encountered human beings before. They are raised by these animals in a strange atmosphere of freedom, in a world not yet contaminated by the presence of men. After many vicissitudes they are freed by an old aunt and brought home. At home, because of their habits, they get up to all sorts of tricks. Finally they go to Venice and during a competition they are elected "doges" of the carnival, that is, leaders of the celebrations. Whilst they dance and enjoy themselves they see a little girl crying bitterly; she has lost her doll in the lagoon. How can they amuse themselves when someone is suffering? This is, in fact, one of the moral teachings of the picture produced with a great sense of humour and freshness of invention. The three Dinamites are the leaders of the carnival; they order that the festivities be interrupted until the doll is found. The crowd rebels and wants to lynch the three brothers, but they dive into the water, find the doll and return it to the crying girl who smiles happily. In spite of the difficulties, the three Dinamites, these gay and determined heroes, have been successful; they have brought back the smile to the little girl's face. And Din, Don and Dan go home satisfied.

English title:	THE SPADES
Original title:	I PICCHIATELLI (They're Crazy)
Year:	1958
Medium:	Animated cartoon/live/ puppets (Ferraniacolour)
Director:	Antoni Attanasi
Animation:	Carlo Bachini, Gianni Giacometos, Gaudi Correti, Niso Ramponi, Ermanno Prastolo, Tito Scappini
Producer:	Antonio Attanasi
Music:	Luigi Malatesta
Production:	Alfa Beta films

Subject:

Two children accidentally enter an animation studio. They find the filmmakers photographing animated cartoon characters.

Animated puppets are also used in this extraordinary film, which took four years to make and 53,000 cels.

Original title:	WEST AND SODA
Year:	1965
Country:	Italy
Running time:	91 mins.
Medium:	Animated cartoon/colour (Eastmancolor)
Direction and screenplay:	Bruno Bozzetto
Collaboration on direction and screenplay:	Attilio Giovannini
Director of animation:	Guido Manuli
Art director and scenography:	Giovanni Mulazzani
Animation:	Guiseppe Lagana, Franco Martelli
Sound effects:	Vittorio Pazzaglia
Music:	Giampero Boneschi

Subject:

A legendary tale, an enticing film in the latest style and technique.

For a long time the Far West has been a legendary and fabulous subject: all its customs, the popular characteristics, good triumphing over evil, the brawls in the 'Saloon', duels to the last drop of blood and the chases on horseback are presented in this amusing film in a satirical, spectacular manner.

West and Soda presents in a new light those characteristics which are already part of our experience as expert spectators: Clementina, the plucky cowgirl who lives on the only fertile field in the valley, the Super Bad Man, a rich land-owner, who aims at possessing Clementina and her ranch; Ursus and Slim, the two sharp-shooters, always ready to oblige with their fists and bullets; Johnny, the good and generous cowboy who is slow to use weapons and violence unless he is forced to do so by his enemies; Esmeralda the charmer of the saloon, ready to give her favours to order; Katy, Ebe and Dolly, Clementina's three gossiping cows; and Socrates, Clementina's endearing mongrel dog, who is always drunk.

English title:	FILLIPO THE CAT
Original title:	GATTO FILIPPO: LICENZA DI INCIDERE
Year:	1965
Country:	Italy
Running time:	65 mins.
Medium:	Animated cartoon, cut-outs and puppets and live action, colour (Eastmancolor)
Director:	Pino Zac (Pino Zaccaria)
Artistic collaboration:	Francesco Maria Guido (Gibba), Nino Conti
Photography:	Carlo Ventimiglia
Music:	Roberto Nicolosi
Live action sequences:	
Director:	Daniele d'Anza
Photography:	Marco Scarpelli
Production:	Telecinema 21—Studio DV3

Subject:

A cat, Gatto Filippo, feels alienated by all the inhabitants of the town. He consults a specialist about this, and he tells the psychoanalyst about his obsessions.

English title:	THE SUPER-VIPS
Original title:	VIP — MIO FRATELLO SUPERUOMO
Year:	1968
Country:	Italy
Running time:	
Medium:	Animated cartoon/colour (Eastmancolor)
Direction and production:	Bruno Bozzetto
Subject by:	Bruno Bozzetto
Head of design and animation:	Guido Manuli
Animation:	Franco Martolli, Giuseppe Lagana, Roberto Vitali
Art director and scenography:	Giovanni Mulazzani
Screenplay:	Bruno Bozzetto, Atillio Giovannini, Guido Manuli
Special collaboration:	Stearn Robinson
Special effects and editing:	Luciano Marzetti
Sound effects and editing:	Giancarlo Rossi
Music composed and directed:	Franco Godi

Subject:

VIPS are a special breed of supermen whose glorious origin goes back to prehistoric times. Its present descendants are two brothers: Supervip, who is a prime specimen of the family tradition and Minivip who, due to a genetic trick of nature, is small, myopic, and has limited powers. These limitations give Minivip an inferiority complex.

Supervip, being very fond of his brother, is concerned about his depressed condition and takes him to consult a group of psychiatrists. They suggest that a relaxing trip would be helpful in warding off neurosis, and Supervip persuades Minivip to embark on a cruise.

As things develop, the cruise turns out to be anything but relaxing. Minivip falls overboard and finds himself adrift at sea on a raft with a strange lion. They finally land on the beach of a lovely island. However, they quickly discover that what appeared to be an uninhabited tropical paradise is, in fact, the secret site of an atomic stronghold created by a warped female tycoon named Happy Betty.

She is developing a project by which she hopes to get an economic clutch on the world. The project involves the use of a stolen scientific discovery for implanting brain-missiles.

Minivip and his lion friend, now revealed as Lisa, a young lady cruise passenger in masquerade costume, are just getting into desperate difficulties on the island when Supervip arrives and rescues his brother. Supervip later locates Lisa who has been locked in the stronghold tower, and falls in love with her.

Meanwhile, Minivip, searching the dungeons, finds Nervustrata, a small gentle girl, who has been used as a guinea-pig in Happy Betty's experiments.

At this moment Supervip, momentarily off his guard and confused by love, is captured, together with Lisa and Nervustrata, by Happy Betty's henchmen, while Minivip is taken captive by Happy Betty herself and destined to be used in the final experiment preceding the launching of the brain missiles on the world.

In a last minute heroic effort Minivip manages to free himself and his brother and together they succeed In turning the destructive weapon against its makers.

Having again upheld their family tradition of protecting humanity against aggression, the two famous brothers carry tradition further by marrying the girls they rescued during their fantastic adventure.

English title:	THE NON-EXISTENT KNIGHT
Original title:	IL CAVALIERE INESISTENTE
Year:	1969
Country:	Italy
Medium:	Live action with animated cartoon and object animation/colour (Eastmancolor)
Director:	Pino Zac
Production:	Istituto Luce
Screenplay:	Tommaso Chiaretti, Pino Zac, based on the novel by Italo Calvino.
Design:	Emanuelle Piccirilli
Animation:	Vincenzo Castrovillari
Animated shots:	Jindrich Hrdina
Special effects:	Jiri Simunek
Actors (live):	Hana Ruziokova, Stefano Oppedisano, Evelina Verhigli-Gori.
Music:	Sergio Battistelli

Subject:

The story takes place in the time of Charlemagne, in the setting of constantly warring armies. Among

Charlemagne's faithful knights, Agilolfe is of special merit. He never takes off his armour, never sleeps and carries out faultlessly all the duties of a knight-errant; in actual fact he is an empty suit of armour.

During a banquet at which Charlemagne presides, another Knight suggests that a lady whom Agilolfe had saved was not noble. Since this exploit had given him the status of a holy knight, Agilolfe undertakes to prove the falseness of the allegation. He sets off, accompanied by a strange squire, who becomes one with everything he touches, and followed at a distance by the heroine Bradamante, who is in love with him, and by Torrismund, a knight who believes himself to be the brother of the 'fair damsel' our hero has saved. Agilolfe comes through a host of difficulties and among other things frees a widow who was being besieged in her castle by bears.

He eventually finds the lady, now the prisoner of a sultan. He frees her and takes her away. By a grotto, in the presence of Charlemagne, the truth is at last revealed: the girl is in fact a princess, and Torrismund is free to love her. for she is not his sister. Meanwhile Agilolfe has left. Rambaud, a knight who deeply admires him, searches for him. But alas, in the wood he finds only scattered pieces of armour.

English title:	PUTIFERIO GOES TO WAR
Original title:	PUTIFERIO VA ALLA GUERRA
Year:	1968
Running time:	80 mins.
Country:	Italy
Medium:	Animated cartoon/colour (Eastmancolor)
Director:	Roberto Gavioli
Producer:	Bruno Paolinelli, for Saba Cinematografica, Rizzoli-Film—Gamma-Film
Screenplay:	Luciano Doddoli, Bruno Paolinelli, based on "La guerriera nera", by Mario Piereghin
Technical director:	Nino Piffarerio
Art director:	Gino Gavioli
Backgrounds:	Adelchi, Galloni, Paolo Albicocco, Franco Paolucci
Music:	Beppe Moraschi
Editing:	Vittorio Sedini
General organisation:	Renato Casini
Distribution:	Cineriz

Subject:

The little owls are setting off, from all corners of the world, to visit their grandfather, Puti-Puti,

who has, though they do not know this, been put in prison for four years in the Calm Valley, for vandalism while drunk. The old owl is ashamed to let his young relatives know that he is in prisgn, so his neighbours hide his prison uniform and tidy up his house. The young owls notice nothing. Puti-Puti tells them of an incident which recently happened in the Calm Valley—the war between the red ants and the yellow ants during the time when they were bringing up their young ones.

The red ants attack the home of the yellow ants while Putiferio is on guard alone. This ant goes off to get help from the neighbouring ants in the mill.

An army is formed and war is declared on the red ants. They set off to attack, while Putifero is carried up into the sky in a bubble of soap She is thought to be dead, but is saved by a patrol of dragon-flies, who take her to Puti-Puti's tree. The two armies are about to engage in battle and it looks as if there will be a great deal of bloodshed. But while all this is going on an ant-eater arrives, destroying everything in its way. The two armies, terrified, take flight, and hide in the roots of trees. Nevertheless, the ant-eater claims a large number of victims. Putiferio and Trin-Trni, the leader of the red ants, miraculously, hand in hand, escape death.

At last the ant-eater goes off. There is no more thought of war, for everything is to be rebuilt and the hands . . . sorry, legs of all the ants will be needed. Time passes, and we see the marriage of Trin-Trin and Putiferio. They go off on their honeymoon amidst the congratulations of ants of all races and all colours.

Original title:	PINOCHIO
Year:	1972
Country:	Italy
Running time:	80 mins. (approx.)
Medium:	Animated cartoon/colour
Director:	Giuliano Cenci
Screenplay:	Giuliano Cenci, based on Carlo Collodi
Advice on the adaptation:	Dr. Mario Lorenzini, nephew of the author
Scenegraphy:	Alberto d'Angelo, Abramo Scortecci
Photography:	Renzo Cenci
Editing:	Giuliano Cenci
Animation:	Giuseppe Conti, Valeria Pronti, Mario Magherini, Roberto Campani, Ferdanda Giomi, Pratrizia Gatto
Production:	Cartoons Cinematografica Italiana, Florence
Colour styling:	Albertina Rainieri, Fiorenza Magherini

Subject:

Another adaptation from the original story by Carlo Collodi.

English title:	A WORLD TOUR MADE BY PEYNET'S "LOVERS"
Original title:	IL GIRO DEL MONDO DEGLI INNAMORATI DI PEYNET
Year:	1974
Country:	Italy/France
Running time:	82 mins.
Medium:	Animated cartoon/colour
Director:	Cesare Perfetto
Screenplay:	Melgari, Paolinelli, Perfetto
Producer:	Bruno Paolinelli for N.O.C.
Original Design:	Raymond Peynet
Animation:	Manfredo Manfredi
Music:	Ennio Morricone

Subject:

This animated cartoon is inspired by the characters of Raymond Peynet's "Les amoureux" and they are identified by him with the youth of today which refuses to accept modern society and looks at it critically instead.

The story of the film, which is naturally in a critical-humoristic key, starts with the "lovers" flight from this world to take refuge in a dream which takes them to visit the main cities and countries in the world.

Each country is seen in a joyous light, in its most characteristic aspect, both with regard to its countryside and its monuments, adapting Peynet's style of drawing to the place, or vice versa. For instance, the Flemish countryside is seen in interpretations as if by Brueghel, or Rembrandt.

Each nation has its characters, its facts, which mainly identify it and characterise it: these people and these facts give the most pleasant and humorous inspirations for the adventures of the "lovers".

The journey ends in Paris, with a great display of lovers who invoke a new life, more peaceful, and happier, under the banner of love.

English title:	THE GOLD MARIA
Original title:	MARIA D'ORO
Year:	1975
Country:	Italy/Germany
Running time:	90 mins.
Medium:	Animated cartoon/colour
Director:	Roberto Gavioli
Screenplay:	Rolf Kauka/Gavioli
Producer:	Rolf Kauka, Germany and Gamma-Studio, Italy
Music:	Peter Thomas

Subject:

Musical fairytale for children with the adventures of a little blue dog "Bello Blue".

English title:	THE WHITE SNAKE ENCHANTRESS
Original title:	HAKUJA DEN
Year:	1958
Country:	Japan
Running time:	78 mins.
Medium:	Animated cartoon/colour (Eastmancolor)
Director:	Taiji Yabushita
Production:	Toei Animation Studio— Toei Motion Pictures Co. Ltd.
Screenplay:	Taiji Yabushita
Executive producer:	Hiroshi Okawa
Associate producers:	Koichi Akagawi, Sanae Yamamoto, Hideyuki Takahashi
Art directors:	Kazuhiko Okabe, Kiyoshi Hashimoto
Original drawings by:	Akira Daikubara, Yasuj Mori
Animators:	Yasuo Otsuka, Yusaku Sakamoto
Backgrounds:	Kazuo Kusano
Music:	Chuji Kinoshita
Photography:	Kokichi Tsukahara
Sound recording:	Takeshi Mori
Editing:	Shintaro Miyamoto
Dialogue:	Seiichi Yashiro

Subject:

Based on an old Chinese legend, this was the first Japanese full-length animated film.

A boy named Hsu Hsien finds a white snake, of which he soon becomes very fond. His parents force him to abandon it. One day Hsu Hsien meets a beautiful young girl, Pai Ning and they fall deeply in love. To the boy's surprise, the girl is the incarnation of the white snake he had abandoned.

A Wizard named Fa Hai attempts to harm the young lovers, but is thwarted by their devoted companions, a panda and a cat. Fa Hai, summoning all his magic power, creates a terrible storm at sea in a final attempt to subdue them. With the lives of the young people in his power, the wizard, moved by the beauty and the purity of their love, finally spares them.

English title:	THE ADVENTURES OF LITTLE SAMURAI (MAGIC BOY)
Original title:	SHONEN SARUTOBI SA-SUKE
Year:	1959
Country:	Japan
Running time:	83 mins.
Medium:	Animated cartoon/colour (Magicolor)
Director:	Taiji Yabushita
Production:	Toei Animation Studio

Subject:

In the mountainous part of Japan, existence is peaceful for a little boy called Saski and his elder sister, Ogu. But when Saski is playing one day with his friends, the forest animals, a huge eagle starts hovering above them. It is the sinister companion of Yaksha, the sorcerer-princess. The eagle swoops down and lifts Trinkle, a little faun, in his terrible talons. Reaching a mountain lake, the eagle drops the faun into the jaws of a giant sea monster. Sashi tries to save Trinkle, but the faun's mother is eaten while Trinkle escapes.

Sashi decides to go and see Hakunnsai, the wise old man of the mountain, the most learned magician in the world. The boy tells him his troubles, and over several years learns magic so that he can defeat Yaksha.

A band of Yaksha's bandits are pillaging the countryside. The prince and the villagers chase them, and Oyu tells the prince of her brother's plan. Saski is now a fully fledged magician, and has an occult battle with Yakshi while the prince fights the brigands.

Both Saski and the prince win their battles and peace returns to the country.

English title:	THE ENCHANTED MONKEY or ALKAZAM THE GREAT
Original title:	SAIYU-KI
Year:	1960
Country:	Japan
Running time:	88 mins.
Medium:	Animated cartoon/colour (Eastmancolor) Toeiscope
Directors:	Taiji Yabushita, Osamu Tezuka
Production:	Toei Animation Studio
Screenplay:	Keinosuke Uekusa
Original drawings:	Yasuji Mori, Akira Daikubara
Photography:	Seigo Otsuka
Music:	Les Baxter

Subject:

When the earth was born there was a strange shaped rock in the country of Gorai. One day this rock is torn apart, with a tremendous flash, and a silver egg emerges, from which emerges a silver monkey.

Isolated from his fellows, the monkey falls in love with a beautiful girl, but later becomes king of the monkeys and becomes known by the name of Goku. Found guilty by the Buddha for practising magic, Goku is sentenced to be trapped in a mountain wilderness for five hundred years, but is released by a priest who is seeking some rare Buddhist sutras.

Goku joins him, but on their journey they are attacked by a monster who is also a magician. Goku overcomes this enemy, and now forgiven by Buddha, returns to his loved ones. The priest succeeds in his mission.

English title:	THE ORPHAN BROTHER
Original title:	ANJU TO ZUSHIO-MARU
Year:	1961
Country:	Japan
Running time:	83 mins.
Medium:	Animated drawing/colour (Eastmancolor) Toeiscope
Director:	Taiji Yabushita
Production:	Toei Animation Studio
Screenplay:	Sumie Tanaka
Original drawings by:	Akiri Daikubara & Yasuji Mori
Producer:	Isamu Takahashi
Photography:	Shinkichi Otsuka
Voices:	Yoshiko Sakuma, Kinya Kitaoji

Subject:

Anju, a lovely young girl, and Zushio, her younger brother, are separated from their father when he is imprisoned for a crime he did not commit. The sister and brother are also compelled to part from their mother, who is cheated by a slave-dealer, and sold to Dayu, the chieftain of a powerful clan. Dayu has two sons, the elder cruel, the younger gentle. The gentle brother takes pity on them and he allows Zushio to escape, Anju is cruelly beaten by Dayu and the elder son. She tries to escape, but is cornered and drowns herself in a pond.

Zushio goes to Kyoto to search for his parents, and learns of his father's death. Encouraged by a samurai he works hard at his sword and pen, grows up to be a fine young samurai and is nominated to be governor of his native country. He subjugates Dayu and his men, and frees all the slaves. The story ends when he meets his aged mother who has become blind.

English title:	THE LIFE OF BUDDHA
Original title:	SHAKA NO SHOGAI
Year:	1961
Country:	Japan
Running time:	70 mins.
Medium:	Animated silhouettes/black and white
Director:	Nobuo Ofuji
Production:	Sanko Studio Co. Ltd.

Subject:

This silhouette film depicts the life of Buddha, incorporating various episodes—for example, his leaving the palace, ascetic exercises in remote mountains, temptations of the Devil, Nirvana and the miracles he performed.

The late Nobuo Ofuji made a dozen silhouette films, among which are such fine works as *Phantom Ship, Whale* and *Legend of the Dragon.*

English title:	ADVENTURES OF SINBAD
Original title:	SHINDBAD NO BADEN
Year:	1962
Country:	Japan
Running time:	81 mins.
Medium:	Animated cartoon/colour (Eastmancolor) Toeiscope
Director:	Taiji Yabushita
Production:	Toei Animation Studio
Screenplay:	Osamu Tezuka, Morio Kita
Animation:	Hideo Furusawa; Akira Daikubara; Yasuo Otsuka

Subject:

Sinbad succumbing to the call of the sea, with his friend Ali, sneaks aboard a ship named the *Golda.* Once discovered, the boys are permitted to join the crew and make friends with two sailors, Abdul and Yassim.

After a long voyage the *Golda* enters the port of Bahrain, and the boys set out in search of amusement. Sinbad is so high-spirited and mischievous that he and his friends are brought before the king and thrown into jail. Ali flees into the room of the young princess Sameel who has been longing for freedom. She takes pity on the boys, sets them free and runs away with them. A minister, Sameel's husband-to-be, commands his soldiers to pursue them. But the young fugitives board the *Golda,* which sets sail for Treasure Island just in the nick of time.

After surmounting many obstacles, including storms, attacks from monsters sent by the minister and a chance encounter with a frightening ghost ship, they reach the island, but are prevented from landing by the appearance of more monsters. In the confusion, Sinbad is separated from his companions. In the meantime, the minister and his soldiers reach the island in a warship. A battle takes place and the minister and his men are defeated. Sinbad finally rejoins Ali, Sameel and the rest of his companions and they discover fabulous treasure in a secret cavern. But the princess Sameel has no desire for riches and reveals her love for young Sinbad.

English title:	A STORY ON A STREET CORNER
Original title:	ARU MACHIKADO NO MONOGATARI
Year:	1962
Country:	Japan
Medium:	Animated cartoon/colour
Producer:	Osamu Tezuka
Planning and organisation:	Osamu Tezuka
Directors:	Eichi Yamamoto, Yusaku Sekamoto
Art director:	Toru Arai
Production:	Mushi Film
Music:	Tatsuo Takai
Original drawings by:	Syuji Konno, Gisaburo Sugii
Animation:	Yurio Sakurai, Shigeru Yamamoto
Backgrounds:	Katzuyuki Hirokaya, Noriyuki Sakura
Special effects:	Yukio Nogi

Subject:

It is an autumn afternoon, the place is a street corner where recently demolished houses face skyscrapers under construction.

A balloon seller arrives, pushing his cart, and one of his balloons floats upwards to a little girl standing at a window. At the sight of the balloon she drops her toy bear out of the window, and it lands in the gutter, by a family of rats.

In the road there is a row of posters, reminding us of the problems of everyday life, sad or joyful. The posters come alive to the people on the street corner.

Through the events inspired by the posters, a contemporary story is told with a great deal of realism. The bear is found, but not before the town is bombed, leaving a closing shot of the little girl standing on a pile of rubble.

English title:	SPARROW IN A GOURD
Original title:	HYOTAN SUZUME
Year:	1962
Country:	Japan
Running time:	55 mins.
Medium:	Animated cartoon/colour (Eastmancolor)

Director:	Ryuichi Yokoyama
Production:	Ryuichi Yokoyama/Otogi-Productions
Distribution:	Toho Co. Ltd.
Music:	Koji Taku

Subject:

The stars here are frogs and sparrows. One day a wicked frog named Danbei comes to a peaceful village of frogs. He is a master with a sling-shot and causes unexpected trouble in the village and even the death of a poor sparrow which lived in a gourd. A kind frog Zensuke buried the dead sparrow on a hill-top.

Danbei throws a police frog, who comes to arrest him, into jail, threatens all inhabitants with his sling and forces them to build a pyramid to establish his own kingdom. But the kingdom is soon upset by a coup d'etat led by Zensuke, and Danbei is dethroned.

A few days later, Zensuke visits the hill where the poor sparrow is buried and to his astonishment finds a strange shoot growing rapidly, with a big gourd. As Zensuke takes it home, rice falls out of it, endlessly. The wicked Danbei hears about this and kills another innocent sparrow to bury on a hill-top. A few days later a shoot comes up as expected and brings him a gourd.

But when Danbei cracks that gourd, a black apparition appears out of it to scare him away.

English title:	TOURING THE WORLD
Original title:	OTOGI NO SEKAI RYOKO
Year:	1962
Country:	Japan
Running time:	94 mins.
Medium:	Animated cartoon / colour (Eastmancolor) Tohoscope
Director:	Ryuichi Yokohama
Producer:	Ryuichi Yokohama/Otigi Film
Animation:	Shinichi Suzuki, Mitsuhiro Machiyama, Hiroshi Shinsenji
Music:	Ikuma Dan

Subject:

Full of interest and wonder for adults and children alike, the film consists of seven parts, each a little story, told by a character in the film, which is set in a fanciful part of a fairyland world. Fantastic rocket launchings, an underwater zoo, waterspouts on a crimson sea, turtles playing golf, Mr. Steam Locomotive and son, a band of bungling gangsters chased by incompetent police, a kingdom of beggars, a trip to the stars—these are but a few of the scenes, characters and events appearing in the film, which took three years to produce.

English title:	LITTLE PRINCE AND THE EIGHT HEADED DRAGON
Original title:	WAN PAKU OGI NO OROCHITALJI
Year:	1963
Country:	Japan
Running time:	86 mins.
Medium:	Animated cartoon/colour (Eastmancolor) Toeiscope
Director:	Yugo Serikawa
Producer:	Toei Animation Studios
Screenplay:	Ichiro Ikeda: Takashi Iijima
Photography:	Hideaki Sugawara, Mitsuaki Ishikawa
Animation:	Yasuji Mori
Music:	Akira Ifukube

Subject:

Based on Japanese mythology, this is the story of Susano, a naughty prince living happily with his kind-hearted parents and animal friends. The death of his mother changes the boy and, ignoring his father, he leaves for an adventurous journey in search of his mother accompanied by Red Nose the rabbit.

His progress is stalled by a monstrous fish and he fights his way through the ocean to the realm of Sea Bottom, ruled by his elder brother, Tsukuyomi, who tells him to hurry home. Angered, Susano heads for the Heavenly Highland, and after a fierce battle with Fire Demon, meets the Sun Goddess, his elder sister.

Though well-meaning, Susano makes so many mistakes that he is banished from his sister's domain.

The prince continues his journey in quest of his mother, and reaches Izumo, where he learns of Kushinada, a beautiful maiden now a captive of the Eight-Headed Serpent.

After a terrific combat, Suzano, riding Pegasus, cuts off the eight fearful heads. Thereupon, dark Izumo under the spell of the serpent glows again and beautiful scenery unfolds.

The young prince now realises he is in his mother's country, and pledges all in his power to build a rich, peaceful land with Princess Kushianada and his friend.

English title:	DOGGIE MARCH
Original title:	WANWAN CHUSHINGURA
Year:	1964
Country:	Japan
Running time:	82 mins.
Medium:	Animated cartoon/colour (Eastmancolor) Toeiscope
Director:	Daisaku Shirakawa

Producer:	Hiroshi Okawa/Toei Studio
Screenplay:	Kei Iijima, Daisaku Shirakawa
Photography:	Kenji Sugiyama, Jiro Yoshimura
Music:	Urato Watanabe

Subject:

In a high mountain and surrounding valley live many small animals, squirrels, rabbits, raccoons, moles, birds, the dog Shiro and her puppy Rock. Their peaceful life is only disturbed by Killer the tiger, and Red Ear the Fox, the only carnivorous animals in the area.

Shiro, however, is young enough to fight the tiger so that the small animals admire her as their protector.

But Shiro falls into a trap set by the tiger and Red Ear, and dies an untimely death. So Rock, the orphan, makes up his mind to go to town to train himself to be able to avenge his mother's death.

In the big town, Rock is befriended by several vagrant dogs, who turn out to be very helpful and promise to assist him. Killer, the tiger, hears of this and sends Red Ear on reconnaissance. Red Ear and Raccoon, who is deceived into helping him, find Rock and decoy him into a warehouse. Rock is trapped and thrown into the water by Red Ear, but is saved.

Then Racoon discovers that he has been used by Red Ear, tells the dogs how he was deceived, and is admitted to their group.

A gigantic dam is to be constructed and surveyors enter the mountain. Wild animals are driven out, captured and sent to the city zoo. Killer begins to rule the animals such as elephants, gorillas, lions and others and becomes their king. Rock, now grown up into a strong dog, is able to find the way into the zoo, thanks to the help of Racoon, followed by forty-seven other dogs and in a fierce fight he avenges his mother's death.

English title:	GULLIVER'S SPACE TRAVELS
Original title:	GARIBAH NO UCHO RYOKO
Year:	1965
Country:	Japan
Medium:	Animated cartoon/colour
Director:	Maseo Kuroda
Production:	Toei Animation Studio
Producer:	Iroshi Okawa
Screenplay:	Shinichy Sekizawa
Planning:	Yutaka Onozawa; Yoshifumi Hatano
Voices:	Kyy Sakamoto, Chiyoko Honma; Seiji Miyaguchi, Schoichi Ozawa

Subject:

Ted is a small homeless boy who has lost all hope in life. Luckily he is befriended by a small wooden soldier and a strong dog, Mack, who give him encouragement. The three set off together for an amusement park. There, they switch on the power and begin to enjoy themselves.

Unfortunately, they are discovered by the guards but manage to escape by a rocket which lands near Gulliver's house.

Gulliver takes a liking to the three visitors and tells them about his plans to make a space flight to a distant planet he calls Hope Star. Ted at once begs to go along.

Gulliver and his friends blast off for Hope Star. Soon they run into a meteor storm which damages their ship. Ted makes repairs. Soon afterwards the group find themselves in a reversed time nebula and are saved only because a strange spaceship helps them. They again set out towards Hope Star, but soon find themselves forced to land on a strange planet by the space patrol. They soon learn that Hope Star is ruled by a group of rebellious robots, who even now plan to attack their former masters. They also learn that it was the princess of this planet who helped them escape the reversed time nebula. While visiting the palace, the robots launch an attack and capture both the princess and Mack the dog. Ted and Gulliver discover that the robot's weak point is water. The group go to Hope Star and completely destroy the robots. Mack and the princess are found unharmed. Ted has given new hope to the planet.

English title:	TARO, THE SON OF DRAGON
Original title:	TATSU, NO KO TARO
Year:	1966
Country:	Japan
Running time:	63 mins.
Medium:	Puppets/colour
Director:	Ichiro Michibayashi
Screenplay:	Takuo Segawa based on an original story by Miyoka Matsutani
Production:	Kyodo Eiga Co. Ltd.
Photography:	Seiichi Kizuka
Puppets:	Takashi Anabuki
Art director:	Genji Uno
Music:	Hiroakazu Sugano

Subject:

In a poor mountain village there was a boy named Taro, the son of Dragon. One day Taro met Aya, a young girl who played a flute. However, she was kidnapped by Red Devil. Taro fought Red Devil and helped her. Then he killed Black Devil. He then went to seek his mother who had been changed into a dragon because she had violated the rule of the villagers. Taro found her and struggled to till the mountain to make a fertile ricefield. Then the dragon changed back into his mother.

English title:	PICTURES AT AN EXHIBITION
Original title:	TENRA KAI NO E
Year:	1966
Country:	Japan
Running time:	50 mins.
Medium:	Animated cartoon/colour
Director:	Osamu Tezuka
Production:	Mushi Productions Ltd., Osamu Tezuka
Screenplay:	Osamu Tezuka
Animation:	Nobuo Onuki
Art director:	Tatsuya Nagahara
Colour designer:	Kazuo Ito
Photography:	Eiji Yamaura
Editing:	Noriyoshi Matsuura
Sound recording:	Atsumi Tashiro

Subject:

In this animated film, already a winner of several Japanese prizes, we have realised a long standing ambition. For several years we have wanted to set the Moussorgsky score to the screen while preserving the original flavour, but updating the pictorial comment. In particular, we wished to comment on our world according to the pictures in an exhibition. Thus we start in a real picture gallery and then accompanied by Moussorgsky, begin exploring the kind of world we live in. In this exhibition several portraits of heroes of our time are displayed, and each one relates his own episode according the Moussorgsky music as follows:
1. Gnomu—Journalist
2. Il Vecdio Castello—Landscape Gardens
3. Tuilleries—Plastic surgeon
4. Bydlo—Big Factory Proprietor
5. Ballet des Poussins dans leurs Coques—Beatnik
6. Samuel Goldenberg et Schmuyle—Boxer
7. Limoges—Le Marché—T.V. Talent
8. Catacombae—Zen Priest
9. La Cabane sur des Pattes de Poule—War and Soldier
10. La Grande Porte de Kiev—Allegorical conclusion

If you were to name our theme you would have to call it an anti-heroic one verging on the satirical and certainly including the ironic, because our world is one which could certainly be bettered. Towards this end, we have used all the latest techniques of animation, and the strongest imag-ination possible. The results have pleased us, as well as those who have seen our picture. (Film Mushi Productions announcement).

English title:	JUNGLE EMPEROR
Original title:	JUNGLE TAITEI
Year:	1966
Country:	Japan
Running time:	82 mins.
Medium:	Animated cartoon/colour
Supervisor:	Shigeyuki Hayashi
Director:	Osamu Tezuka
Production:	Mushi Films
Producer:	Masaki Mori
Author:	Osamu Tezuka
Screenplay:	Masaki Tsuji
Animation:	Hiroshi Saito
Cameraman:	Tatsumasu Shimizu
Sound recordist:	Atsumi Tashiro
Special effects:	Hirokazu Iwata
Music:	Isao Tomita
Art director:	Nobuharu Ito
Production manager:	Eiichi Yamamoto

Subject:

Panja, a male lion with pure white hair, has long ruled over the animal world, but one day he is shot by the hunter Hamegg. Eriza, Panja's wife was caught by humans and put in a cage on the cargo-boat to be sent to the zoo.

One moonlit night on the boat, she gave birth to a white-haired lion cub named Leo, just like father Panja. "Go across the ocean and return to Africa to carry out your late father's wishes" Eriza tells her young child.

Leo arrives in Africa swimming through the Atlantic and is welcomed by animals in the Jungle. On his way back home, deepening his understanding of human society and power, Leo establishes a theory that a happy life for animals should be based on civilisation. Burning with his theory, Leo starts to build a farm, so that they are no longer dependent on natural food. And all the animals eventually help.

Suddenly in the middle of these happy days, there appear three "Death Wanderers"—elephant, baboon and fangy cat. They do a great deal of mischief and try to destroy the jungle. They are too big and strong for Leo and the other animals and old Mandy says "Once Death comes to Jungle, that's the end of it! The best thing we can do is to run away from this jungle before all of us are eaten up..." But Leo does not give up and Parrot Koko trains Leo so that he is strong enought to fight with Death. The animals then receive the news that Koko has been caught by Death and is going to be eaten up.

Leo rises. "I'll go and save Koko even if I'm not strong enough to fight against them. Give me one more chance to try." Old Mandy cannot say anything except "Good Luck!" Leo runs like a white arrow. Leo and Death face each other. Fangy cat and baboon are smashed down in an instant. And finally elephant collapses and falls from a steep cliff.

Old Mandy and the animals shout for joy. "Let's go back home and make a happier jungle from now on!"

English title:	THE KUROHIME STORY
Original title:	HUROHIME MONOGATARI
Year:	1967
Country:	Japan
Running time:	61 mins.
Medium:	Animated puppets/colour
Director:	Miyoji Ieki
Screenplay:	Takuo Segawa, Ysaku Yamagata, original story Takuo Segawa
Production:	Kyodo Elga Co. Ltd.
Puppets:	Ishiro Kumoro
Photography:	Shunichiro Nakao
Art director:	Jira Ariga
Music:	Hirokazu Sugano

Subject:

This puppet film tells of Kurohime, Princess of a small mountainous province who meets and falls in love with a good-looking young man, even after he turns out to be an incarnation of Black Dragon.

Meanwhile, a Government minister learns of her beauty, wants to marry her and orders the young man to be killed. Furious, the young man changes into a dragon and causes a great storm and floods.

But the pure love of Kurohime changes the dragon back into the young man she loves and they live happily ever after.

English title	CYBORG 009
Original title:	SAIBOGU 009
Year:	1966
Country:	Japan
Medium:	Animated cartoon/Eastmancolor
Director:	Yugo Serikawa
Production:	Toei Animation Studios
Screenplay:	Takashi Iijima and Yugo Serikawa
Chief Animator:	Keiichiro Kimura
Original story:	Shotaro Ishimori
Artistic Director:	Tomoo Fukumoto

Photography:	Shigeyoshi Ikeda
Music:	Taichiro Kosugi

Subject:

The Black Ghosts, a group of evildoers having their base on Ghost Island somewhere in the Pacific, plot to cause another world war and profit by taking advantage of the confusion.

They produce various new weapons in an underground factory of the island, the most amazing of which are the cyborgs, robots with intricate mechanical brains.

Dr. Gillmore, inventor of the cyborgs, is suffering a guilty conscience over his involvement in the plot designed by Beagle, leader of the Black Ghosts. So when the last CYBORG 009, his masterpiece, is completed, he escapes from the island taking all of his cyborgs with him.

English title:	CYBORG 009—UNDERGROUND DUEL
Original title:	SAIBOGU 009—KAIJU SENSO
Year:	1967
Country:	Japan
Running time:	60 mins.
Medium:	Animated cartoon/colour (Eastmancolor) Toeiscope.
Director:	Yugo Serikawa
Production:	Toei Animation Studio
Screenplay:	Kei Iijima, Yugo Serikwa, Daisaku Shirakawa
Photography:	Shigeyochi Ikeda
Art director:	Tomoo Fukumoto
Music:	Tiachiro Kosugi

Subject:

Though they have successfully vanquished the Black Ghosts, Dr. Gilmore and his robot Cyborg friends realise that a few must be left, because there is a great monster creating havoc in the nearby sea.

Sure enough, the monster is a new robot, controlled by Beagle, leader of the Black Ghosts. Gathering his Cyborgs about him, Dr. Gilmore prepares to attack.

He has quite a few other robots. One of them can think amazingly well, another is a supersonic runner, another has finger machine-guns, another can spit fire-rays, another is an expert underwater swimmer and 009, the best model, is the leader of them all.

Chasing the monster they come across a pretty girl on a submarine who asks them to join her, but it soon develops that she is an agent working for the Black Ghosts. Thanks to her, however, they discover the new headquarters of their foes, and attack and finally destroy the new base.

English title:	JACK AND THE WITCH
Original title:	SHONEN JACK TO MA-HOTSUKAI
Year:	1967
Country:	Japan
Running time:	80 mins.
Medium:	Animated cartoon/colour (Eastmancolor)
Director:	Taiji Yabushita
Production:	Toei Animation Studio
Screenplay:	Shinichi Sekizawa and Susumu Takahisa
Photography:	Hideaki Sugawara
Art director:	Teiji Koyama
Music:	Seiichiro Uno

Subject:

Jack, while out with his animal friends, meets a nice little girl named Kiky. At least she seems nice. It soon turns out, however, that she is really working for an evil witch who makes her kidnap children so that she can turn them into devils by running them through her devil-producing machine.

Jack's friend, the mouse, is turned into a demon but the rest escape, Kiky in pursuit. Later they creep back into the old castle to release their friend and are caught.

Jack is saved, however, when his friends prevent the machine from working, and they then set about destroying it. In the meantime the old witch is furious at Kiky for her failure and imprisons her in a glacier. Jack saves her but is killed.

The little girl starts to cry and her tears are so potent that Jack is brought back to life. Together, they brave thunder, storm and flood, to pursue the old witch. They find that her crystal ball is really the source of her magic. When it is destroyed she is a powerless old woman, Kiky is disenchanted, all the devils return to their former selves, and they all rush happily back home.

English title:	THE MADCAP ISLAND
Original title:	HYOKKORI HYOTAN JIMA
Year:	1967
Country:	Japan
Running time:	61 mins.
Medium:	Animated cartoon/colour (Eastmancolor) Toeiscope
Director:	Taiji Yabushita
Production:	Toei Animation Studio
Screenplay:	Hiroshi Inoue, Morihisa Yamoto
Photography:	Miki Shirao
Art director:	Hideo Chiba
Music:	Seiichiro Uno

Subject:

This full-length animated cartoon is a satire about a country which, after a volcanic explosion simply drifts out to sea. Finally it arrives at a continent inhabited entirely by man-hating dogs who immediately attack the humans. Though the president, Don Gavacho, tries to negotiate with the animals, he is taken prisoner and sentenced to death. His friends disguise themselves as horses and enter dog-land to save their leader. Using a secret weapon—flea bombs—they attack the beasts. Also they hoist the flea-eggs aloft in balloons and then puncture the carriers when they are over the dog capital. Eventually, the most intrepid of the saviours, Machine-gun Dandy, has it out with the dog leader, Commander Spitz, in a spirited gun battle on the deserted streets of the local ghost town.

English title:	FABLES FROM HANS CHRISTIAN ANDERSEN
Original title:	ANDERSEN MONOGATARI
Year:	1968
Country:	Japan
Running time:	80 mins.
Medium:	Animated colour/cartoon (Eastmancolor) Toeiscope
Director:	Kimio Yabuki
Production:	Toei Animation Studios
Screenplay:	Hiroshis Inoue & Morhisa Yamamoto
Art direction:	Tadashi Koyama
Animation:	Akira Diakubara
Photography:	Morihisa Yamamoto
Music:	Seiichiro Uno

Subject:

This full-length animated cartoon is taken from the fairy-tales of Hans Christian Andersen, who is shown as a young man, good friend of a little girl named Eliza.

One day Uncle Oley, the man who gives beautiful dreams to children, visits the village. Hans wants to learn about them so that he can tell lovely dream-like stories to other children, especially Eliza.

But she and her grandmother have been evicted from their home, and must leave the village. Hans can do nothing but hopes to meet her again. In the meantime a dancing contest is to be held. Hans' father, a shoemaker, has been given some magic leather by Uncle Oley and makes a lovely pair of slippers. The spoiled daughter of the mayor, Karen, insists on having them, however, and so the prize money which would have been theirs is lost.

Hans, who had planned to use the money to go to the city and see the opera, goes anyway, works hard, and finally has enough money for an opera ticket. Just then he meets Eliza again—now working as a match-girl. So he gives her the money and buys all her matches, and so is unable to go to the opera. This is just as well because Karen is appearing in her red shoes and cannot stop dancing. Then Uncle Oley appears and saves her, to make her a better girl in the process. In the meantime, Hans has been entertaining Eliza with a story and when he is finished there is a burst of applause because all the city-folk have been listening too.

So it is decided that Hans shall go to school in Copenhagen and learn how to write his lovely stories.

English title:	LITTLE NORSE PRINCE VALIANT
Original title:	TAIYO NO OGI, HORUSO, NO DIABOKEN
Year:	1968
Country:	Japan
Running time:	82 mins.
Medium:	Animated cartoon/colour (Eastmancolor)
Director:	Isao Takahata
Production:	Toei Animation Studio
Screenplay:	Kazuo Fukazawa
Art director:	Mataji Urata
Photography:	Jiro Yoshimura
Animation:	Yasuo Otsuka
Music:	Yoshio Mamiya

Subject:

Hols, a small boy, lives with his friend, a small bear—both sworn enemies of the terrible Grunwald who tries in various ways to get rid of little Hols but never succeeds.

When the boy goes out into the world he discovers that Grunwald is making life difficult for everyone. He sends out hordes of man-eating wolves, and puts giant barracuda in the streams. Hols kills the giant fish and then meets a beautiful girl named Hilda, not knowing she is Grunwald's sister.

She is under orders from her wicked brother but is really fond of Hols and refuses to enter into the plots against him.

He tries to save her but lands himself in dire trouble when Grunwald attacks.

Grunwald sacrifices his own sister but does not count on Hols' determination. The boys chase him back to his ice castle and there, using the newly-made sword of the sun, Hols finally succeeds in killing him.

When he returns he finds that Hilda is herself again, his bear friend is safe, and all ends happily.

English title:	THE FOX WITH NINE TAILS
Original title:	"SESSHO-SEKI" or KYUBI NO KITSUNE TO TOBI-MARU
Year:	1968
Country:	Japan
Running time:	81 mins.
Medium:	Animated cartoon/colour (Fuji Colour)
Director:	Shinichi Yagi
Production:	Japan Animated Film Co./ Nihon Doga Co. Ltd.
Producer:	Gentaro Nakajima
Distribution:	Daei Motion Picture Co. Ltd.
Original story:	Kido Okamoto
Screenplay:	Michio Yoshioka
Animation:	Taku Sugiyama
Photography:	Masayoshi Kishimoto
Art director:	Isamu Kageyama
Music:	Shigeru Ikeno
Background:	Isamu Kageyama

Subject:

Once, over a thousand years ago, there lived a girl named Tamamo, and she was so lovely that to see her was to love her. She grew up with a handsome youth named Tobimaru and they loved each other as brother and sister.

One day, however, she discovered that she was really a nine-tailed fox in disguise and that her purpose on earth was to captivate the people of the land and turn it over to the King of Darkness.

Terrified, she fled to Kyoto, but there her beauty made all people want to be near her and did nothing to solve her problem, In addition, her destiny was becoming manifest and her evil deeds began.

She ordered all the images of Buddha in the city of Kyoto to be destroyed. In their place was to be erected an enormous statue of herself. Once this was accomplished the King of Darkness would move in and civilization would fall.

Tobimaru, who had come in search of her, saw what was happening and, though he loved the girl, it was he who found the sacred Halberd and, using it, destroyed the great statue just before it was finished.

Fleeing, the lovely Tamamo returned to the scene of her youth, hoping to find Tobimaru waiting. But as she fled she was turned to stone and one may still see this Death Stone which was once the beauteous Tamamo.

English title:	THE MIGHTY TARO
Original title:	
Year:	1968
Country:	Japan

Running time:	65 mins.
Medium:	Animated puppets/colour
Director:	Myoji Ieki
Production:	Kyodo Eiga Co. Ltd.
Distribution:	Sanyo Shoji Co. Ltd.

Subject:

Once upon a time a poor woodcutter in Northern Japan had a very strange child whom he called Taro. He ate ten times as much as other babies and slept when he wasn't eating. But he grew large and strong and soon set off on his travels. In so doing he met two others just like himself and the three boys set out to kill a great monster which was keeping a number of worthy people prisoner in its castle.

When they succeed they set the prisoners free.

English title:	PUS'N BOOTS
Original title:	NAGAGUTSU O HAITA NECKO
Year:	1969
Country:	Japan
Running time:	80 mins.
Medium:	Animated cartoon/colour (Eastmancolor) Toeiscope.
Director:	Kimio Yabuki
Production:	Toei Animation Studio
Original story:	Charles Perrault
Screenplay:	Hisashi Inoue, Morihisa Yamamoto
Animation:	Koji Mori
Music:	Seiichiro Uno

Subject:

Pero is a very clever and brave cat. One day he saves some mice and is driven out of the cat's world. Under the eaves of a farmer's house he meets Pierre, the youngest of three brothers, who has been driven from home by his greedy brothers.

Pero cheers up Pierre and they start on a journey, and at last arrive in a town with a castle where the king is searching for a husband for his daughter. At first glance Pierre is enamoured with the princess, and Pero decides to help him marry her. Suddenly a storm breaks out and the Devil King appears, and tries to curry favour with the princess by changing the castle into gold and the rooms of the palace into diamonds. But she is terrified. At this the Devil King becomes angry and changes the castle into ruins.

He then flies away vowing to return and take the princess away.

The Devil King reappears and snatches the princess away in a whirlpool. Pierre, Pero and the mice follow in pursuit riding white horses. They arrive at the Devil King's castle, as a wedding

party is about to be held. Pero goes before the Devil King and asks him to perform his magic. He changes himself into a lion, then an elephant and even to a mouse. At this moment Pierre attacks. The Devil King tries to escape and drops his skull pendant by which he is able to perform his magic. But he retrieves it and confines Pierre and the others to a dungeon. Princess Rosa agrees to his proposal on the condition that he does not kill them. Then in an unguarded moment she takes the pendant away from him and throws it into the dungeon. Pierre holds the pendant high up over his head and climbs up to the tower of the castle. Then a beam of sunlight shines down from the mountains and the Devil King and his castle are destroyed.

Peace returns to the kingdom and Pierre, the princess and Pero, live happily ever after.

English title:	FLYING PHANTOM SHIP
Original title:	SORA TOBU YUREISEN
Year:	1969
Country:	Japan
Running time:	60 mins.
Medium:	Animated cartoon/colour (Eastmancolor) Toeiscope
Director:	Hiroshi Ikeda
Production:	Toei Production Studio
Original story:	Shotaro Ishimori
Screenplay:	Masaki Tsuji
Animation:	Yoichi Otabe
Art director:	Isamu Tsuchida
Music:	Kosuke Onozaki

Subject:

A ghost clipper with tattered sails appears from out of the fog to attack ships connected with the Kuroshio Conglomerate.

When Hayato goes fishing with his father, they see a car fall off a cliff, and rescue Mr. Kuroshio, the Board Chairman of the Kuroshio Conglomerate, and his wife.

Soon after, Giant Robot Ghorem, known as Ghost Clipper's Robot, appears and begins to destroy cities. The defending forces jets and tanks attack but are all destroyed by the missiles of Ghorem.

Hayato's father is badly hurt and before he dies he discloses that he found Hayato floating on a raft some twelve years before with a photo of his real parents.

When Hayato visits Kuroshio and sits on a chair, it descends underground through a weapons factory. Under the sea, many more Giant Ghorem robots are in the process of production. A large television screen shows the Giant Ghorem destroying all the port facilities. Suddenly, the Ghost Clipper rises from the sea and pursues it into the sky, and after a fierce duel Giant Ghorem is shot down.

Hayato manages to escape and runs into a police station to inform the policemen what is taking place, but nobody listens to him. Then he runs into the TV station where he reveals that he is Kuroshio who manipulates the giant robot. Giant crabs and lobster-like monsters appear and begin to destroy the buildings and melt people with their BOA juice foam, but Hayato is saved by Ghost Clipper.

The captain of the clipper proves to be Hayato's real father who explains that the sea monsters are nothing more than the tools of the Undersea Empire, whose headquarters are 10,000 metres under the sea.

The captain is hurt but Hayato operates the Ghost Clipper, and counter-attacks the enemy head-quarters.

The sea-bottom city is completely destroyed and the Earth is once again secure.

English title:	*A THOUSAND AND ONE NIGHTS*
Original title:	*SENYA ICHIYA MONOGA-TARI*
Year:	1969
Country:	Japan
Running time:	2 hours 30 mins. cut to 90 mins. for export
Medium:	Animated cartoon/colour (Animerama)
Director:	Osamu Tezuka
Designer:	Eiichi Yamamoto
Production:	Mushi Films
Executive producer, general supervisor and co-screenplay:	Osamu Tezuka
Asst. supervisor, and co-screenplay:	Kazuo Fukazawa
Distribution:	Nippon Herald Motion Pictures Co. Ltd.
Artistic director:	Takahi Yanase
Photography:	Akira Rsuchiya
Music:	Isso Tomita
Chief animator:	Kazuko Nakamura
Other collaborators:	Morio Kita Soichi Ohya, Sakyo Komatsu

Subject:

The film claims to be "the first animated film for adults".

The use of a multiplane camera has added some good special effects. The montage of animation drawings with photography taken from life is another technical achievement utilized in the film.

Story:

Aldin, a poor water-vendor, comes to Bagdad and is attracted to a beautiful slave woman Milliam, who is being auctioned at the market place.

Hubbaslum, the spoilt son of the police superintendent, is ready to buy her at any cost. Aldin snatches Milliam and flees with her. They spend a passionate night together in a luxurious house.

The next morning, Shalieman, the rich owner of the house and a lecherous peeper, is found murdered and the police arrest Aldin and Milliam. The police superintendent throws Aldin into jail as Shalieman's killer.

The superintendent is impotent and spiritless. His wife, Halimar, is a wanton woman who indulges in the pleasures of lust with Kamhakim, the boss of a band of robbers. Badli, an ambitious policeman, had Kamhakim raid Shalieman's house to get Milliam back for Hubbaslum and has succeeded in gaining the superintendent's trust Badli is so bad that he not only raped Kamhakim's daughter, Madia, while she was bathing, but even committed bestiality hoping to realice the Arab legend that a man who has intercourse with a crocodile shall become a king.

Hubbaslum is overjoyed to get Milliam and in a careless moment of exultation, falls off a high building to his death. Badli then takes Milliam to his house.

In the meantime Aldin, who refuses to confess, has been continuously tortured. The chief jailor admires his tenacious attachment to life and gives him a plan to get out. Following his advice, Aldin. feigns death and is carried out. He immediately starts looking for his beloved Milliam and soon discovers her whereabouts. He hurries to Badli's house only to learn that she died after giving birth to a female baby. Aldin, in tears, sees Badli come out on horseback and tails him to Kamhakim's hide-out in the mountains. "Open sesame!," he cries, and a rock opens to let Badli in. Later, Aldin steals into the cave and finds it filled with gold and jewels. He is about to take some bags full of gold when Madia returns alone and finds him. She is struck by his strange charm and asks him to take her with him. They get a flying horse and take off to travel. They fly over an ocean and land on an island which is inhabited by women only. After a fight with the Queen of the island, Madia is beaten and forced to leave.

Aldin has a very good time for a few days until overcome by curiosity, he steals into a forbidden room of the queen's palace, where he sees her turn into a huge python. Frightened, Aldin runs out and manages to escape to the open sea in a row-boat.

After a few days drifting he is saved by a merchant ship. The ship is wrecked in a tempest and blown to an eerie island inhabited by a giant goblin. The crew fall its prey but when a huge bird attacks it only Aldin is fortunate enough to survive, and the two monsters, struggling viciously, fall into the sea. The turbulence caused by them makes a sunken ship rise to the surface. It is a magic ship with a hold full of treasures. Thus Aldin gets riches and begins to dream of something more.

Years have passed.

Gin and Ginnie, a couple of imps, have respectively been attracted to Aslan, a young and handsome shepherd in the Black State, and Jallis, a beautiful girl in Bagdad. The imps bet on which of their discoveries has more human beauty. Aslan and Jallis are brought together in their sleep. Gin and Ginnie decide to awaken them together and see which will fall in love with the other. The young couple wake up, look at each other and fall in love simultaneously. The bet is a draw, and the imps make them sleep again and take them back to their places of origin.

Back in Bagdad Jallis wakes up. She is Milliam's daughter, being brought up by Badli. She cannot think of anything but Aslan now. She assumes man's attire and leaves for the Black State alone. On arriving at the capital of the Black State, Jallis receives the King's favour. Believing Jallis is a man, the king has her marry his princess daughter. In the matrimonial bed Jallis confesses and the princess is pleased to know that Jallis is a woman because she has a taste for lesbian love. The Princess tells Jallis to behave like her prince consort in the daytime and they enjoy themselves as women at night. One day when Jallis is making an inspection round, she runs into Aslan whom she has never forgotten. They leave the Black State for Bagdad together.

At about this time, a famous merchant named Sinbad is leading his wealthy fleet along the Tigris River towards Bagdad. Sinbad and his crew reach land and halt at an oasis to rest. Kamhakim and his forty robbers are preparing to attack them when a troop led by Badli surprises and kills them all. Badli, who is the commander of the garrison at Bagdad has heard of Sinbad's enormous wealth and decided to take sides with him for the time being. On meeting him, Badli suspects that he has seen Sinbad somewhere. Later Sinbad sees Milliam in Jallis and utters a cry, which reminds Badli of Aldin the water-vendor. Badli plots to entrap him some day. He sends Aslan, who is in his way, into the army.

Sinbad ventures into a treasure competition with the King of Bagdad but loses to the King's unfair trick. He then has the King and his Ministers aboard the magic ship and sinks it deep in the sea. Thus Sinbad reaches the throne, but he has no idea what to do as a king. All he can do is order the construction of a skyscraper which will symbolise his power and dignity. Badli feigns loyalty and awaits his chance to take over.

Madia, the bandit's daughter, mingles with the tower construction workers to take her revenge on Badli.

Aslan deserts from the front, wanting to see Jallis, but is caught. He is to be executed in the valley of the lions. When a lion approaches him, Ginnie comes to his rescue.

Badli tells Jallis that Aslan was killed and persuades her to enter the king's harem. King Sinbad takes her to his bed. Badli chuckles to himself over the thought that the throne has as good as fallen into his hands.

Early next morning Badli calls the people of Bagdad to the square in front of the palace and announces before them that the King has had sexual connection with his daughter. However, his accusation is denied by Aslan who actually shared the bed of Jallis with Ginnie's help.

His wicked plot exposed, Badli tries to throw a serpent at the king, when an arrow from Madia's bow hits him. She aims a second arrow at the king but cannot shoot him. Recognising that he is Aldin, her love is rekindled. The second arrow hits the skyscraping tower and it collapses in a flash of lightning.

Aldin, alias Sinbad, understands now that the throne meant nothing to him. He throws the crown away and goes on a journey in search of something better than the throne. Aslan and Jallis, arm in arm, watch him disappear over the horizon.

English title:	HANAKO, THE ELEPHANT
Original title:	
Year:	1969
Country:	Japan
Running time:	63 mins.
Medium:	Puppets/colour (16 mm)
Director:	Hiroshi Matsumoto
Production:	Kyodo Eiga Co. Ltd.
Distribution:	Sanyo Shoji Co. Ltd.

Subject:

Adapted freely from a true story that took place in Japan shortly before its surrender in the Pacific War. Because of food shortages and intensifying air-raids the fierce animals in zoos had to be killed. However out of pity a few people hid an elephant in the mountains and helped it survive. And the army, who ordered the death of the animals, feigned ignorance of this fact.

The film emphasises the absurdity of war as well as a little boy's courage and love for animals.

English title:	CLEOPATRA, QUEEN OF SEX
Original title:	CLEOPATRA
Year:	1970
Country:	Japan

Medium:	Animated cartoon/colour (Animerama)
Director:	Osamu Tezuka
Co-director:	Eiichi Yamamoto
Creator of characters:	Koh Kojima
Screenplay:	Shigemi Satoyoshi
Voices:	Chinatsu Nakayama (Cleopatra), Hajime Hana (Caesar)
Production:	Mushi Films
Distribution:	Nippon Herald

Subject:

Cleopatra, the voluptuous beauty who twisted the invaders round her little finger, and saved her country, has a series of romps with Julius Caesar and other Romans.

The film intends to emphasise erotism in animation.

Title:	KYOJIN NO HOSHI
Year:	1969
Country:	Japan
Running time:	88 mins.
Medium:	Animated cartoon/colour
Director:	Tadao Nagahama
Production:	Toho Company

Subject:

A drama about a baseball hero. The first of a series of several animated films aimed primarily at television.

Title:	KYOJIN NO HOSHI, YUKE HYUMA
Year:	1969
Running time:	71 mins.
Country:	Japan
Medium:	Animated cartoon/colour
Director:	Tadao Nagahama
Production:	Toho Company

Subject:

A drama about a baseball hero.

Title:	KYOJIN NO HOSHI, DAIRIGU BORU
Year:	1970
Running time:	70 mins.
Country:	Japan
Medium:	Animated cartoon/colour
Director:	Tadao Nagahama
Production:	Toho Company

Subject:

A drama about a baseball hero.

Title:	KYOJIN NO HOSHI, SHUMEKEI NO TAIKETSU
Year:	1970
Running time:	61 mins.
Country:	Japan
Medium:	Animated cartoon/colour
Director:	Tadao Nagahama
Production:	Toho Company

Subject:

A drama about a football hero.

English title:	TREASURE ISLAND
Original title:	DOBUTSU TAKARAJIMA
Year:	1971
Country:	Japan
Running time:	78 mins.
Medium:	Animated cartoon(Eastmancolor), Toeiscope
Director:	Hiroshi Ikeda
Animator:	Yasuo Meri
Music:	Nanzumol Yamamoto
Production:	Toei

Subject:

Based on Robert Louis Stevenson's famous story, this feature was made to mark the twentieth anniversary of the establishment of the Toei company. Scenario from original by Hiroshi Jyima.

English title:	THE FANTASTIC WORLD OF UKIYOE
Original title:	MARHUI GEKIGA, UKIYOE SENICHIYA
Year:	1969
Country:	Japan
Running time:	70 mins.
Medium:	Animated cartoon/colour
Director:	Leo Nishimura
Production:	Toei

Subject:

The main character runs through sadism, eroticism and fantasy in an unprecedented crystallisation of present-day live-action trends in the cartoon medium.

Title:	ATAKKU NANBA WAN NO. 1
Year:	1970
Country:	Japan
Running time:	63 mins.
Medium:	Animated cartoon
Production:	Toho Company

Subject:

A drama about a girl's volley-ball team. A series of animated feature films mainly for television.

Title:	*ATAKKU NANBA WAN, NAMIDA NO KAITEN RESIBU. NO. 2*
Year:	1970
Running time:	59 mins.
Country:	Japan
Medium:	Animated cartoon
Production:	Toho Company

Subject:

Another series of animated feature films mainly for television.

Title:	*ATAKKU NANBA WAN, NAMIDA NO SEKAI SENSHUKEN. NO. 2*
Year:	1970
Running time:	51 mins
Country:	Japan
Medium:	Animated cartoon
Production:	Toho Company

Subject:

Another series of animated feature films mainly for television.

English title:	*NOBODY'S BOY*
Original title:	*CHIBIKKO REMI TO MEI-KEN CAPI*
Year:	1970
Country:	Japan
Running time:	81 mins.
Medium:	Animated cartoon/colour
Production:	Toei Animation Studio
Producer:	Hiroshi Okawa
Original story:	"Sans Famille" by Hector Malot
Director:	S. Fukumoto
Planning:	C. Yamanashi; K. Ito, K. Lijima
Screenplay:	Shoji Sewaga
Designer:	A. Diakubara
Music:	T. Kinoshita

Subject:

Remi is living in the small village of Chavanon, France, poor but happy, with his good friends Capi and Pepe, the parrot, and his dear mother, Barbarin. But all this comes to a sudden end with the return of his father Jermoe, who had hurt his leg in Paris. Remi was a foundling picked up in front of the Notre Dame eight years ago. Jerome sells Remi to Vitalis.

Vitalis was once a famous singer at L'Opera in Paris but has turned to becoming a travelling entertainer since he lost his voice. Remi becomes very good friends with the Vitalis troupe's stars, Joli-Coeur the monkey, Zerbino and Dolce, the dogs. Capi joins the troupe as well and they travel from one place to another.

There were good times and there were bad times and the troupe often had to sleep on the ground with empty stomachs.

When they stopped overnight in a cottage, Joli-Coeur, Zarbino and Dolce, who went to fetch firewood, were attacked by the wolves.

Losing all his companions, Vitalis has to sing again himself, but he is jailed for 3 months because he was entertaining without a police permit.

Remi and Capi are saved by Mrs. Milligan while she is searching for her child who was abducted when he was a baby. They live on a river boat, the *White Swan*, with Lise and the pet dog Beatrice. Vitalis gets out of jail and Milligan wishes him to stay on the *White Swan* with Remi, but Remi follows Vitalis, leaving his one treasured item, a rosary, with Lise. However, Vitalis passes away in the shattered windmill-house, holding Remi's hand.

Mrs. Milligan now knows by the rosary that Remi is the child she was looking for and asks her brother-in-law James to bring Remi to their castle in Rouen, but he finds Remi in Paris and locks him up at the castle so that he can inherit the property himself. He informs Mrs. Milligan that Remi fell into the river Seine and drowned. Remi and Capi manage to escape and finally catch up with Mrs. Milligan on board the ship going from France to England.

Happy days follow for Remi and Capi with a real mother and sister. But Remi, decides to leave because Barberin is now alone and poor. He informs his mother that once he does everything he can for Barberin he will return home again, and leaves for Chavanon.

English title:	*30,000 MILES UNDER THE SEA*
Original title:	*KAITEI 30,000 MARU*
Year:	1971
Country:	Japan
Running time:	60 minutes
Medium:	Animated cartoon/colour
Production company:	Toei
Art director:	Makoto Yamayazi
Animator:	Sadahiro Okuda
Scenario:	Katsumi Okamoto
Original story:	Shotaro Ishimori
Music:	Takeo Watanabe

Subject:

Isamu goes with Cheetah to see the crater where he meets Angel, the princess of Submarine Kingdom. She arrives in a fantastic vessel named the Seethrough, accompanying lamp-post Octopus and plump Turtle.

All of a sudden, monstrous dragons appear out of the crater with the rumble of the ground and begin to spit lava from their mouths to melt the surroundings. Tanks and jet fighters which come to attack the flaming dragons, are destroyed.

The flaming dragons are robots made by Magma VII of the Subterranean Empire. Thousands of years ago, the Subterreanean people lived on the land. Now, Magma VII makes the flaming dragon invade the countries on the earth.

The Seethrough finds a flaming dragon and secretly chases it until the vessel gets into the Subterranean territory. Isamu, Angel and the others are captured, but they kill the guards and break out of prison.

In the Submarine Kingdom, the king proclaims that he will make an assault on the Subterranean Empire unless the emperor gives up invading the countries on the land. The Submarine fleet of Soapbubble discharge electric eels, sea anemone and starfish, and overwhelm the flaming dragons.

Seeing that Magma VII is left alone in the control office, Isamu attacks and knocks him down. He presses the red button, and the flaming dragons turn against the Subterranean army and the whole Empire is blown up by an immense explosion caused by the flaming dragons.

English title :	***ALI-BABA AND THE FORTY THIEVES***
Original title :	***ARI-BABATO YONJUPPIKI NO TOZOKU***
Year :	1971
Country :	Japan
Running time :	56 mins.
Medium :	Animated cartoon/colour
Production :	Toei Company
Director :	Hiroshi Shidara
Art director :	Saburo Yokoi
Animation :	Akira Daikubara
Music :	Selichiro Uno

Subject:

In the small kingdom named Ali-Baba, the king is a scoundrel who has spent all the nation's treasures.

Only an old oil lamp remains. Rubbing it by accident one day a genie appears before the king and vows to do his bidding, but confesses that he is afraid of cats. So King Ali-Baba orders his soldiers to round up all the cats in the Kingdom and imprison them in the 'open sesame' cave.

But Al Huck, who carries a small rat on his shoulder named Kajiru, helps many stray cats escape.

Dora, leader of the stray cats tells Al Huck not to run away. "Your ancester was the leader of the forty thieves. This is your chance to topple the wicked king from his throne!", he says.

One night Al Huck, the cats and the rats meet. Kajiru brings an old carpet and tells them, "This is a magic carpet. It was the only treasure my ancestors saved from being taken by King Ali-Baba."

Al Huck and Kajiru leave for the king's castle, but the carpet has engine trouble and they are caught by the genie.

In the meantime, the cats turn themselves into birds through self-hypnosis and the genie flees in terror. The cats then attack the soldiers and after a fierce battle they defeat the king and his soldiers and peace returns to the kingdom of Ali-Baba.

Title :	*BELLADONNA*
Year :	1974
Country :	Japan
Running time :	102 mins.
Medium :	Animated cartoon/colour
Production :	Mushi-Nippon
Director :	Eiichi Yamamoto
Producer :	Katsumi Furukawa
Art Director :	Kuni Fukai
Screenplay :	Yoshiyuki Fukuda
Original story :	"The Witch (1862)" by Jules Michelet
Lyrics :	Yu Aku, Asei Kobayashi
Music :	Masahiko Sato

Subject:

The story of Jeanne, the beautiful wife of a poor peasant, who has sold her body and soul to the devil, is based on a novel by the French historian Jules Michelet, in which the witches of the Middle Ages appear as the first women who have rebelled against the so often absurd laws of the church and have fought for their liberty.

Jean and Jeanne live in a small village. They got married, their happiness seems to be perfect. But Jean does not succeed in convincing his master, the count, to renounce his "jus primae noctis", the right conceding him the first night with the wife of his bondsman. Jeanne, fighting tooth and nail, is raped by the count and his henchmen. The next morning the young couple try to forget the nightmare, but even their passionate love does not help them to forget. Jeanne endeavours desperately to find a way out for herself and her husband from this dilemma and their misery. Behold, the devil appears in the guise of a goblin and promises Jeanne every possible help under the condition that she sells him her body and soul. Jeanne succumbs to the temptation and soon attains prosperity and success in her village. This rouses the envy and ill-will of the countess, who insinuates to her husband that Jeanne is a witch. With the help of the devil the young woman, chased about, once again finds refuge in a lonely valley, dotted with Belladonna plants. In the meantime the village is stricken by the pest. The villagers call on Jeanne for help. She prepares a medicine from the belladonna plant which helps to defeat the illness.

The count orders Jean to wrench the secret of the medicine from Jeanne. Jeanne refuses to reveal it and being a witch she is burnt to death. Jean too is killed by the guards when trying to help his wife.

But the spirit of rebellion lives on in the villagers, their faces bearing the imprint of Jeanne.

Title:	JACK AND THE BEAN-STALK
Year:	1974
Country:	Japan
Running time:	82 mins.
Medium:	Animated cartoon (East-mancolor)
Production:	Nippon Herald Films Inc. and Group TAC
Director:	Gisaburo Sugii
Producer:	Katsumi Furukawa
Art directors:	Takao Kodama, Yoshiyuki Uchida, Koji Abe, Shiro Fujimoto
Screenplay:	Shuji Hirami
Executive producer:	Mikio Nakada
Assist. producer:	Makoto Kato
Music coordinator:	Yuh Aku
Music director:	Morihisa Shibuya
Sound director:	Atsumi Tashiro
Composers:	Takashi Miki, Tadao Inoue, Shunichi Tokura
Animators:	Shigeru Yamamoto, Yasuo Maeda, Teruhito Kamiguchi, Takateru Miwa, Kazuko Nakamura, Toshio Hirata, Kanji Akabori, Sadao Tsukioka
Celluloid work:	Masaharu Arai
Photography:	VAC
Editing:	Masashi Furukawa
Sound effects:	Mitsuru Kashiwabara

Subject:

Based on the famous traditional British folktale, interpreted as a musical fantasy for children.

Title:	ROUND THE WORLD WITH BOLEK AND LOLEK
Year:	1975
Country:	Poland
Running time:	80 mins.
Medium:	Animated cartoon/colour
Direction:	Wladyslaw Nehrebecki and Leszek Mech
Production:	Bielsko-Biala

Subject:

Another adaption of Jules Verne's subject, this time with the children's characters Bolek and Lolek—both the main figures of a successful television series produced by the same directors and studio.

English title:	THE NEW GULLIVER
Original title:	NOVII GULLIVER
Year:	1935
Country:	Russia (Mosfilm)
Running time:	73 mins.
Medium:	Puppets and live action/ black and white
Director:	Alexander Ptuschko
Screenplay:	Alexander Ptuschko, and G. Roshal
Photography:	N. Renkov
Composer:	L. Schvartz
Puppet master:	S. Mokil
Animation:	G. Yalev
Art director:	Yu Shvetz
Actor:	V. Konstantinov as "Gulliver Pioneer Peter"

Subject:

The film uses various elements of Johnathan Swift's *Gulliver's Travels Book 1, Voyage to the Country of the Lilliputians*. The satire is directed against Fascism and militarism.

Story:

Pioneer Peter, on holiday at Artek, receives *Gulliver's Travels* as a present. Peter is greatly influenced by the book and one day he falls asleep on the seashore. He dreams that he is a bold traveller like Gulliver. A ship with Peter-Gulliver on board is wrecked. A wave casts Peter onto the shores of Lilliputia, where he is taken prisoner by the tiny inhabitants. After a stormy debate, the Lilliputian Parliament decides to use the 'man mountain' for militaristic purposes.

Peter sees scenes of Lilliputian life as they prepare for war. The Lilliputian proletariat rises in revolt and Peter helps them. He tows the Government's ships out to sea. Detachments of armed workers celebrate their victory.

Peter declares that henceforth Lilliputia is a free country . . . and wakes up.

English title:	THE LITTLE GOLDEN KEY
Original title:	SOLOTOJ, KLUJUTSCHIK
Year:	1939
Country:	Russia (Mosfilm)
Running time:	84 mins.
Medium:	Puppets and live action/ black and white
Director:	Alexander Ptuschko
Screenplay:	Alexander Tolstoi, from the book of the same name, the Russian "Pinnochio"
Artist:	Yu Shvetz
Puppets:	B. Kadatchnikov
Photography:	N. Renkov
Composer:	L. Schvartz
Actors:	A. Shchagin as "Kambas-Barabas," S. Martinson as "Duremap", G. Urarov as "Papa Karlo."

Subject:

An unusual talking log comes into the possession of the organ-grinder Papa Karlo and in his skilful hands it is turned into a wooden boy, Buratino. Karabas-Barabas's wooden puppet theatre comes to town. He rules his puppet people with a rod of iron.

Karabas has a little golden key to a secret door where he hopes to find a huge treasure. The dog Artemon steals the magic key from him, and with Buratino, the two puppets Melvina and Pierrot and Papa Karlo, runs away to the secret door.

Karabas pursues them but the puppets manage to open the door with the golden key, and a magic boat carries the heroes of the story away to a happy country where "all the children study in schools and the old people live gloriously".

English title:	THE HUNCH-BACKED HORSE
Original title:	KONJOK-GORBUNOK
Year:	1947
Country:	Russia (Soyuzmultfilm)
Running time:	57 mins.
Medium:	Animated cartoon/colour
Director:	Ivan Ivanov-Vano
Supervision:	A. Snezhko-Blotskaya
Artists:	L. Michin, V. Rodzhero, I. Troyanova, A. Belyakov
Screenplay:	J. Pomestschikov, N. Roshkov
Photography:	N. Voinov
Composer:	V. Oransky

Subject:

From the fairy story of the same name by P. Jerschov.

Story:

Ivan the Silly becomes owner of a miraculous hump-backed horse. With its help he brings a magic firebird into the Czar's palace and then a beautiful Princess. The old Czar asks her to become his wife, but she says that first he must grow young by bathing in three baths—one of boiling water, one of milk and one of cold water. The Czar is suspicious, and gets Ivan to test the effet of the baths. When Ivan is bathed he turns into a beautiful Prince Ivan. But the stupid and envious Czar is cooked in the boiling water. The hump-backed horse carries Ivan and the Princess to a new palace.

English title:	THE NIGHT BEFORE CHRISTMAS
Original title:	NOCE PERED ROSHDEST-VOM
Year:	1951
Country:	Russia (Soyuzmultfilm)
Running time:	50 mins.
Medium:	Animated cartoon/colour
Directors:	V. and Z. Brumberg
Screenplay:	V. and Z. Brumberg, M. Yanshin
Art directors:	N. Stroganova, A. Belyakov, P. Repkin
Photography:	N. Voinov
Music:	V. Oransky

Subject:

From the story by N. V. Gogol.

Story:

The proud beauty Oksana laughs at the lovelorn smith Vakula and asks him to bring her the Tsarina's shoes. When he arrives home Vakula finds some big sacks in the hut. Inside the sacks are three guests of his mother Solakha—the devil, an official, and a Cossack. Vakula mounts astride the devil and goes to the Tsar's palace. The Tsarina gives him the shoes and when he returns to the village, Vakula presents the shoes to Oksana who now loves him.

English title:	THE LITTLE SNOW MAIDEN
Original title:	SNEGUROTCHKA
Year:	1952
Country:	Russia (Soyuzmultfilm)

Running time:	67 mins.
Medium:	Animated cartoon/colour
Director:	Ivan Ivanov-Vano
Screenplay:	Ivan Ivanov-Vano, A. Snesh-ko-Blozkaya, O. Leonidov
Artistic supervision:	N. Stroganov
Artists:	L. Milchin, W. Nikitin
Music:	Rimsky-Korsakov
Musical arrangement:	L. Schvartz
Photography:	N. Voinov

Subject:

From a fairy story by A. N. Ostrovsky and an Opera by Rimsky-Korsakov.

Story:

With the onset of spring the heart of the cold and passionless Snow Maiden awakens to a dream of love and happiness. The Snow Maiden's mother Spring, gives her a garland in which is hidden the great strength of love. The Snow Maiden falls in love with a merchant's son, Misgir.

But the Sun, hating the snow maiden's grandfather Frost, destroys her. Now Frost has lost his power over the country of the Berends and it is covered with thick foliage and flowers.

English title:	THE TWELVE MONTHS
Original title:	DWENADZAT MESSJAZEW
Year:	1956
Country:	Russia (Soyuzmultfilm)
Running time:	55 mins.
Medium:	Animated cartoon/colour
Director:	Ivan Ivanov-Vano
Screenplay:	S. Marshak, N. Erdman
Producer:	M. Botom
Artists:	A. Belyakov, K. Karpov, A. Kuritsyn
Photography:	N. Voinov, E. Petrova
Composer:	M. Vineberg
Sound:	N. Prilutsky

Subject:

A film version of S. Marshak's own story of the same title.

Story:

A capricious queen will give gold to anyone who can bring her a basket of snowdrops on the night of New Year's Eve. A modest hardworking young girl is sent to collect snowdrops for this purpose by her evil stepmother and stepsister. In the forest, the girl meets the Twelve Months. The Brother Months help her to collect the flowers.

The stepmother takes the flowers to the queen, and is given the gold. The queen is greedy to see the flowers, and the girl leads her into the forest with her stepmother and stepsister. There, the Brother Months punish the queen, turn the stepmother and stepdaughter into dogs, and reward the girl with all the gifts of nature.

English title:	THE SNOW QUEEN
Original title:	SNESHAJA KOROLEWA
Year:	1957
Country:	Russia (Soyuzmultfilm)
Running time:	55 mins.
Medium:	Animated cartoon/colour
Director:	Lev Atamanov
Screenplay:	Lev Atamanov, G. Grebner
Artists:	A. Vinkurov, I. Schwarzman

Subject:

From the tale by Hans Christian Andersen.

English title:	THE ADVENTURES OF BURATINO
Original title:	PRIKLUTSCHENIJA BURATINO
Year:	1959
Country:	Russia (Soyuzmultfilm)
Running time:	67 mins.
Medium:	Animated cartoon/colour
Directors:	Ivan Ivanov-Vano, Dimitri Babichenko
Screenplay:	N. Erdman
Artists:	P. Repkin, S. Rusanov
Photography:	M. Druyan
Composer:	A. Lepin

Subject:

The same as *Solotoj, Klujutschnik (The Little Golden Key)*, except that when the heroes pass through the secret door they become directors and artists of a puppet theatre.

English title:	I DREW THE MAN
Year:	1960
Country:	Russia (Soyuzmultfilm)
Running time:	55 mins.
Medium:	Animated cartoon/colour
Directors:	V. and Z. Brumberg
Screenplay:	M. Volpin, N. Erdman
Artists:	L. Azarch, V. Lalayantz
Composer:	N. Bogoslovsk

Subject:

A new version of a film of 1949, *Fedja Saizew*.

Story:

Fedja has not confessed to his teacher that he drew the picture of a man on the classroom wall. The picture comes to life, leading all sorts of adventures and showing Fedja his guilt for not owning up. Eventually Fedja confesses his crime.

English title:	*THE KEY*
Year:	1961
Country:	Russia (Soyuzmultfilm)
Running time:	55 mins.
Medium:	Animated cartoon/colour
Director:	Lev Atamanov
Screenplay:	M. Volpin
Artists:	A. Vinokurov, I. Schvartzman
Photography:	M. Druyan
Composer:	L. Solin
Sound:	N. Prilutsky

Subject:

The fairies give a young boy a magic ball, which will take him to the Land of Happiness whenever he so desires. But his parents take away the ball and his grandfather, helped by Volshebnikov the magician, puts a lock on the gates of the Land of Happiness.

The boy grows up at magical speed, and one day comes to the locked gates of the Land of Happiness. He discovers that only a key made by his own hands will open the lock, so he goes to his grandfather, who gives him locksmith's tools. His grandfather also explains that true happiness can only come from knowledge, ability and generosity.

English title:	*THE BATH*
Original title:	*BANJA*
Year:	1962
Country:	Russia (Soyuzmultfilm)
Running time:	52 mins.
Medium:	Puppets and live action/colour/Cinemascope
Direction and screenplay:	Sergei Yutkievitch, Anatoli Karanovitch
Artist:	F. Zbarsky
Animation:	V. Kotenochkin
Composer:	R. Shchedrin
Narration:	A. and E. Raikin

Subject:

From a play by Vladimir Mayakovsky.

Story:

A stupid bureaucrat and lover of red tape, Pobedonosikov, constantly interferes with the work of inventors and scientists, even when Professor Velocipedkin invents a time machine. Velocipedkin cannot get funds to develop his machine. But he refuses to sell it to Pomkitch, the rich English capitalist, and with the aid of his assistants eventually succeeds in making a woman of the future appear. She is empowered to select a company of worthy people for a journey into the future. They see the glorious future of the Soviet people, but Pomkitch and Pobedonosikov fall into a dustbin when they return from the journey.

English title:	*THE WILD SWANS*
Original title:	*DIKIJE LEBEDI*
Year:	1962
Country:	Russia (Soyuzmultfilm)
Running time:	60 mins.
Medium:	Animated cartoon/colour/cinemascope
Directors:	M. and V. Tsekhanovsky
Art directors:	N. Lernev, M. Zherebchevsky
Composer:	A. Varlamaov

Subject:

From elements of the story of the same name by Hans Christian Andersen.

Story:

Eliza and her eleven brothers live happily with their father the king, a widower. A witch, Machecka, turns Eliza's brothers into swans and makes Eliza so ugly that her father does not recognise her and drives her off. A kind old lady cares for Eliza.

After bathing in a boiling lake and emerging as a beautiful maiden, Eliza is told by an old crow that to turn the swans back into men she must weave a net from nettles and throw it over them. She must also keep quiet about her identity.

The king sees Eliza and decides to make her his bride. But his enemies tell the witch, who arranges that Eliza be burnt at the stake. Up to the last moment of her life, Eliza weaves the net, and just as she dies throws it over the swans who turn back into beautiful young men and kill the witch.

English title:	*THE MECHANICAL FLEA*
Original title:	*LEVSHA*
Year:	1964
Country:	Russia (Soyuzmultfilm)
Medium:	Animated cut-outs/colour
Director:	Ivan Ivanov-Vano
Screenplay:	Ivan Ivanov-Vano
Art directors:	A. Yurin, M. Solokova, A. Kuritsyn

Animation:	Y. Norchtein, A. Malianto-vitch, L. J. Danov, C. Zolo-tovskaia, M. Botov
Music:	A. Alexandrov
Voices:	D. Jouraviev

Subject:

From a story by Nicholai Leskov

Story:

Levsha is a superhumanly ingenious Russian craftsman. A rich foreigner commissions a toy from him—a mechanical flea which dances in the heart of a diamond. Levsha makes the toy but refuses all reward and dies unnoticed in a poor hospital.

English title:	THE BLUE BIRD
Original title:	SINJAJA PTIZA
Year:	1972
Country:	Russia
Medium:	Animated cartoon/colour
Director and screenplay:	V. Livanov

Subject:

Adapted from a book by Maeterlink, completed, but not released yet.

English title:	THE KNIGHT GARBANCITO
Original title:	GARBANCITO DE LA MANCHA
Year:	1947
Country:	Spain
Running time:	72 mins.
Medium:	Animated cartoon/colour
Executive director:	Arturo Moreno
Production:	Balet y Blay
Screenplay:	Julian Permartin
Music:	Maestro Guerrero
Director:	José Maria Blay

Subject:

A brave little peasant, Garbancito, protected by a fairy, becomes a valiant knight. He victoriously defends his village and the children from the schemes of a giant.

English title:	HAPPY HOLIDAYS
Original title:	ALEGRES VACACIONES
Year:	1948
Country:	Spain
Running time:	65 mins.
Medium:	Animated cartoon/colour (Dufaycolour)

Executive director	Arturo Moreno
Production:	Balet y Blay
Director:	José Maria Blay
Music:	Maestro Ferres
Screenplay:	Ramon de Castro

Subject:

The characters of *Garbancito de la Mancha*, even the bad ones, travel about Spain in a motor coach.

Original title:	SUENOS DE TAI PY
Year:	About 1950
Country:	Spain
Running time:	70 mins.
Medium:	Animated cartoon/colour (Dufaycolour)
Screenplay:	F. Winterstein
Animation:	Armando Tosquellas
Director:	José Maria Blay, P. Winter-stein
Production:	Balet y Blay
Songs:	Artor Kaps, Augusto Alguero, jun.
Music and musical direction:	Augusto Alguero, jun.

Subject:

A musical show. The songs are sung by animals made up and dressed to look like film stars.

English title:	ONCE UPON A TIME
Original title:	ERASE UNA VEZ
Year:	1950
Country:	Spain
Running time:	75 mins.
Medium:	Animated Cartoon/colour (Cinefotocolor)
Screenplay:	Alexandre Cirici-Pellicer, Maestro Rafael Ferrer
Music:	Maestro Rafael Ferrer
Executive directors:	José Escobar, Alexandre Cirici-Pellicer, Ferrandiz, Frezquet, Tur, Ferran
Production:	Estela Film
Director and art director:	Alexandre Cirici-Pellicer

Subject:

An adapted version of the story of Cinderella.

English title:	THE MAGI OF DREAMS
Original title:	EL MAGO DE LOS SUENOS
Year:	1966

Country:	Spain
Running time:	80 mins.
Medium:	Animated cartoon/colour (Eastmancolor)
Presented:	By UNICEF to the United Nations Organisation
Directed:	Francisco Macian
Production:	Estudios Macian
Distribution (Spain):	Interpeninsular Film
Backgrounds:	J. Blasco
Music:	José Sola
Songs and Voices:	Andy Russel, Tito Mora, Pinocho, Chicho, Gordillo, Los Tres Sudamericanos, Ennio Sanguisto, Teresa Maria, Los Quatro de la Torre.

Subject:

Night after night a fantastic figure is seen among stars. It is the Magus of Dreams. He tells fairy tales to Cleo, Tete, Maripi, Colitas, Pelusin and Cuquil in the Telerin family.

The characters were originally created by José Luis Moro for a programme on Channel 1 of Spain's television in which the children are wished goodnight.

English title:	SCOPE, COLOUR, MUDA 75
Original title:	ERE ERERA BALEIBU ICIK SUBUA ARVAREN
Year:	1970
Country:	Spain
Running time:	75 mins.
Medium:	Painted directly on the film/colour/Scope/silent
Director, editing:	José Antonio Sistiaga
Producer:	Aldolfo Oliete
Executive producer:	J. Ma. Gonzales Sinde
Presented by:	X Films
Distribution:	X Films/Narvaez-Madrid
Laboratory:	Fotofilm, Madrid
Copyright:	M.21.391-69
Production time:	17 months, October 1968–February 1970

Subject:

This production entirely painted directly on to the film by J. A. Sistiaga alone, because of its abstract form cannot be explained rationally, just as its title has no meaning:

It is a visual film, which sets in motion the imagination, and the powers of meditation and of reflection.

This film was featured in the X Certamen Internacional de Cine Documental in Bilbao, and it won the Christu de Plata Prize for experimental films with its first 10 mins.

In its completed form it was entered in the Cinema Incontri, Abano, Terme, Italy (March 1970), Oberhausen, Germany (April 1970), Festival del Cine en color, Barcelona, Spain (October 1970) and the Festival Sigman Bordeaux, France (November 1970).

English title:	CINDERELLA
Original title:	CINDELITA
Year:	In production
Country:	Spain
Medium:	Animated cartoon/colour
Director:	Francisco Macian
Production:	Estudios Macian
Animation team:	Salvador Mestres, José Mira

Subject:

Another adapted version of Cinderella still in production.

English title:	MAGIC ADVENTURE
Original title:	MAGICA AVENTURA
Year:	1975
Country:	Spain
Running time:	1 hr. 11 min.
Medium:	Animated cartoon/Eastmancolor
Director:	Cruz Delgado
Producer:	Cruz Delgado Produccion
Free adaptation:	Gustavo Alcalde, Cruz Delgado, Felix Cascajo
Animation:	Basilio Gonzalez, Carlos Alfonso y Vicente G. Sangrador
Photography:	Jose Maria Sanchez, Rafael Catalan
Background:	Jose Luis Berlanga
Music:	Antonio Areta
Design:	Angel S. Chicharro, Mauro Cacéres, Jose Zumel

Subject:

Tito and Tita are running after their kite and go into the wood. There they come across a castle in which a Puss-in-Boots dwells. It tells them how it managed to overcome the ogre so that its master could marry a princess.

The children continue to look for their kite and reach some reefs crowned by a lighthouse and the lighthouse keeper tells them the adventures of a fantastic boat.

The lighthouse becomes lost in the mist. The

children find their kite and go back home with it, helped by the wind, which becomes their friend. But the kite becomes caught up on the weathervane of the writer Andersen's house, and he shows them his last story.

The Magician Wind comes back to tell them that in a distant land, children are not allowed to play. Tito and Tita fly to "Never-play-land" aboard their kite and helped by many toys they overcome the enemies of children's toys.

English title:	OUT OF AN OLD MAN'S HEAD
Original title:	I HUVET PA EN GAMMEL GUBBE
Year:	1968
Country:	Sweden
Running time:	76 min. (Animation 55 mins.)
Medium:	Animated cartoon and live action/colour (Eastmancolor)
Written by:	Swedish Words, Inc., Hans Alfredson, Tage Danielsson
Director:	Per Ahlin
Screenplay:	AB Svenska Ord (Hans Alfredson, Tage Danielsson)
Music:	Gunnar Svensson
Animation cameraman:	Conny Marnelius
Live action:	Bo Wanngard
Sound recordist:	Louis Anselmi
Editing:	Lars Ogenklev
Actors:	Hans Alfredson (as the old man, Johan Bjork) with Fatima Eckman, Gosta Eckman, Monica Eckman, Monica Nielson, Ernst Gunther, Rolf Bengtsson, Gus Dahlstrom, Gunnel Wadner
Production:	GK-Film Inc., (Gunner Karlson)
Distribution:	AB Svensk Filmindustri
1st showing:	6th December, 1968 in Stockholm

Subject:

Hans Alfredson and Tage Danielsson, the most important laughter-makers in Sweden, and the founders of the company Swedish Words Inc., have introduced a new branch to the Swedish film industry. Anybody can film a person's exterior, but they decided to film the inside of a person, or, more precisely, the inside of someone's head. The character, Johan Bjork, is admitted to an old people's home, and as he lives there, he thinks of the events of his life and, rather more, of the things he would like to have happened.

The old man is shown realistically in a contemporary setting, while memories and fantasies of his past career are shown in caricature. Johan's most carefree memories are the ones he dwells on—his romantic childhood and his boring apprenticeship to a beer-swilling mason. From these he creates fantastic dreams of a life as gay as Don Juan's, where he is well-known in brothels and seduces girls with ease. This is a strong contrast to his married life, which passes lightning-fast through his memory, with a bang and a sigh.

English title:	THUNDERING FATTY
Original title:	DUNDERKLUMPEN!
Year:	1974
Country:	Sweden
Running time:	90 mins.
Medium:	Animation combined with live action/colour
Directors:	Per Ahlin
Producer:	Gunnar Karlson
Production:	GK Film, and Sveriges Radio
Animators:	Per Ahlin, Beppe Wolgers, Jens Wolgers
Screenplay:	Beppe Wolgers
Music:	Toots Thielemans

Subject:

In a fantastic mixture of animated and live sequences, strange adventures are portrayed in a fabulous natural setting in northern Sweden, the land of the midnight sun, where toys, fairy-tale spirits, and real people participate in a thrilling chase after a treasure chest.

Title:	SNOW WHITE AND THE SEVEN DWARFS
Year:	1938
Country:	U.S.A.
Running time:	83 mins.
Medium:	Animated cartoon/colour
Direction:	Walt Disney
Production:	Walt Disney
Director of sequences:	Wilfred Jackson
Directors:	P. Pearce, L. Morey, W. Cottrell, B. Sharpenstein
Supervision:	David Hand
Direction assistant:	John Hubley
Screenplay:	Earl Hurd
Animators:	Arthur Babitt, Ward Kimball, Joshua Meader, Maurice Noble

Music :   Frank Churchill, Leigh Har-
line, Paul Smith

Subject:

Inspired by one of the Grimm Fairy Tales.

Story:

Once upon a time there lived a lovely little Princess named Snow White. Her vain and wicked stepmother, the queen, feared that someday Snow White's beauty would surpass her own. So she dressed the little princess in rags and forced her to work as a scullery maid. Each day the vain queen consulted her magic mirror—"Magic mirror, on the wall, who is the fairest of them all?" And as long as the mirror answered, "you are the fairest one of all," Snow White was safe from the queen's cruel jealousy. However, one day the mirror answered, "Snow White!"

When the queen saw a handsome young prince admiring Snow White, she instructed her hunts-man to take her to the forest and kill her. But the huntsman's courage failed. As he watched her stoop to help a little lost bird he told her to run far into the woods and never return. Friendly birds and animals comforted her and led her to a charm-ing little cottage, the home of the seven dwarfs. There Snow White found such an untidy state of affairs, she thought it belonged to children, so, with her forest friends helping, she cleaned up the house.

When the dwarfs came back home from work and found the rooms tidied, they thought a monster was in the house, but only found Snow White sleeping. They were delighted when she asked to stay and keep house for them. She found great happiness with her friends until the queen con-sulting her Magic Mirror found that the princess was not dead. Disguising herself as an old pedlar woman the queen visited Snow White and tempted her to bite a magic apple. Snow White fell to the floor as if dead. The little birds and animals having recognised the queen warned the dwarfs. They gave chase and finally drove the wicked queen to the top of a cliff. Trapped, she toppled to her death. The dwarfs, heart-broken, made Snow White a glass coffin, because, even in death (as they supposed) she remained so beautiful. Night and day, they kept watch over it.

Eventually the prince, who had fallen in love with Snow White, discovered the coffin. He dismounted and kissed her. Immediately, the princess' eyes opened, for the spell could only be broken by love's first kiss. Snow White and the prince rode off together amid the cheers of the happy dwarfs.

Title :   *FANTASIA*
Year :   1939
Country :   U.S.A.

Running time :   124 mins.
Medium :   Animated cartoon/colour
Director :   Walt Disney
Production :   Ben Sharpenstein
Screenplay :   Joe Grant, Dick Huemer
Musical direction : Edward H. Plumb
Director of orchestra : Leopold Stokowsky
Editor :   Stephen Ceillag
Recording :   William E. Garrity, C. O. Slyfield, D. N. A. Hawkings

Subject:

Eight different pieces of music are each given a visual interpretation by teams of Disney artists. The last two pieces of music run together, so there are seven animation sequences all told, plus a short visualisation of the soundtrack, linked by live-action sequences in which Deems Taylor, as Master of Ceremonies, introduces each theme.

(1) Toccata and Fugue in D minor (J. S. Bach)

Direction: Samuel Armstrong

Story development: Lee Blair, Elmer Plummer, Phil Dyke

Art direction: Robert Cormack

Backgrounds: Joe Stahley, John Hench, Nino Carbe

Animation: Cy Young, Art Palmer, Daniel Mc-Manus, George Rowley, Edwin Aardal, Joshua Meador, Cornett Wood .

Story:

Gigantic coloured shadows of the musicians fill the screen. Shapes like violin bows flit across, move in circles, divide and cross. Heavy cloud forms drift along, and vapourous shapes that wind and undulate. Then a rippling mass of colour, across which bursts something like a comet. Another comet bursts in the opposite direction. Cloud masses gather into what might be organ pipes. The clouds dissolve into bright light, against which stands the silhouette of the con-ductor.

(2) The Nutcracker Suite (P. I. Tchaikovsky)

Direction: Samuel Armstrong

Story development: Sylvia Moberly-Holland, Norman Wright, Albert Heath, Bianca Majolie, Graham Heid

Character designs: John Walbridge, Elmer Plummer, Ethel Kulsar

Art direction: Robert Cormack, Al Zinnen, Curtiss D. Perkins, Arthur Byram, Bruce Bush-man

Backgrounds: John Hench, Ethel Kulsar, Nino Carbe

Animation: Art Babitt, Les Clark, Don Lusk, Cy Young, Robert Stokes

Story:

A sequence of dances on the theme of nature: Dance of the sugar plum fairy (fairies and flowers), Chinese dance (mushrooms), Dance of the flutes (blossom on a stream), Arab dance (underwater plants and goldfish), Russian dance (thistle and orchids), Dance of the flowers (autumn trees and fairies).

(3) The Sorcerer's Apprentice (P. Dukas)

Direction: James Algar

Story development: Perce Pearce, Carl Fallberg

Art direction: Tom Codrick, Charles Philippi, Zack Schwartz

Backgrounds: Claude Coates, Stan Spohn, Albert Dempster, Eric Hansen

Animation supervision: Fred Moore

Animation: Les Clark, Riley Thomson, Marvin Woodward, Preston Blair, Edward Love, Ugo D'orsi, George Rowley, Cornett Wood

Story:

Mickey Mouse tries to perform his master's spells, with disastrous results.

(4) The Rite of Spring (I. Stravinsky)

Direction: Bill Roberts, Paul Satterfield

Story development and Research: William Martin, Leo Thistle, Robert Steiner, John Fraser McLeish

Art direction: McLaren Stewart, Dick Kelsey, John Hubley

Backgrounds: Ed Starr, Brice Mack, Edward Levitt

Animation supervision: Wolfgang Reitherman, Joshua Meador

Animation: Philip Duncan, John McManus, Paul Busch, Art Palmer, Don Tobin, Edwin Aardal, Paul B. Kossoff

Special camera effects: Gail Papineau, Leonard Pickley

Story:

The history of the world up to the extinction of the dinosaurs.

(5) Pastoral Symphony (L. van Beethoven)

Direction: Hamilton Luske, Jim Handley, Ford Beebe

Story development: Otto Englander, Webb Smith, Erdman Penner, Joseph Sabo, Bill Peed, George Stallings

Character designs: James Brodrero, John P. Miller, Lorna S. Soderstrom

Art direction: Hugh Hennesy, Kenneth Anderson, J. Gordon Legg, Herbert Ryman, Yale Gracey, Lance Nolley

Background paintings: Claude Coates, Ray Hufine, W. Richard Anthony, Arthur Riley, Gerald Nevius, Roy Forkum

Animation supervision: Fred Moore, Ward Kimball, Arthur Babitt

Animation: Berny Wolf, Jack Campbell, Jack Bradbury, James Moore, Milt Neil, Bill Justice, John Elliotte, Walt Kelly, Don Lusk, Lynn Karp, Murray McCellan, Robert W. Youngquist, Harry Hamsel

Story:

A pageant of Disneyesque mythological creatures: Winged horses, fauns, unicorns, male and female Centaurs, followed by the entry of Bacchus, a thunderstorm from Zeus, a rainbow from Iris, Apollo in his sun-chariot, and Artemis with a new moon and a constellation of stars.

(6) Dance of the Hours (A. Ponchielli)

Direction: Tee Hee, Norman Ferguson

Character designs: Martin Provensen, James Rodrero, Duke Russel, Earl Hurd

Art direction: Kendall O'Connor, Harold Doughty, Earnest Nordli

Background paintings: Albert Dempster, Charles Connor

Animation supervision: Norman Ferguson

Animation: John Lounsbery, Howard Swift, Preston Blair, Hugh Fraser, Harvey Toombs, Norman Tate, Hicks Locky, Art Elliot, Grand Simmons, Ray Patterson, Franklin Grundeen

Story:

The progress of a day in the formal garden of the Duke of Alvise, with dances by ostriches, hippopotami, elephants and alligators.

(7) Night on Bald Mountain (M. Moussorgsky) and *Ave Maria* (F. Schubert)

Direction: Wilfred Jackson

Story development: Campbell Grant, Arthur Reinemann, Phil Dyke

Art direction: Kay Nielsen, Terrell Stapp, Charles Payzant, Thir Putnam

Background paintings: Merle Cox, Ray Lockrem, Robert Storms, W. Richard Anthony

Animation supervision: Vladikmir Tytla

Special animation effects: Joshua Meador, Miles E. Pike, John F. Reed, Daniel McManus

Animation: John McManus, William N. Shull, Rob. W. Carlson, Jr., Lester Novros, Don Patterson

Special camera effects: Gail Papineau, Leonard Pickley

Ave Maria Chorus Direction: Charles Henderson

Soloist: Julietta Novis

Story:

Evil spirits gather at night. Chernabog, Lord of Evil, appears out of Bald Mountain, plays with spirits, and throws them into the fiery pit. He disappears back into the mountain as dawn rises. Below the mountain, a vast host of worshippers, all carrying tapers, makes its way through the forest into the light of the morning.

Title:	*GULLIVER'S TRAVELS*
Year:	1939
Country:	U.S.A.
Running time:	80 mins.
Medium:	Animated cartoon/colour (Technicolor)
Director:	Dave Fleischer
Producer:	Max Fleischer
Distribution:	Paramount (Germany)
Screenplay:	Dan Gordon, Cal Howard, Ted Pierce, Isidore Sparber, Edmond Seward
Photography:	Charles Schettler
Music:	Leo Robin, Ralph Rainger

Subject:

The film is based on the romance by Jonathan Swift. Lemuel Gulliver is shipwrecked upon the shore of an uncharted island. He falls into a deep sleep, sprawled full length on the sandy beach. The island is the strange little kingdom of Lilliput, inhabited by a race of tiny people, the tallest of whom is no more than six inches high. Everything on the island is on the same diminutive scale. We see Gulliver escape from various plans to catch him while sleeping and later see the favours bestowed on him by the king who finds himself at war with the kingdom of Brobdingnag, although the children of the two kings were about to marry. Thanks to Gulliver the Brobdingnag fleet is defeated and as a reward the king has a boat built to take Gulliver back to his homeland.

Title:	*MISTER BUG GOES TO TOWN*
Year:	1940
Country:	U.S.A.
Running time:	80 mins.
Medium:	Animated cartoon/colour
Director:	Dave Fleischer
Screenplay:	Dan Gordon, Ted Pierce, Isidore Sparber, William Turner, Carl Mayer, Graham Place, Bob Wickersham, and Cal Howard, from the original story by Dave Fleischer, Dan Gordon, Ted Pierce and Isidore Sparber

Music and lyrics:	Hoagy Carmichael, Frank Loesser and Sammy Timberg
Directors of animation:	Willard Bowsky, Myron Waldman, Thomas Johnson, David Tendlar, James Culhane, H. C. Ellison, Stan Quackenbush and Graham Place
Atmospheric music created and conducted:	Leigh Harline
Voices:	Kenny Gardner, Gwen Williams, Jack Mercer, Ted Pierce, Carl Mayer, Stan Freed and Pauline Loth

Subject:

C. Bagley Beetle, a meanie at heart, and his hoodlum henchmen, Swat the Fly and Smack the Mosquito, represent the weaknesses and vices of the insect family. Beetle is a first class Simon Legree, too, and for a time comes close to marrying lovely Honey Bee whose heart really belongs to a grasshopper named Hoppity. But mostly this film is about the never-ending fight against the human menace waged by an insect colony just forty-five inches off Broadway. Their location is admittedly bad, so perhaps their harsh mode of life is not typical.

Title:	*PINOCCHIO*
Year:	1940
Country:	U.S.A.
Running time:	87 mins.
Medium:	Animated cartoon/colour
Director:	Walt Disney
Story adaption:	Aurelius Battaglia, Ted Sears, Webb Smith, Joseph Sabo, Otto Englander, William Cottrell, Erdman Penner
Supervising directors:	Ben Sharpenstein, Hamilton Luske
Sequence directors:	Tee Hee, Wilfred Jackson, Bill Roberts, Jack Kinney, Norman Ferguson
Animation direction:	Fred Moore, Milton Kahl, Ward Kimball, Eric Larson, Franklin Thomas, Vladimar Tytla, Arthur Babbitt, Wolfgang Reitherman
Music and lyrics:	Leigh Harlin, Ted Washington, Paul J. Smith
Character design:	Joe Grant, John P. Miller, Martin Provenson, Albert Hurter, Campbell Grant, John Walbridge

Art directors:	Charles Philippi, Hugh Hennesy, Kenneth Henderson, Dick Kelsey, Kendall O'Connor, Terrell Stapp, Thor Putnam, John Hubley, McLaren Stewart, Al Zinnen
Backgrounds:	Claude Coats, Merle Cox, Ed. Starr, Ray Hufine
Animators:	Jack Campbell, Olivier M. Johnston, Berny Wolf, Don Lusk, John Lunsbery, Norman Tate, John Bradbury, Lynn Karp, Charles Nichols, Art Palmer, Don Tobin, Georges Rowley, Don Patterson, Les Clarck, Hugh Fraser, Joshua Meador, Robert Martsch, John McManus, Preston Blair, Marvin Woodward, John Elliotte, Don Gowsley

Subject:

Pinocchio is Disney's second attempt at feature-length story-telling, and succeeds in presenting a better illusion of 3-D than Snow White. A new painting process called "the blend" gives a rounded appearance to the characters and the multiplane camera technique is much extended. The opening scene of the rooftops of a village at night is a great tour-de-force of cinematic illusion. Disney's film is the only cartoon version of Collodi's story that has yet been completed.

Story:

An old, toymaker named Geppetto has created a delightful puppet, which he calls Pinocchio. He wishes it were a real live boy. That night the Blue Fairy gives life to the puppet and appoints Jiminy Cricket as his conscience. Pinocchio is sent to school, but Honest John the fox and Giddy the cat spirit him away and sell him to Stromboli, an unscrupulous showman. The Blue Fairy and Jiminy Cricket rescue him, but once again he gets into trouble. This time the fox sells him to the villainous coachman who takes wayward boys to Pleasure Island, from which they never return as boys.

Jiminy follows and finds Pinocchio and Lampwick, a tough boy, gorging themselves on the good things of life while they are slowly being turned into donkeys. Pinocchio has grown long ears and a tail before he and Jiminy manage to swim to the mainland.

They learn that Geppetto has gone in search of his live puppet and has been swallowed by Monstro the Whale. Jiminy and Pinocchio dive to the bottom of the sea and are also swallowed by Monstro. After a joyous re-union with Geppetto and his pets, Figaro the kitten and Cleo the goldfish, Pinocchio builds a fire in the whale's belly.

This causes him to sneeze and they are all blown free.

After a chase in which Monstro smashes their raft, Pinocchio saves Geppetto at the risk of his own life, and thereby proves himself brave and unselfish and worthy of becoming a real, live boy.

Title:	DUMBO
Year:	1941
Country:	U.S.A.
Running time:	64 mins.
Medium:	Animated cartoon/colour
Director:	Walt Disney
Supervision:	Ben Sharpenstein
Art direction associate:	John Hubley
Sequence director:	Wilfred Jackson
Animation directors:	Arthur Babitt, Ward Kimball
Screenplay:	Aurelius Battaglia
Character designs:	Maurice Noble

Subject:

Spring comes to the circus, and storks begin dropping new tiger cubs, baby hippos, seals, monkeys and all the rest in parachutes. All get babies except Mrs. Jumbo, the mama elephant. The circus entrains and Mrs. Jumbo grieves in her compartment. The youngster for whom she pines is in the charge of a stork who has lost his way. The messenger eventually locates the train and drops the parachute for Mrs. Jumbo. It lands, and her baby tumbles out. Everybody laughs, for the infant's ears are as large as sails. But Mrs. Jumbo ignores the hilarity: she loves her baby.

As time goes on, the youngster becomes such a figure of fun that he is named Dumbo and is the constant victim of teasing. One day, during a parade, a boy pokes his tongue out at Dumbo and Mrs. Jumbo snatches him up and spanks him. The crowd panics and Mrs. Jumbo is chained and imprisoned. Dumbo is left on his own. He is befriended by Timothy Mouse, who cannot bear to see the motherless baby provoked and insulted. Timothy and Dumbo decide that if the latter were to become famous, the ringmaster would release his mother. They plan a sensational ring trick, but Dumbo, no thanks to his ears, succeeds only in wrecking the performance.

Dumbo is in disgrace and Timothy tells his sad story to the forest birds. The feathered sages give the baby confidence to fly with the use of his ears, and Dumbo scores a spectacular success with his aerial feats. He has triumphed at last. The first thing he does is to get his mother out of jail. Timothy becomes his manager, and he, the baby and Mrs Jumbo set off on a special streamlined train for Hollywood, where new triumphs await the Flying Elephant.

Title:	THE RELUCTANT DRAGON (sub-title): THE WALT DISNEY STORY
Year:	1941
Country:	U.S.A.
Running time:	73 mins.
Director, animation:	Hamilton Luske
Medium:	Animated cartoon/and live action/colour
Director/producer:	Walt Disney
Live-action director:	Alfred Werker
Commentary:	Robert Benchley
Actors and animators:	Ward Kimball, Fred Moore, Norman Ferguson

Subject:

The story of *The Reluctant Dragon* itself occupies the last ten minutes of the film, and it is a cartoon from a Kenneth Grahame story about a dragon who dislikes terrorising people and comes to a compromise with a knight who dislikes fighting dragons. The other animation sequences include *Baby Weems* in story sketch stage, a sequence starring Goofy, a sequence showing sound effects being synchronised to a sequence from *Dumbo*, and a short scene of Donald Duck. The rest of the film consists of a guided tour of the Disney studio conducted by Robert Benchley.

Title:	BAMBI
Year:	1942
Country	U.S.A.
Running time:	69 mins.
Medium:	Animated cartoon/colour
Director/Producer:	Walt Disney
Art director:	David Hilberman
Associate art director:	John Hubley
Backgrounds:	Robert Mackintosh
Animator:	Joshua Meador

Subject:

From a story by Felix Salten.

Story:

In the heart of the forest, a baby deer, Prince Bambi, is born. All the other animals come and do him honour. Under the guidance of his mother, and sometimes helped by Thumper the rabbit, Bambi learns to walk and talk and get to know his domain. He is cold in winter, and suffers greatly when his mother is killed. But in spring he re-discovers the young doe whom he met the previous year, and in due time she gives birth to Bambi's baby in a remote hollow of the woods. There is a forest fire, and Bambi is pursued by dogs, but he escapes and takes over from his father as leader of the herd.

Title:	VICTORY THROUGH AIR-POWER
Year:	1943
Country:	U.S.A.
Running time:	65 mins.
Medium:	Live action combined with animation/colour
Story director:	Perce Pearce
Director and Supervisor:	David Hand
Production:	Walt Disney Studios

Subject:

During the Second World War it was essential to provide some information regarding the strategy of the U.S.A. The Disney Organisation have, with experts, projected how air-power could destroy the enemy. The film is a highly dramatic work of the period.

Title:	THE THREE CABALLEROS
Year:	1945
Country:	U.S.A.
Running time:	72 mins.
Medium:	Animated cartoon and live action/colour
Director/Producer:	Walt Disney
Production supervisor:	Norman Ferguson
Live action director:	Harold Young
Animators:	John McManus, Ward Kimball
Live action photography:	Ray Rennahan
Special effects:	Ub Iwerks

Subject:

A musical with sixteen songs, *The Three Caballeros* is a combination of live action personalities and cartoon figures on the same screen. The actors are mostly pretty girls, and in keeping with the Latin-American setting they include a Brazilian singer, Aurora Miranda, and two Mexican ones, Carmen Molina and Dora Luz.

Story:

Donald Duck receives three packages for his birthday. One is a film about a penguin called Pablo who is always trying to get to a warm climate. The second is a film about rare South American birds, including a flying donkey. The third is José Carioca, an old friend of Donald's. He takes Donald to Baia where Donald falls in love with a beautiful saleslady, but José whisks him away to

Mexico where he meets Panchito, a convivial rooster, who is the third caballero. Panchito takes Donald and José aboard a magic flying serape, and they go through Mexico seeing children celebrating Christmas, a famed dancer doing the "Jesusita" and other events. Donald has fallen in love again, but is taken to Vera Cruz for a festival, to Acapulco for a frolic on the sand, and finally to Mexico City, where the film climaxes in a bullfight and fireworks.

Title:	*MAKE MINE MUSIC*
Year:	1946
Country:	U.S.A.
Medium:	Animated cartoon/colour
Running time:	75 mins.
Director/Producer:	Walt Disney
Supervision:	Joshua Meador
Story:	Tee Hee
Animator:	Ward Kimball, John Mc-Manus
Special effects:	Ub Iwerks

Subject:

This film consists of ten episodes, unconnected except that they are all based on singing or music and most introduce new Disney characters. The titles of the various episodes are:

(1) The Martins and the Coys, (2) Without You, (3) Casey at the Bat, (4) Blue Bayou, (5) Peter and the Wolf, (6) Johnny Fedora and Alice Bluebonnet, (7) All the Cats join in, (8) After you've gone, (9) The Silhouettes, (10) The Whale who wanted to sing at the Met.

Title:	*SONG OF THE SOUTH*
Year:	1946
Country:	U.S.A.
Running time:	94 mins.
Medium:	Animated cartoon and live action/colour
Director/Producer:	Walt Disney
Animation Director:	Wilfred Jackson
Animators:	Rudy Larriva, Joshua Meador
Special effects:	Ub Iwerks

Subject:

The Georgia family of John and Sally and their little boy Johnny, go back to the grandmother's plantation from Atlanta to escape ostracism because of John's newspaper editorials. Distressed by conditions at home, the parents having become estranged, Johnny makes an attempt to run away.

Uncle Remus relates a fable of Brer Rabbit, shelters Johnny in his cabin, and keeps him interested by telling him other fables while word can be sent to the lad's mother.

Johnny is taken home and meets the Favers family, poor white neighbours, and a friendship springs up between him and their little girl Ginny. However, he gets into trouble with her rowdy brothers, Joe and Jake, when he endeavours to save a puppy from their cruelty. Uncle Remus interposes, and diverts the children with the fable of Brer Rabbit and Tar Baby.

Ginny dressed in her best party clothes, gets pushed into a mud puddle. Uncle Remus, searching for Johnny, finds that he is unwilling to go to his birthday party because Ginny's dress has been ruined. To cheer the children, Uncle Remus tells them a tale about the Laughing Place. Johnny's mother, angered because of the children's absence from the party, forbids Uncle Remus to tell Johnny any more stories.

Uncle Remus, saddened by the mother's misunderstanding of his motives, starts to wander from the plantation. The boy tries to intercept his old friend by cutting across a pasture, but is attacked and seriously hurt by an angry bull.

While Johnny appears to be hovering between life and death, his father returns home and a reconciliation between the parents occurs at the boy's bedside. The lad seems to have lost the will to live, until Uncle Remus volunteers to try reviving him with a reminder of the stories. Johnny recovers, his mother realises the good influences of Uncle Remus and the children once again return to his knee to hear further wonderful adventures of Brer Rabbit.

Title:	*SINBAD THE SAILOR*
Year:	1946
Country:	U.S.A.
Running time:	50 mins.
Medium:	Animated cartoon/colour
Director:	Dave Fleischer
Method:	This production makes excellent use of three dimensional illusion by utilising the different panning capabilities of the rostrum camera. The foreground moves more slowly than the background, and the relation between various planes give the illusion of depth

Subject:

The film uses the character of Popeye as Sinbad in an Arabian nights adventure.

Title:	FUN AND FANCY FREE
Year:	1947
Country:	U.S.A.
Running time:	72 mins.
Medium:	Animated cartoon and live action/colour
Director:	Walt Disney
Animation director:	Ward Kimball
Animator:	Arthur Babitt
Special effects:	Ub Iwerks

Subject:

Jiminy Cricket tells the story of Bongo, a little circus bear who escapes from the circus on his monocycle to seek the love of Lulubelle, a little female bear.

Lulubelle loves Bongo, and smacks him to show him her love. Bongo doesn't realise what she means, and ducks so that she hits Lumpjaw, the villain. Bongo then leaves sadly as Lulubelle and Lumpjaw prepare to marry, then realises what Lulubelle meant, returns, has a fight with Lumpjaw, and wins Lulubelle.

Then Jiminy hops to (live action) Edgar Bergen's house, where Bergen tells the story of Happy Valley. Mickey Mouse, Donald Duck and Goofy are three peasants, who lose their magic harp and have to sell their cow. In exchange Mickey gets some magic beans, which grow into a huge beanstalk that leads the peasants up to a giant's castle. The giant has the harp, which is rescued after a chase in which the giant falls down the beanstalk and is killed.

Back in Edgar Bergen's house, one of his guests complains that he liked the giant. Bergen is explaining that he is a figment of the imagination when the giant puts his face to the window and asks where Mickey the mouse is. Bergen faints, and the giant walks away across Hollywood.

Title:	SO DEAR TO MY HEART
Year:	1948
Country:	U.S.A.
Running time:	82 mins.
Medium:	Animated cartoon and live action/colour
Director:	H. Luske, Harold Schuster
Production:	Walt Disney Studios

Subject:

This film has only 15 per cent animation, and is based on Sterling North's best-seller of the same name. A boy called Jerry Kincaid adopts a black lamb, Tildy, his little girl friend, helps him groom it for the County Fair, but it escapes and there is a terrifying search for it. It is found, given the Special Award by the judges at the County Fair, and returns home in triumph with Jerry and Tildy.

Title:	MELODY TIME
Year:	1948
Country:	U.S.A.
Running time:	75 mins.
Medium:	Animated cartoon and live action/colour
Director/Producer:	Walt Disney
Sequences director:	Wilfred Jackson
Animation director:	Ward Kimball
Animators:	Robert Canon, Rudy Larriva, Joshua Meador, Dan McManus

Subject:

A musical fantasy in seven episodes, starring Ethel Smith and Roy Rodgers. 1. *Once upon a Wintertime*, where a couple dance with some rabbits. 2. *Bumble Boogie*, inspired by Rimsky Korsakoff's "Flight of the Bumblebee". 3. *Johnny Appleseed*, the story of the American folk hero. 4. *Little Toot*, the story of a New York tugboat. 5. *Trees*. 6. *Blame it on the Samba*—Ethel Smith does a samba with Donald Duck. 7. *Pecos Bill*, a complaint about a horse who jumps up to the moon.

Title:	ALICE IN WONDERLAND
Year:	1948
Country:	U.S.A.
Running time:	70 mins.
Medium:	Animated puppets and live action/colour
Director:	Dallas Bower
Puppetry:	Lou Bunin
Cast:	Pamela Brown, Felix Aylmer Stephan Murray, Carol Marsh
Production:	Leo Hurwitz
Method:	A combination of puppet animation with live action photography. Although the technique was successful the film was not a box office triumph.

Subject:

Based on the famous story by Lewis Carroll of a little girl's adventures in Wonderland.

Title:	THE ADVENTURES OF ICHABOD AND MR TOAD
Year:	1949
Country:	U.S.A.
Medium:	Animated cartoon/colour
Production:	Walt Disney Studios
Directors:	Jack Kinney, Clyde Geronimi, James Algar

Narration:	Bing Crosby & Basil Rathbone
Colour and styling:	Claude Coates, Mary Blair, Don Da Gradi, John Hench
Layout:	Charles Philippi, Al Zinnen, Tom Codrick, Thor Putnam, Hugh Hennesy, Lance Nolley
Background:	Ray Huffine, Merle Cox, Art Riley, Brice Mack, Dick Anthony
Directing animators:	Frank Thomas, Ollie Johnston, Wolfgang Reitherman, Milt Kahl, John Lounbsery, Ward Kimball.
Character animators:	Fred Moore, Harvey Toombs, John Sibley, Hal King, Marc Davis, Hugh Fraser, Hal Ambro, Don Lusk
EFX animators:	George Rowley, Jack Boyd
Special processes:	Ub Iwerks
Sound director:	C. O. Slyfield
Sound recording:	Robert O. Cook
Film editor:	John O. Young
Music editor:	Al Teeter
Musical direction:	Oliver Wallace
Vocal arrangements:	Ken Darby
Ichabod songs by:	Don Raye, Gene De Paul
Voices:	Eric Blore, Pat O'Malley, John Ployardt, Colin Campbell, Campbell Grant, Claud Allister and the Rythmaires
Distribution:	RKO

Subject:

Disney combines two separate stories, Washington Irving's *Legend of Sleepy Hollow* and part of Kenneth Grahame's *Wind in the Willows*, adapted to represent their heroes as "the most fascinating scapegraces of literature". An argument between Bing Crosby, who narrates *Ichabod*, and Basil Rathbone, who narrates *Mr. Toad*, links the two stories and establishes this theme.

Story:

1. *Ichabod*. Ichabod is an itinerant Yankee schoolmaster who becomes the laughing stock of a Hudson River village through his clumsy efforts at social climbing. He woos Katrina Van Tassel, intending to gain possession of her father's rich lands by marrying her. But he has a rival in Brom Bones, the husky bully of the region. Katrina prefers Brom, but is an incurable coquette and shamelessly encourages the schoolmaster.

Ichabod attends a big dance at Katrina's home, far from the village. Brom Jones is also there, and as the guests talk of local legends and superstitions he realises that Ichabod is terrified of

ghosts. So Brom tells Ichabod the legend of the "Headless Horseman" who rides about the area looking for his head. The party breaks up, and the schoolmaster heads back towards his lodgings.

True to his worst anticipations, Ichabod hears demoniacal laughter and sees a headless apparition galloping after him. There is a terrifying chase, and Ichabod gets back to the village just in time. But though schoolboys discover that the ghost was a hoax, Ichabod leaves the district forever.

2. *Mr. Toad*. Toad is careering about the countryside in a Gipsy caravan, with the aid of his horse, Cyril. His friends, MacBadger, Water Rat and Mole are concerned about him, and creditors are besiegeing his ancestral home. Toad takes no notice of all this, and gives his manor house to a gang of weasels in exchange for their powerful red motor car.

The car is a stolen one, and Toad is jailed for possessing it. He escapes with the aid of his horse, and is chased by the police through city and country, outrunning his pursuers by hijacking a railway engine. He nearly drowns in a pond, but finally arrives at the home of Water Rat. The weasels have taken over Toad Hall, but with the aid of his friends Toad recovers his property and is exonerated of stealing the motor car. But Toad's mania for excitement continues and he is last seen flying a flimsy aeroplane above his mansion and knocking its steeples to pieces.

Title:	CINDERELLA
Year:	1950
Country:	U.S.A.
Running time:	74 mins.
Medium:	Animated cartoon
Production:	Walt Disney Studios
Animation director:	Ward Kimball
Sequences director:	Wilfred Jackson
Directors:	Hamilton Luske, Clyde Geronimi
Supervision:	Ben Sharpenstein
Music:	Oliver Wallace, Paul Smith
Animator:	Joshua Meador
Editing:	Donald Halliday
Songs:	Mack David, Harry Livingston, A. C. Hofman

Subject:

From a story by Charles Perrault.

Story:

Cinderella, an orphan, lives with her stepmother and her two daughters, who make her slave for them while they live in luxury. But thanks to her friendship with small animals, Cinderella endures her hardship with a good temper.

The King wants to find a wife for his son, so he holds a ball at his castle and invites all the prettiest girls in the kingdom. Cinderella is only allowed to go if she finishes her housework, and she has far too much to do. The animals make her a robe, but her stepsisters tear it. Cinderella's fairy godmother comes to her rescue, and gives Cinderella fine clothes and a coach to take her to the ball. But she must leave at midnight. At the ball, the Prince falls in love with Cinderella, but midnight strikes and she makes her escape, leaving behind one of her slippers. Next day, the prince searches the realm for the owner of the slipper, finds Cinderella, and marries her.

Title :	*ALICE IN WONDERLAND*
Year :	1951
Country :	U.S.A.
Running time :	75 mins.
Medium :	Animated cartoon/colour
Production :	Walt Disney Studios
Animation director :	Ward Kimball
Sequences director :	Wilfred Jackson
Directors :	Clyde Geronimi, Hamilton Luske
Supervision :	Ben Sharbenstein
Animator :	Joshua Meador
Special effects :	Ub Iwerks

Subject:

From Lewis Carroll's two books, "Alice in Wonderland" and "Through the Looking Glass."

Alice's sister is reading to her in a garden, but Alice is not listening and goes into a dream. She sees a white rabbit consulting a watch, complaining that he is late, and disappearing down a hole. Alice follows, falls through space for some time, arrives in a room from which she only escapes by swimming through the tears she wept when she was giant sized, dances the Lobster quadrille, is told the story of the Walrus and the carpenter and has several adventures before being directed to the Queen by the disappearing Cheshire cat. Earning the Queen's disapproval by failing to show her enough respect, Alice is put on trial, but the whole court turns into a pack of cards and Alice finds herself back in the garden with her sister.

Title :	*PETER PAN*
Year :	1953
Country :	U.S.A.
Running time :	76 mins.
Medium :	Animated cartoon/colour
Production :	Walt Disney Studios
Animation director :	Ward Kimball
Sequence director :	Wilfred Jackson
Animation :	Joshua Meador
Special effects :	Ub Iwerks
Music :	Oliver Wallace
Editing :	Donald Halliday

Subject:

From a book by Sir James Barrie.

Story:

Wendy, Michael and John, the children of Mr. and Mrs. Darling of Bloomsbury, London, have a fairy-tale hero, Peter Pan. The parents go out one evening leaving the children in the care of the nursemaid dog, Nana.

Peter Pan, who listens to Wendy reading stories to her younger brothers, steals into their bedroom in search of his lost shadow. With him is his tiny friend, Tinker Bell. Wendy sews Peter's shadow on to him and soon earns the dislike of jealous Tinker Bell.

Wendy and the boys are taught to fly, and all leave for Peter's home. Here their adventures begin, when Captain Hook, chief of the pirates, tries to shoot them down.

Hook is trying to find Peter's hiding place. In his turn he is pursued by the hungry crocodile of which he is hysterically afraid.

The children go to Peter's home where they meet the Lost Boys. Later, Peter strengthens his friendship with the local Red Indian tribe when he saves the chief's daughter from Hook's hands.

When Hook tricks the jealousy-stricken Tinker Bell into revealing the hide-out, he captures the children and plants a time bomb in Peter's home. Tinker Bell nearly dies while saving Peter. She is revived when Peter tells her she means more to him than anyone else in the world.

Peter saves the children, and Hook is chased over the horizon by the crocodile. Tinker Bell covers the ship with pixie dust and it sails back to London, Bloomsbury and home.

Title :	*THE LADY AND THE TRAMP*
Year :	1955
Country :	U.S.A.
Running time :	75 mins.
Medium :	Animated cartoon/colour (Cinemascope)
Production :	Walt Disney Studios
Producers :	Walt Disney and Erdman Penner
Directors :	Hamilton Luske, Clyde Geronimi, Wilfred Jackson
Special effects :	Ub Iwerks, G. Rowley, D. MacManus
Screenplay :	E. Penner, J. Rinaldi, R. Wright, D. Da Gradi

Animation:	M. Kahl, F. Thomas, O. Johnston, J. Lousbery, W. Reitherman, E. Larson, H. King, L. Clarck	Directors:	Eric Larson, Wolfgang Reitherman, Les Clark
		Supervision:	Clyde Geronimi
Layout:	K. Anderson, T. Godrick, A. Zinnen, A. O'Connor, H. Hennesy, L. Nolley, J. Rupp, M. L. Stewart, D. Griffith, T. Putnam, C. Campbell, V. Haboush, B. Bosche	Chief artists:	Milt Kahl, Marc Davis, Frank Thomas, Ollie Johnston, John Lousbery, Hal King, Blaine Gibson, Ken Hultgren
		Artists:	Hal King, Blaine Gibson, Ken Hultgren, George Nitchilas, Henry Tanous, Hal Ambro, John Sibley, Bob Youngquist, John Kennedy, Don Lusk, Bob Carlson, Fred Kopietz, Eric Cleworth, Ken O'Brien, Harvey Toombs
Backgrounds:	C. Coates, D. Anthony, R. Hulette, A. Dempster, T. Witmar, E. Earle, J. Trout, R. Huffine, B. Mack		
Characters:	G. Nicholas, H. Ambro, K. O'Brien, J. Hathcock, E. Cleworth, M. Woodward, E. Aardal, J. Sibley, H. Toombs, C. Nordberg, D. Lusk, G. Kreisl, H. Traser, J. Freeman, J. Campbell, B. Carlson.		
		Effects:	Ub Iwerks, Eustache Lycett
		Animators:	Don MacManus, Joshua Meador, Jack Boyd, Jack Buckley
Music:	Oliver Wallace	Layout:	McLaren Stewart, Don Griffith, Basil Davidovitch, Joe Hale, Jack Huber, Tom Codrick, Erni Nordli, Victor Haboush, Homer Jonas, Ray Aragon
Music played by:	E. Plumb, S. Fine		
Songs:	Peggy Lee, Sonny Burke		
Sound recordings:	A. J. Steck, R. O. Cook		
Sound mixing:	G. Rowley, D. MacManus		
		Backgrounds:	Frank Armitage, Al Dempster, Bill Layne, Dick Anthony, Richard H. Thomas, Thelma Witmer, Walt Peregoy, Ralph Hulett, Fil Mottola, Anthony Rizzo

Subject:

From a story by Warde Greene.

Story:

Jim gives his wife a pretty feminine cocker spaniel for Christmas, called Lady. Everybody loves her, especially Jock and Caesar, the neighbour's dogs, and the Tramp, a stray who values his liberty above all else. A baby in the household gives Lady some trouble, but it is the arrival of Aunt Sarah and her Siamese cats which causes catastrophe. Lady is muzzled, and escapes. She is nearly eaten by some mastiffs, but the Tramp puts them to flight. The Tramp takes her to the zoo, where the muzzle is removed, but in the morning Lady is captured and taken to the pound, where she learns about the Tramp's bad character. She goes back home, spurning the Tramp, but the Tramp kills a rat who threatens the baby, and he is accepted into the household, settling down and fathering four puppies.

		Production manager:	Ken Peterson
		Production:	Don La Gardi, Ken Anderson
		Design:	Tom Oreb
		Editing:	Roy M. Brewer Jr., Donald Halliday
		Colour:	Eyvind Earle
		Music:	Piotre Tchiakowsky, adapted by George Bruns, Erdman Penner, Tom Adair, Sammy Fain, Winston Hibler, Jack Lawrence, Ted Sears
		Choral arrangement:	John Rarig
		Dialogue:	Joe Rinaldi, Bill Peet, Ralph Wright, Winston Hibler, Ted Sears, Milt Banat

Title:	SLEEPING BEAUTY
Year:	1959
Country:	U.S.A.
Running time:	75 mins.
Medium:	Animated cartoon/colour Technirama (70mm)
Production:	Walt Disney Studios
Producers:	Walt Disney, Erdman Penner

Subject:

From a story by Charles Perault, adapted by Erdman Penner.

Story:

In the fourteenth century, good king Stephen and his wife are celebrating the baptism of their daughter Aurora, and her betrothal to Prince Philip. Three good fairies give her beauty, goodness and charm, but the bad fairy casts a spell on her that she will prick her finger on a spindle when she is sixteen and die. One of the good fairies changes the spell before it reaches Aurora and makes her fate sleep rather than death. She will awaken with a loving kiss.

Under the name of Eglantine, Aurora is being brought up by the three good fairies. On the day of her sixteenth birthday she meets Philip and they fall in love. Then she pricks her finger on the sole remaining spindle in the castle and falls asleep, as does the whole court.

Philip has been imprisoned by the bad fairy, but is released by the good fairies, and armed with the sword of truth and the shield of virtue he destroys the bad fairy, awakens Aurora and marries her.

Title:	A THOUSAND AND ONE ARABIAN NIGHTS
Year:	1959
Country:	U.S.A.
Running time:	76 mins.
Medium:	Animated cartoon/colour
Director:	Jack Kinney
Production:	UPA (United Pictures of America) Stephen Bosustow
Associate directors:	Rudy Larriva, Gil Turner, Osmond Evans, Tom Macdonald, Alan Zaslove
Director of animation:	Abe Levitow
Screenplay:	Czenzi Ormonde, based on stories by Dick Kinney, Leo Salakin, Pete Burness, Lew Keller, Ed Nofziger, Ted Allan, Margaret Schneider, Paul Schneider
Distribution:	Columbia
Head cameraman:	Jack Eckes
Animation:	Harvey Toombs, Phil Duncan, Clarke Mallery, Bob Carlson, Hank Smith, Ken Hultgren, Jim Davis, Casey Onaitis, Sanford Strother, Ed Friedman, Jack Campbell, Herman Cohen, Rudy Camor, Stan Wilkins
Colour styling:	Jules Engel, Bob Macintoch
Music:	Georges Duning
Production manager:	Bud Getzler
Sound:	John Livadary, Marne Fallis
Voices:	Jim Backus, Kathryn Grant, Dwayne Hickman, Hans Conried, Herschel Bernardi, Alan Reed, Daws Butler, Clark Sisters

Subject:

The daughter of the Sultan of Bagdad, Yasminda, is loved by the sinister Wazir, but she loves Aladdin, the nephew of Abdul Aziz Magoo, a lamp-seller.

Wazir deceives Magoo into thinking he is his long lost brother and succeeds in getting Aladdin to hunt out the magic lamp for him. When it has been found, Wazir throws Aladdin into an underground cave.

A blunder by Magoo helps Aladdin to recover the lamp and subsequently he discovers its magic power. In order to recover this valuable prize, Wazir kidnaps Yasminda to make Aladdin give the lamp to him. Aladdin has been captured and is about to be executed when Magoo rescues him on his flying carpet and saves both Aladdin and Yasminda. Aladdin and Yasmind amarry and Wazir is punished.

Title:	ONE HUNDRED AND ONE DALMATIANS
Year:	1960
Country:	U.S.A.
Running time:	80 mins.
Medium:	Animated cartoon/colour
Production:	Walt Disney Studios
Direction:	Wolfgang Reitherman, Hamilton S. Luske, Clyde Geronimi
Screenplay:	Story by Dodie Smith, adapted by Bill Pee
Animation:	Milt Kahl, Marc Davis, Ollie Joynston, Frank Thomas, John Lousbery, Eric Larson
Characters:	Hal King, Les Clark, Cliff Nordberg, Blaine Gibson, Eric Cleworth, J. Sibley, A. Stevens, J. Sendsen, Hal Ambro, T. Berman, Bill Keil, Don Lusk, Dick Lucas, Amby Paliwoda
Effects:	Ub Iwerks, Eustache Lycett
Music:	Georges Bruns
Arrangements:	Franklyn Marks
Music editing:	Evelyn Kennedy
Sounds:	Robert O. Cook
Editing:	Donald Halliday, Roy M. Brewer Jr.
Supervision:	Ken Anderson

Subject:

From a novel by Dodie Smith.

Story:

Like most human bachelors, Roger believes his the ideal way of life. He smokes a treasured, but foul pipe, composes inferior, but loud music, and lives in an untidy bachelor apartment in an unfashionable London suburb.

Roger owns a dalmatian dog named Pongo. The dog is really the master. Pongo, with considerable crafty manoeuvring, arranges for his pet human (Roger of course) to meet Anita, a lovely, shapely human. It is love at first sight—marriage at first chance. But, in addition to the new human bride to brighten their lives, Roger and Pongo acquire Anita's dalmatian dog, Perdita. Oh, what a beautiful spotted animal she is! Pongo loses his mind with love. They, too, decide that love is wonderful.

Time passes . . . To Pongo and Perdita are born fifteen beautiful dalmatian puppies. Life is complete.

Enter Cruella De Vil-rich, rich, rich—and evil—very evil—and cunning. She loves furs. Any furs, but for dalmatian furs she has a passion! The puppies must be hers! At any or no price!

Crafty Cruella hires two unhandsome, real bad'uns to dognap the pups. They do their dirty duty, and hide the pups in a very haunted old English manor house filled to overflowing with dalmatians—one hundred and one of them—all alive and kicking, and potential fur coats for Cruella.

Roger and Anita appeal to the police for help. Top men of Scotland Yard are baffled by the dognapping. There are no clues. The police cannot help. But Pongo calls for assistance from the dogs of London. By a noisy but secret system known only to dogs, they relay news of the crime across the English countryside. The message reaches deepest Suffolk, and a certain colonel (a very shaggy colonel), has a suspicion where the criminals have imprisoned the stolen pups. Orders go to the captain (a very wise horse), to the sergeant (a very efficient cat), and soon plans are underway for a rescue. After a long trek through the winter snow, all ninety nine puppies are rescued and brought home to Roger and Anita on Christmas Eve.

Title :	OF STARS AND MEN
Year :	1961
Country :	U.S.A.
Running time :	52 mins.
Medium :	Animated cartoon/colour (Eastmancolor)
Production :	John and Faith Hubley
Screenplay :	Adapted by John and Faith Hubley from the book by Harlow Shapley in collaboration with the author
Director :	John Hubley
Key animators :	William Littlejohn, Gary Mooney
Backgrounds and Animators :	John Hubley, Patricia Byron, Faith Hubley, Nina Di Gangi

Music :	Petzel, Gabrielli, Bach, Handel, Mozart, Beethoven
Commentary :	Harlow Shapley
Children's voices :	Mark and Hampy Hubley
Musical direction :	Walter Trampler

Subject:

This film attempts to create the scientific world and locate man's place in it, in an amusing and intelligible manner. A new form was sought combining painting in motion with music and humour, and the world of the scientist.

The central character, Man, who is revealed as king of the animals, helps locate man's place in the universe. His place in Space, Time, Matter and Energy is pinpointed and Man discovers he is no longer centre of the universe. He is shaken. He ponders the meaning of life.

The dance of life on earth is visualised and life on other planets is considered. The conclusion is that Man is not enough and that life flourishes throughout the universe. Man is left thinking deep thoughts.

The scientist's world of electrons, the ever changing motion of matter, the expanding galaxies have presented new views of the surrounding cosmos. Today the artist sees nature with fresh eyes. The animated film is a means of interpreting the restless motion, the vast distances, the velocities, the relationship within the material universe.

A small group of six artists completed the film using super-imposition, optical diffusion, and reticulations to free the animation medium from its old restrictive methods. It was a co-operative venture, creatively and economically, and was two years in preparation and ten months in production. The work was carried out in Hollywood and New York simultaneously.

Title :	MR MAGOO'S CHRISTMAS CAROL
Year :	1962
Country :	U.S.A.
Running time :	50 mins.
Medium :	Animated cartoon/colour Television special (NBC Television)
Director :	Abe Levitow
Production :	UPA for U.S. Time Corporation
Executive producer :	Henry G. Saperstein
Producer :	Lee Orgel
Production manager :	Earl Jonas
Adaptation :	Barbara Chain
Colour stylists :	Phil Norman, Gloria Wood, Bob Inman, Jack Heiter, Dave Weidman

Animation:	John Walker, Hank Smith, Xenia, Ed Solomon, Tom McDonald, Casey Onaitis
Editing:	Sam Horta, Earl Bennett, George Probert, Wayne Hughes
Sequence continuity:	Steve Clark, Gerrard Baldwin, Duane Crowther
Production designers:	Lee Mishkin, Bob Singer, Richard Ung, Corny Cole, Sam Weiss
Music:	Jules Styne, Bob Merrill
Voices:	Jim Backus, Morey Amsterdam, Jack Cassidy, Royal Dano, Paul Frees, Joan Gardner, John Hart, Jane Kean, Marie Matthews, Laura Olsher, Lee Tremayne

Subject:

Taken from Charles Dickens' famous story *A Christmas Carol*. Mr Magoo plays the role of Ebenezer Scrooge.

Title:	*GAY PURR-EE*
Year:	1962
Country:	U.S.A.
Running time:	85 mins.
Medium:	Animated cartoon/colour (Technicolor)
Director:	Abe Levitow
Executive producer:	Henry G. Saperstein
Executive directors:	Dorothy and Chuck Jones
Art director:	Victor Haboush
Associate producer:	Lee Orgel
Production manager:	Earl Jones
Production design:	Robert Singer, Richard Ung, Corny Cole, Ray Aragon, Edward Levitt, Ernest Nordli
Editorial supervisor:	Ted Baker
Sequence continuity:	Steve Clark
Editing:	Sam Horta, Earl Bennett
Additional dialogue:	Ralph Wright
Animation:	Ben Washam, Phil Duncan, Hal Ambro, Ray Patterson, Grant Simmons, Irv Spence, Don Lusk, Hank Smith, Harvey Toombs, Volus Jones, Ken Harris, Art Davis, Fred Madison
Music:	Harold Arlen
Lyrics:	E. V. Harburg
Musical direction and arrangement:	Mort Lindsay
Voices:	Judy Garland, Robert Goulet, Red Buttons, Hermione Gingold, Paul Frees, Morey Amsterdam, Mel Blanc, Julie Bennett, Joan Gardner
Production:	UPA (United Pictures of America)
Distribution:	Warner Brothers

Subject:

Spurning a mouse brought to her by Jaune-Tom (Robert Goulet), her boyfriend, Mewsette (Judy Garland) announces that she is tired of just peasant-type cats and is leaving the farm on the next train to Paris. Accompanied by a tiny companion, Robespierre (Red Buttons), Jaune-Tom follows her on foot.

Arriving in Paris, the naive country girl cat is led astray by Meowrice (Paul Frees), a suave city slicker cat. He takes her to a beauty salon run by Madame Rubens-Chatte (Hermoine Gingold) to be glamorised. Meowrice plans to marry Mewsette off for a price to a rich old coal cat in Pittsburg. Meowrice orders his dastardly minions, the cat-nappers, to keep an eye on the place so that Mewsette doesn't escape.

Meowrice takes Mewsette out for a night on the town and after a dinner at a sidewalk cafe, a stroll down the boulevards and a drive through the park, Mewsette is determined to stay in Paris and become beautiful and famous.

Jaune-Tom and Robespierre comb Paris looking for her. They come to Madame Rubens-Chatte's salon for felines and stop to go in, but a cat-napper shoves Robespierre down a manhole and Jaune-Tom goes to his rescue. Jaune-Tom climbs back out of the sewer, spots a mouse and catches it. Meowrice, who is just posting a letter to his client about his bride-to-be recognises Jaune-Tom as Mewsette's boyfriend and offers him and Robespierre a drink. Soon they are drunk and the next day they wake up to find themselves out at sea on a boat for Alaska. Back in Paris, Mewsette has obviously arrived. All the top cats of the period, Cezanne, Monet, Braque, Seurat, Modigliani, Degas, Toulouse-Lautrec, Rousseau, Gauguin, Van-Gogh, Renoir and Picasso paint her portrait in their particular styles.

Jaune-Tom and Robespierre return to France rich after finding gold in Alaska and again start to search Paris for Mewsette. Meowrice tells Mewsette of his plan to marry her to the rich American cat and she refuses to go through with it and runs away.

A cat-napper overhears Jaune-Tom and Robespierre calling Mewsette's name and has her taken in a basket to a train but she is first able to scratch a message on the wall which is found by Jaune-Tom. He and Robespierre rush to the station but the train has gone.

Jaune-Tom catches the train and rescues

Mewsette, beats up Meowrice and puts him in the basket instead headed for Pittsburg. Jaune-Tom and Mewsette return to Paris together.

Title:	THE SWORD IN THE STONE
Year:	1963
Country:	U.S.A.
Running time:	80 mins.
Medium:	Animated cartoon/colour
Production:	Walt Disney Studio
Direction:	Wolfgang Reitherman
Screenplay:	Bill Peet
Music editing:	Evelyn Kennedy
Backgrounds:	Ken Anderson, W. Peregoy, B. Layne, A. Rizzo, A. Dempster, R. Hulett, F. Mottola
Animators:	Frank Thomas, Ollie Johnston, Milt Karl, John Lousebery
Characters:	M. Kahl, B. Peet, H. King, E. Cleworth, C. Nordberg, E. Larson, J. Sibley, H. Ambro, D. Lucas
Layout:	D. Griffith, V. Gerry, D. Barnhart, B. Davidovitch, S. Cobb, H. Jonas.
Effects:	Don McManus, Jack Boyd, Jack Buckley
Editing:	Donald Halliday
Songs:	Richard M. Sherman, Robert B. Sherman
Supervision:	Robert O. Cook

Subject:

From the novel *The Sword in the Stone* by T. H. White.

Story:

Wart, the foster-son of Sir Ector, comes upon Merlin's cottage in the middle of a wood. Merlin decides to take charge of Wart's education, and takes up residence in Sir Ector's castle, where he teaches Wart both conventional knowledge and inside experience of the life of various animals. Wart falls into the hands of a sorceress, but is rescued by the magic skill of Merlin.

It is announced that a tournament is to be held in London. Sir Ector and his son Sir Kay attend the tournament, with Wart acting as Kay's squire. As they set off from their lodgings to go and joust, Kay finds that he has forgotten his sword, and sends Wart back to get it. But the lodging house is locked up. Wart sees a sword sticking out of an anvil, and pulls it out to give it to Kay, little knowing that only the man who is the rightful king of all England can pull the sword from the anvil. When Sir Ector discovers the source of the sword, Wart is proclaimed king, Merlin reveals that his real name is Arthur, and that he is destined to be head of the heroic round table.

Title:	HEY THERE, IT'S YOGI BEAR
Year:	1964
Country:	U.S.A.
Running time:	90 mins.
Medium:	Animated cartoon/colour (Yogicolor)
Directors:	William Hanna, Joseph Barbera
Production:	William Hanna, Joseph Barbera
Distribution:	Columbia
Screenplay:	Joseph Barbera, Warren Foster, William Hanna
Music:	Marty Paich, Ray Gilbert, Doug Goodwin, David Gates
Key animator:	Charles A. Nichols
Cameraman:	Bud Myers
Co-production:	Alex Lovy
Production manager:	Howard Hanson
Voices:	Daws Butler (Yogi), Don Messick (Boo-Boo) and Smith

Subject:

In Jellystone Park, Yogi Bear is king as long as ranger Smith is not reminding him of the regulations.

Yogi is accompanied everywhere by his friend Boo-Boo and girl friend Cindy. Thinking that Yogi has been sent away to a zoo, Cindy arranges to get out of the park, but Yogi has not really gone.

So Yogi and Boo-Boo set off across the United States looking for Cindy who has been captured by the organisers of a circus. The three friends have many adventures and finally meet up at the top of a New York skyscraper, where Smith comes to their rescue.

Title:	THE MAN FROM BUTTON WILLOW
Country:	U.S.A.
Running time:	81 mins.
Year:	1965
Medium:	Animated cartoon/colour (Eastmancolor)
Director:	David Detiege
Producer:	Eagle Film Ltd./Phyllis Bounds, Dietiege

Animation:	Ken Hultgren, Don Towsley, Don Lusk, George Rowley
Voices:	Dale Robertson, Howard Keel, Edgar Buchanan, Barbara Jean Wong
Music:	George Stoll

Subject:

The action takes place in 1869 and tells the story of the first US Government undercover agent Justin Eagle. His adventures take him to the Barbary Coast where he is shanghied, but he trounces the whole crew of the boat, rescues a kidnapped government official and foils a plan to sabotage a state railroad.

Title:	THE JUNGLE BOOK
Year:	1967
Country:	U.S.A.
Running time:	78 mins.
Medium:	Animated cartoon/colour
Production:	Walt Disney Studio
Direction:	Wolfgang Reitherman
Screenplay:	Larry Clemmons, Ralph Wright, Ken Anderson, Vance Gerry
Animation direction:	Milt Kahl, Frank Thomas, Ollie Johnston, John Louebery
Character animation:	Hal King, Eric Larson, Walt Stanchfield, Eric Cleworth, Fred Hemlich, John Ewing, Dick Lucas, Dan McManus
Layout:	Don Griffith, Basil Davidovitch, Tom Codrick, Dale Barnhart, Sylvia Roemer
Head of production:	Don Duckwall
Music:	George Bruns
Voices:	Phil Harris, Sebastian Cabot, Louis Prima, George Sanders, Sterling Holloway, Pat O'Malley, Bruce Reitherman
Background styling:	Al Dempster
Background:	Bill Layne, Ralph Hulett, Art Riley, Thelma Witner, Frank Armitage
Effects animation:	Dan McManus
Sound:	Robert O. Cook
Distribution:	M.G.M. Walt Disney Productions

Subject:

From *The Jungle Book* by Rudyard Kipling.

Story:

Bagheera, a dignified but pompous Indian pan-ther, finds an abandoned baby boy and leaves it to grow up with a wolf family.

Ten years later, the wold pack elders decide that as Shere Khan, the tiger, is in the district, the boy, Mowgli, must go back to the man village. Bagheera agrees to guide him there. On the way both of them are nearly hypnotised by Kaa, the snake, but escape. Next day they meet a herd of elephants under Colonel Hathi, who is annoyed with Mowgli's play. Mowgli breaks away from Bagheera to fend for himself, and spends some time with Baloo, a carefree bear.

Mowgli is kidnapped by a band of monkeys, and Baloo gets Bagheera to help him rescue the boy. After some confusion, they succeed. While Mowgli is asleep, Bagheera convinces Baloo that Mowgli must go back to the man village, but Mowgli runs away from both of them and is trailed by Shere Khan. He is captured by Kaa, but escapes while Kaa is talking to Shere Khan.

After Mowgli has talked to some vultures, Shere Khan catches up with him. His attack is delayed by Baloo, who is knocked out, and as the helpful vultures harass the tiger Mowgli ties a burning branch to his tail. Shere Khan runs away.

Now Mowgli can safely stay in the jungle, but he sees a young Indian girl and follows her into the man village of his own accord.

Title:	A MAN CALLED FLINT-STONE
Year:	1967
Country:	U.S.A.
Running time:	60 mins.
Medium:	Animated cartoon/colour
Directors:	William Hanna, Joseph Barbera
Production:	Hanna-Barbera
Screenplay:	Harvey Bullock, Ray Allen
Songs:	John McCarthy, Doug Goodwin
Director of animation:	Charles A. Nichols
Art director:	Bill Perez
Music:	Marty Paich, Ted Nichols

Subject:

Fred Flintstone bears a striking resemblance to the spy, Rock Slag, who is wounded in a fight while chasing the international spy, Green Goose and his girl friend Tanya. Because of his resemblance Fred is asked to take Rock's place and somewhat reluctantly accepts. The whole Flintstone family goes off on holiday.

Tanya is in Paris when Fred arrives to learn that she has just left Rome. He follows with his family, but in Rome he finds that the whole thing was a trap; The real spy, Rock Slag, now recovered, arrives in Rome. He rescues Flintstone who returns to the United States and puts paid to the schemes of Tanya and Green Goose.

Title:	JACK AND THE BEAN-STALK
Year:	1967
Country:	U.S.A.
Running time:	60 mins.
Medium:	Animated cartoon and live action in dramatic form for television/colour
Directors:	William Hanna, Joseph Barbera
Cast:	Gene Kelly

Subject:
Based on the classic fairytale.

Note:
This is one of the more polished television specials but is nevertheless a routine type of production.

Title:	MAD MONSTER PARTY
Year:	1968
Country:	U.S.A.
Running time:	94 mins.
Medium:	Puppets/colour
Production:	Videocraft International Ltd., Rankin-Bass Production
Director:	Jules Bass
Producer:	Arthur Rankin, Jr.
Screenplay:	Len Korobkin and Harvey Kurtzman
Executive producer:	Joseph E. Levine
Music and Lyrics:	Maury Laws and Jules Bass,
Cast:	Boris Karloff, Ethel Ennis, Gale Garnett, Phillis Diller

Story:
Famed for his discovery of creation, Dr. Frankenstein's famous career comes full circle when he discovers the secret of *total destruction*! Living on a Caribbean island with The Monster, his mate and his ward Francesca—Frankenstein finds himself growing older and plans to retire. He decides to hold a convention of all the renowned monsters in the world. The best qualified to take his place as head of the Worldwide Organization of Monsters, will inherit his awesome secret.

Attending the historic confab are The Wolfman, Dracula, The Mummy, The Creature, It, The Invisible Man, Dr. Jekyll and Mr. Hyde ... and also Felix, Frankenstein's nephew. Felix never seems to know exactly what is happening during all the double-dealing, triple-crossing, plotting, planning and politics involved in the maneuvring for top spot. Somehow, he and Francesca fall in love, which will really confound him, for she's a "machine" created by Doctor Frankenstein! Francesca on the other hand, is also in for a surprise—for she does not know what Felix will turn out to be—as the sun sinks slowly in the west.

Title:	ALICE IN WONDERLAND
Year:	1968
Country:	U.S.A.
Running time:	60 mins.
Medium:	Animated cartoon for television/colour
Directors:	William Hanna, Joseph Barbera
Voices:	Zsa Zsa Gabor, Bill Dana, Howard Morris, Hedda Hooper, Harvey Kormann, Janet Waldo

Subject:
Based on the famous story by Lewis Carroll.

Title:	A BOY NAMED CHARLIE BROWN
Year:	1969
Country:	U.S.A.
Running time:	80 mins.
Medium:	Animated cartoon/colour (Technicolor)/scope
Director:	Bill Melendez
Production:	Lee Mendelson, Bill Melendez
Music and songs:	Rod McKuen
Voices:	Peter Robbins, Pamelyn Ferdin, Glenn Gilger, Andy Pforsich, Sally Dryer, Anne Altieri, Erin Sullivan, Linda Mendelson, Christopher DeFaria, David Carey, Guy Pforsich, Bill Melendez
Key animators:	Ed Levitt, Dean Spille, Bernard Gruver, Ellie Bonnard, Evert Brown, Jan Green, Ruth Kissane, Al Shean, Charles McElmurry
Animators:	Don Lusk, Spencer Peel, Frank Smith, Hank Smith, Rudy Zamora, Sam Jaimes, Bob Carlson, Maggie Bowen Bill Littlejohn, Herm Cohen, Ken O'Brien, Lew Irwin, Bob Matz, Bror Lansing, Russ Van Neida, Jay Sarbry, Barry Nelson, Gerry Kane, Ken Champin

Editors:	Robert T. Gillis, Charles McCann, Steve Melendez, Alice Keillor
Musical arrangement:	Rod McKuen, Vince Guaraldi, John Scott-Trotter

Subject:

Charlie Brown takes part in a spelling bee—a children's spelling contest. Due to the machinations of Lucy, he gets to the finals of the contest, and goes to New York for the event. Snoopy, the beagle, goes to New York to look for him. Linus follows Snoopy, and they all attend the final contest. Charlie Brown's spelling is terrible and he fails the contest, but when he goes home he receives a hero's welcome anyway. The film is interspersed with fantasy sequences—Snoopy ice-skating, Shroeder being Beethoven, etc.

Title:	THE PHANTOM TOLL BOOTH
Year:	1969
Country:	U.S.A.
Running time:	90 mins.
Medium:	Animated cartoon with live action/colour (Metrocolor)
Directors:	Chuck Jones, Abe Levitow
Director of live sequences:	Dave Monahan
Co-Production	Abe Levitow, Les Goldman
Screenplay:	Chuck Jones, Sam Rosen based on the book by Norton Juster
Music:	Lee Pockriss, Paul Vance
Supervising animators:	Ben Washam, Hal Ambro, George Nichols
Animation:	Irven Spence, Bill Littlejohn, Richard Thomson, Tom Ray, Philip Roman, Carl Bell, Alan Zaslove, Ed Aardal, Ed De Mattia, Xenia, Lloyd Vaughan
Production design.:	Maurice Noble
Animation camera:	Jack Stevens
Typographics:	Don Foster
Layout:	Tony Rivera, Don Morgan, Oscar Dufau, Rosemary O'Connor, Corny Cole, Phyllis Graham
Backgrounds:	Philip DeGuard, Irving Weiner, Robert McIntosh
Film editor:	Jim Faris
Production manager:	Earl Jonas
Distribution:	Metro-Goldwyn-Mayer

Subject:

The adventures of a bored little boy named Milo, who does not know what to do with himself, finds nothing interesting, and thinks almost everything is a waste of time ... at least until he drives through a mysterious toll booth in a toy car.

His bored attitude lands him in the Doldrums, but he is rescued by a dog that ticks, named Tock. Together they embark on a journey through the Kingdom of Wisdom. They meet new friends, a weatherman, a not-so-wicked witch, a spelling bee and a humbug who tells them about the feud between the king of Dictionopolis, a city of words and Digitopolis, a city of numbers.

Milo, Tock and Humbug start on a perilous journey to rescue the Princesses of Rhyme and Reason who have been imprisoned in a castle-in-the-air. To reach them they must do battle with an army of monsters who guard the Mountains of Ignorance.

When Rhyme and Reason are at last returned to their kingdom, the feuding Kings hold a great celebration, ending their battle and admitting that words and numbers are of equal importance in a world of Wisdom.

Regretfully Milo leaves his new friends and returns through the toll booth to his room. Convinced that he has been away for weeks, he discovers that it has only been a matter of minutes. Breathlessly he dashes outside, anxious to become involved in the world he has just discovered.

Title:	THE ARISTOCATS
Year:	1970
Country:	U.S.A.
Running time:	78 mins.
Medium:	Animation cartoon/colour
Director:	Wolfgang Reitherman
Producer:	Wolfgang Reitherman, Winston Hibler
Story by:	Larry Clemons, Vance Gerry Frank Thomas, Julius Svendsen, Ken Anderson, Eric Cleworth, Ralph Wright. Based on a story by Tom McGowan, Tom Rowe
Music:	George Bruns
Editor:	Tom Acosta
Sound:	Robert O. Cook
Songs:	"The Aristocats" "Scales and Arpeggios" "She Never Felt Alone" by Robert Sherman, Richard M. Sherman
Voices:	Phil Harris (O'Malley), Eva Gabor (Duchess), Sterling Holloway (Roquefort), Scatman Crothers (Scat Cat), Paul Wincell (Chinese Cat),

Voices—cont.

Lord Tim Hudson (English Cat), Vito Scotti (Helian Cat), Thurl Ravenscroft (Russian Cat), Dean Clark (Berlioz), Liz English (Marie), Gary Dublin (Toulouse), Nancy Kulp (Frou Frou), Pat Buttram (Napoleon), George Lindsey (Lafayette), Monica Evans (Abigail), Carole Shelley (Amelia), Charles Lare (Lawyer), Hermione Baddeley (Madame), Roddy Maude-Roxby (Edgar) Bill Thomson (Uncle Waldo). "The Aristocats" sung by Maurice Chevalier.

Subject:

The aristocats are Duchess and her three well-bred kittens, Berlioz, Toulouse and Marle. They are the "family" of Madame Bonfamille, an elderly and very wealthy Parisian widow. The four cats are to be left Madame's entire estate in her will, but Edgar the butler and the second beneficiary angrily decide to get rid of them. Having drugged their milk he takes the cats out into the country late at night. Confronted and chased by a pair of farm dogs Edgar leaves the cats' basket in a marsh.

The next day Duchess and her kittens meet Thomas O'Malley, a carefree alley cat. He offers to escort them back to Paris, having fallen for Duchess who reproves his somewhat ungentlemanly advances. Nevertheless his rescue of Marie from the river affirms his essentially honourable nature and he and the cats set off joined by the Gastle sisters, a pair of British spinster Geese, on a walking tour.

Edgar's bragging of his apparently successful catnapping is overheard by Roquefort, the housemouse and friend of the cats.

The cats return to Paris and meet O'Malley's friends Scatcat and his Jazz-playing alleycats, offer a jam session in O'Malley's garret, he proposes to Duchess, who regretfully refuses him out of loyalty to Madame Bonfamille.

Edgar is in the middle of celebrating his future inheritance when the cats return home and leave O'Malley at the gate. Once inside the house Edgar drops them into a sack and hides them in the (unlit) kitchen stove. Roquefort sees it all and chases after O'Malley who sends him to bring the other alleycats from the other side of town.

Duchess and the kittens are locked up in a trunk addressed to Timbuktoo when the Edgar–O'Malley battle begins. Scatcat and the band arrive, Roquefort frees the prisoners and Frou-Frou the horse kicks Edgar into the trunk, just in time for his collection by the carriers.

Madame adopts O'Malley into the family and makes a new provision in her will. She also establishes a foundation for the homeless alleycats of Paris. Scatcat and Co finally celebrate with the song "Everybody Wants to be a Cat".

Title:	SHINBONE ALLEY
Year:	1970
Country:	U.S.A.
Running time:	125 mins.
Medium:	Animated cartoon/colour
Director:	John Wilson
Production:	Fine Arts Film
Production Assistant:	Dan Anderson
Screenplay and design:	Based on the stories of Don Marquis, (the drawings of George Herriman) and the operetta, "Shinbone Alley"
Backgrounds:	Gary Lund, Marsha Gartenbach
Producer:	Preston M. Fleet
Layout:	Tom Baron
Supervision:	David Detiege
Production co-ordination:	Christine Decker
Lyrics:	Joe Darion
Music:	George Kleinsinger
Animation assistant:	Robert Zamboni
Voices:	Carol Channing, Eddie Bracken, John Carradine, Allan Read, Snr., Hal Smith, Sal Delano, Ken Sanson, Byron Kane, The Jackie Ward Singers

Subject:

The love of a cockroach for a sexy street cat.

The story starts when the poet drags himself out of the river, falls into a knothole and threatens to sue the city for leaving the cover off a manhole, says "hallo" to a rat and finally becomes conscious that he has transmigrated into the body of Archy the cockroach.

A list of some of the scenes can give a better impression than can a synopsis of the various settings of the film:

—Alley scenes with Archy, Mehitabel, Big Bill and others.

—The old trouper and the old theatres.

—Cats out on the town.

—Surrealistic sequence: Archy and Mehitabel as "flotsam and jetsam on the sea of life" float along on a garbage can lid as the city becomes a sea.

—Archy becomes inebriated and winds up in a jewel box bordello as a guest of the "ladybugs of the evening".

—Archy declares war, as he rallies the insects to battle with the thoughtless humans who massacre insects indiscriminately.

Title:	*UNCLE SAM MAGOO*
Year:	1970
Country:	U.S.A.
Running time:	60 mins.
Medium:	Animated cartoon/colour. Television special for NBC Television
Director:	Abe Levitow
Production:	UPA Pictures Inc.
Screenplay:	From an original idea by Henry G. Saperstein
Music:	Supervised, arranged and conducted by Walter Scharf
Writer:	Larry Markes
Executive Producer:	Henry G. Saperstein
Producer:	Lee Orgel
Additional Dialogue:	Sam Rosen
Sequence continuity:	Steve Clark, G. M. Nevius
Layout:	Pete Alvardo, Moe Gollub, Tony Rivers, Don Morgan, Margaret Nichols
Storyboard:	Lee Mishkin, Marty Murphy, Bob Ogle
Background:	Ron Dias, Dave High, David Wiedman
Animation:	Hal Ambro, Ray Patterson, Phil Roman, Hank Smith, Irv Spence, Dick Thomson, Xenia

Subject:

Uncle Sam Magoo begins his story with the multiple discoveries of America. Did you know that America was discovered by mistake? Leif Ericson and Christopher Columbus both deviated from their proposed courses.

Finally, with John Smith, and a few years later, the Pilgrims, America was on its way to really being on the map.

Uncle Sam Magoo is present in many events and turning points in the story of "America the Beautiful". This song, by the way, is only one of the many story telling classics. Uncle Sam Magoo is with Paul Revere when he begins his famous midnight ride. He admires and approves Bets Ross's first American flag.

Poor peace-loving Uncle Magoo sees man wars. "Yankee Doodle Dandy" meets the Tennessee dandy "Davy Crockett" at the Alamo. The fight between "Dixie" and the "Battle Hymn of the Republic" is another event he witnesses: "Wouldn't it be nice if someday when they gave a war nobody came" he muses.

One of his more philosophical moments is followed by a discussion about universal power and the invention of bifocals—you can never guess which is more significant for Uncle Sam Magoo.

Uncle Sam Magoo opens the gates to the Wild West and introduces Kit Carson "Darling Clementine" and "Oh Susannah". You will find out that the discovery of gold, just like the discovery of America, was an accident.

Larger-than-life characters such as Paul Bunyan and Johnny Appleseed don't escape the determined myopic Uncle Sam Magoo. Actually he had the foresight to see that Johnny Appleseed may well have been the first hippie with his shoulder-length hair and beard. Uncle Sam Magoo meets many characters, including Tom Sawyer, Huck Finn and their creator Mark Twain.

Uncle Sam Magoo has a new way to jump down, turn around, pick a tale of America.

Title:	*SNOOPY, COME HOME*
Year:	1972
Country:	U.S.A.
Running time:	82 mins.
Medium:	Animated cartoon
Director:	Bill Melendez
Producers:	Lee Mendelson and Bill Melendez
Screenplay:	Charles M. Schulz
Graphics:	Ed Levitt, Sam Jaimes, Beverly Robbins, Bill Littlejohn, Lou Robards, Bernard Gruver, Jacques Vausseur, Eleanor Warren, Phil Roman, Joanne Lansing, Evert Brown, Rod Scribner, Faith Kovaleski, Jim Pabian, Debbie Zamora, Frank Smith, Hank Smith, Manon Washburn, All Pabian, Gwenn Dotzler, Dean Spille, Ruth Kissane, Don Lusk, Adele Lenart, Chandra Poweris, Ellie Bogardus, Emery Hawkins, Rudy Zamora, Joice Lee Marshall, Celine Miles, Al Shean, Carole Barnes, Bob Carlson, Dawn Smith
Photography:	Dickson/Vasu
Editing:	Robert T. Gillis, Charles McCann, Rudy Zamora, Jr.
Music and Lyrics:	Richard M. Sherman and Robert B. Sherman
Music arrangements:	Donald Raike
Voices:	Chad Webber, Robin Kohn, Stephen Shea, David Carey, Johanna Baer, Hilary Momberger, Chris De Faria, Linda Ercoll, Linda Mendelson, Bill Melendez

Subject:

From her hospital bed, a little girl sadly writes a letter that tells us of her loneliness and yearning (*Song:* "Lila's Theme [Do You Remember Me?]"), then drops the letter into a mail chute.

At the beach (*Song:* "At The Beach") Snoopy rides a surfboard, then meets Peppermint Patty and they build a sand castle, frolic in the water and make plans to meet there again on the morrow. The next day, Snoopy fails to see the sign reading "NO DOGS ALLOWED ON THE BEACH" (*Song:* "No Dogs Allowed") and he and his beach gear are flung past the sign.

An irate Snoopy dictates a "Letter to the Editor" to his secretary-typist, Woodstock, protesting the sign at the beach. After a few false starts in the air, Woodstock manages to post the letter. Snoopy then accompanies Charlie Brown and Sally to the library and once more is ejected past a sign reading: "NO DOGS ALLOWED IN LIBRARY" (*Song:* "No Dogs Allowed"). This so angers Snoopy that he starts a fight with Linus over his blanket, then engages in a boxing match with Lucy Van Pelt by inserting his muzzle into a boxing glove and launching a "one-fisted" attack.

Asleep atop his doghouse, Snoopy has a letter delivered by Charlie Brown. Snoopy is overjoyed at its contents, packs his bag and dog dish and sets off with Woodstock in tow, leaving behind a puzzled Charlie Brown. (*Song:* "The Best of Buddies"). Their journey is harsh and unpleasant. They're thrown off a bus with a sign reading: "NO DOGS ALLOWED." They trudge on afoot, then try hitchhiking.

Happening upon an unregenerate little girl, he is captured and tied with a huge rope in the backyard. When Woodstock tries to untie him, he too is captured and caged (*Song:* "Fundamental-Friend-Dependability"). When the little girl takes Snoopy to the veterinarian "to be checked out", he manages to escape, rescues Woodstock and they flee (*Song:* "Gettin' it Together").

Meanwhile, back home, Charlie Brown accompanies Peppermint Patty to a carnival where she out-performs him in the Dart Throw, Baseball Throw, and other games of skill. Then, in answer to Patty's question on the definition of love, Charlie Brown discourses on what love is, based on his father's experience with a cute girl and a 1934 two-door sedan.

Still on their journey, Snoopy and Woodstock are thrown from a railroad coach to the train platform where a sign reads: "NO DOGS ALLOWED" (Song). They trudge along the tracks and spend the night in a hobo jungle. On finally reaching the hospital where Lila had posted her letter, they find a sign reading: "HOSPITAL—QUIET. NO DOGS OR BIRDS ALLOWED IN HOSPITAL" (Song). Snoopy sneaks in the rear entrance, dons a surgeon's robe and mask, but is caught and ejected past the sign. Once more

Snoopy manages an entrance and is able to make his way to Lila's room. When she awakens they have a joyful reunion and Lila is contented.

Back at Charlie Brown Town, the clan gathers to discuss Snoopy's disappearance (*Song:* "Snoopy, Come Home" Reprise). Linus decides to investigate Snoopy's past at the "Daisy Hill Puppy Farm", where Charlie Brown had purchased the bumptious beagle. Linus learns some startling news and reveals that Snoopy had been bought first by a girl named Lila: "You got a used dog, Charlie Brown!"

Snoopy and Woodstock are living high in Lila's hospital room, are fed from her tray and hide each time the nurse or doctor enters. Lila tells Snoopy that her mother agrees Snoopy can come home with her. Snoopy looks so hangdog that Lila suggests he return "to settle your affairs", and they bid a tearful farewell to each other.

Charlie Brown finds Snoopy atop the doghouse typing out his "Last Will and Testament," leaving his belongings to Linus, Schroeder, and the American Humane Association and to Charlie Brown, "my previous owner", he leaves "best wishes for the future".

Linus proposes a farewell party and all the gang attend, with Linus the master of ceremonies. A pile of gifts are unwrapped to reveal a pile of bones. Snoopy puts a "For Sale or To Let" sign on his doghouse, bids goodbye to Charlie Brown and Woodstock, then walks off into the sunset as Charlie Brown acts out a farewell song (*Song:* "It Changes").

Snoopy dawdles on his return to Lila and slowly approaches the apartment building where she lives. He rings the doorbell, then notes a sign reading: "NO DOGS ALLOWED IN BUILDING." He does a happy dance. Lila greets him, but Snoopy points to the sign and Lila is aghast. Snoopy shakes her hand, then races away as Lila sadly waves goodbye.

At home, Charlie Brown and Linus are talking and Woodstock is pecking for seeds. Woodstock hears faint off-stage music and discovers Snoopy returning triumphantly. They have a joyous reunion and march on to music (*Song:* "The Best of Buddies"). The saddened children—Snoopy's coterie—sit on a curb wishing he were back. They see the figures of Snoopy and Woodstock approaching. They do a dance of joy around their favourite beagle, then lift him to their shoulders and Woodstock hitches a ride on Snoopy's dogdish hat.

At the doghouse, Snoopy imperiously snaps his fingers at Woodstock, who flies up and types three letters. Snoopy hands the papers to Linus, Schroeder and Charlie Brown—written demands for the return "in good condition" of his belongings bequeathed to them. An incensed Lucy says: "That does it, Charlie Brown. He's your dog, and you're welcome to him." The kids depart angrily, while Snoopy, unperturbed, returns to his dictation (*Song:* "Snoopy, Come Home." Reprise).

Title:	*BEDKNOBS AND BROOM-STICKS*
Year:	1971
Country:	U.S.A.
Running time:	95 mins.
Medium:	Live action/cartoon combined/colour
Director:	Robert Stevenson
Production:	The Walt Disney Studio
Producer:	Bill Walsh
Screenplay:	Bill Walsh and Don Dagradi
Musical score:	Richard M. and Robert B. Sherman

Subject:

Based on the book by Mary Norton. A believable and magic history how an amateur sorcerer saved England from German invasion. The magic produces a number of Disney type animal characters. The mixed media is handled with a great deal of technical ingenuity and sense of entertainment.

Title:	*POPEYE MEETS THE MAN WHO HATED LAUGHTER*
Year:	1972
Country:	U.S.A.
Running time:	60 mins.
Medium:	Animated cartoon/colour
Directors:	Jack Zander and Hal Seeger
Production:	King Feature Syndicate

Subject:

"Popeye Meets the Man who Hated Laughter" features a bumper crop of comic-strip favourites: Blondie and Dagwood, the Katzenjammer Kids, the Little King, Steve Canyon, Flash Gordon, the Phantom, Tim Tyler, Beetle Bailey, Jiggs and Maggie.

This television film is the work of New York animators under the guidance of the veterans Jack Zander and Hal Seeger.

Title:	*ROBIN HOOD*
Year:	1973
Running time:	82 mins.
Country:	U.S.A.
Medium:	Animated cartoon/colour (Technicolor)
Director:	Wolfgang Reitherman
Producers:	Walt Disney Studio
Screenplay:	Larry Clemmons, Eric Cleworth, Vance Gerry, Ken Anderson and Frank Thomas based on the tales of Sherwood Forest
Characters:	Ken Anderson
Music and songs:	Roger Miller
Voices:	Brian Bedford as Robin Hood, Peter Ustinov as Prince John, Terry Thomas as Sir Hiss, Phil Harris as Little John and Roger Miller as Allan-A-Dale.
Distribution:	Buena Vista Distribution

Subject:

All the familiar characters are played by animated cartoon animals. Among the Sherwood Forest creatures are Robin Hood, a sly benevolent fox, the scheming Prince John, a scrawny lion, King Richard, a regal lion, Little John, Robin's friend—a burly bear, Sir Hiss, a snake counseller to Prince John, Maid Marion, a silver Vixen with her companion, Lady Cluck, a chicken, Friar Tuck, a portly Badger, Allan-A-Dale, a rooster minstrel, and the Sheriff of Nottingham, a wolf.

Title:	*THE POINT*
Year:	1971
Country:	U.S.A. (Murakami-Wolf)
Running time:	88 mins.
Medium:	Animated cartoon/colour
Director:	Fred Wolf
Producers:	Harry Nilsson, Jerry Good, Fred Wolf, Larry Gordon
Screenplay:	Norman Lenzer
Production design:	Gary Lund
Film editor:	Rich Harrison
Additional story development:	Fred Wolf
Production manager:	Sherman Thomson
Graphic production:	Kunimi Terada, Fumiko Roche, Elizabeth Wright, Wilma Guenot, Ann Oliphant
Additional animation:	Vincent Davie, Charles Swenson
Photography:	Wally Bulloch, Michael Gersham, Louis Niemeyer, Paul Marron, Jan Keisser
Narrator:	Dustin Hoffman
Songs written and sung by:	Harry Nilsson
Music arranged and conducted by:	George Tipton
Voices:	Paul Frees, Lenny Weinrib, Bill Martin, Buddy Foster, Joan Gerber, Mike Lookinland

Subject:

From a story by Harry Nilsson.

In a world where everyone's head is pointed is born a child without it. His head is round. This basic difference leads to conflicts with philosophical content.

Title:	*FRITZ THE CAT*
Year:	1972
Country:	U.S.A.
Running time:	75 mins.
Medium:	Animated cartoon/colour
Director:	Ralph Bakshi
Producer:	Steve Krantz/Cinema Industries
Characters:	R. Crumb
Screenplay:	Ralph Bakshi
Music:	B. B. King, Billie Holliday and others. Original rock and jazz.
Distribution:	Black Ink Films Ltd.

Subject:

Fritz and his buddies are messing around Washington Square Park in New York hoping to attract some chicks. Nothing works with the pretty ones, so Fritz makes a play for some young innocents. He entices them—all three—to the crash pad in the East Village where he hopes to bed them down. "Four in a bed is a kick I haven't tried yet".

In the crash pad assorted quasi students are smoking grass. Fritz, in desperation, moves into the bathtub as the only horizontal place available. The giggling and the noise brings the whole gang into the bathtub where the girls develop into a centre of attraction. The noise and the confusion brings on the cops—one a rookie, and the other a pro.

Fritz, in the confusion, grabs one of the cop's guns and shoots the toilet which explodes in a geyser of majestic proportions. He heats it out and hops into an Orthodox synagogue where the congregation is in prayer. The two cops break into the synagogue; one being Jewish, cautions the other, "Don't make any trouble, these are my people". The two of them stumble around the synagogue for Fritz who is entertaining a Jewish chick in the ladies' room.

After a scuffle, a radio the chick has been listening to, broadcasts a special announcement: "Israel Defense Minister and the United States Secretary of State have today concluded a mutual defense pact, a principal point of which calls for the cities of New York and Los Angeles to be returned to the United States". In the joyous dancing and singing that follow, the cops get caught up in the Hora, and Fritz beats it out again.

Fritz decides that the world is passing him by.

He has rivers to cross, poems to write and most important, girls. He sets fire to his schoolbooks and sets out for Harlem, to experience.

In a bar he lights on Duke, shooting pool. Fritz tries to spread his contagion of white liberal platitudes: "My heart cries out to you in this racial crisis". Duke says: "No shit!" After continuing to bug Duke, Fritz accidentally shoves his arm, which causes Duke to sink every one of the 15 balls on the table. Duke gets Fritz out before the crows at the bar cut him to pieces.

After a car chase and a terrific crash, the two of them go off to Big Bertha's pad—a remnant of old time Harlem when white money came up for a good time—where a pot party is in progress. Bertha gets Fritz high on marijuana, and chasing her into a junkyard, he finally grabs her and they start to make love.

In the midst of the lovemaking, Fritz is beset by the idea that he is now a part of the Black lifestyle. He rushes off to a street corner and berates the crows for not rising up and revolting against their white oppressors. A riot ensues. The cops come. Duke again tries to save Fritz, but is killed in the process. Once again, Fritz leaves it all behind to hit the road with an old girlfriend, Winston. The cross country jaunt that was to be full of romance, adventure and poetry for Fritz, turns into a nightmare of carping and complaining by Winston.

When their Volkswagen runs out of gas, Fritz meets up with a group of bike riding Hells Angels. They convince him that revolution is the only way out. Apart from being on hard drugs and from combining sadistic urges against society and each other, Fritz is persuaded to help them blow up a power plant . . . but the sudden beating and rape of Harriet, one of the bikers' chicks, turns Fritz cold on the group.

While planting the dynamite, he realises that their brutality is too much and that this kind of destruction will do no one any good. Too late! KABOOM!

In a hospital room Fritz is swathed in bandages as the girls come sobbing to his bedside. Painfully he talks, a kind of deathbed confession, in which he gets them to come closer. Finally, he takes command and directs the girls into various positions of undress. While Fritz's bandages come flying off, the girls go bounding up and down on the hospital bed in perfect slow motion. The giggling and heavy breathing take over.

Title:	*CHARLOTTE'S WEB*
Year:	1972
Country:	U.S.A.
Running time:	95 mins.
Medium:	Animated cartoon/colour
Directors:	Charles A. Nichols and Iwao Takamoto

Producers:	Hanna and Barbera
Executive producer:	Edgar Bronfman
Story by:	Earl Hamner, Jr.
Based upon the Book "Charlotte's Web" by:	E. B. White
Music and lyrics:	Richard M. Sherman, Robert B. Sherman
Art direction:	Bob Singer, Ray Aragon, Paul Julian
Animation co-ordinators:	Jerry Hathcock, Bill Keil
Key animators:	Hal Ambro, Ed Barge, Lars Galonius, Dick Lundy, Irv Spence
Animation:	Ed Aardal, Lee Dyer, Bob Gow, George Kreisl, Don Patterson, Carlo Vinci, O. E. Callahan, Hugh Fraser, Volus Jones, Ed Parks, Ray Patterson, Xenia
Background supervision:	F. Montealegre
Backgrounds:	Lorraine Andrina, Fernando Arco, Lyle Beddes, Venetia Epler, Ronald Erickson, Martin Forte, Bob Gentle, Al Gmuer, Joseph Griffith, Jr., Gino Giudice, Richard Khim, Tom Knowles, Gary Niblett, Rolando Oliva, Eric Semones, Jeannette Toews, Peter Van Elk
The voices:	Debbie Reynolds, Paul Lynde, Henry Gibson, Rex Allen, Martha Scott, Dave Madden, Danny Bonaduce, Don Messick, Herb Vigrant, Agnes Moorehead, Pam Ferdin, Joan Gerber, Robert Holt, John Stephenson, William B. White

Subject:

On a New England farm in the 1930s, eight-year-old Fern Arable (Pamelyn Ferdin) begs her father (John Stephenson) not to slaughter a new spring pig that was born a runt. The farmer agrees to let Fern raise the pig. She names him Wilbur (Henry Gibson) caring for him like a baby, and singing him lullabies, such as "There Must Be Something More". Fern and her neighbour, ten-year-old Henry Fussy (Bill White) share mischievous adventures with Wilbur, but when the pig grows to full size, Mr. Arable sells him to Homer Zuckerman (Bob Holt).

Wilbur is unhappy at the Zuckerman residence. It is while the stuttering goose (Agnes Moorehead) tries to cheer him up that Wilbur discovers he has the power of speech ("I Can Talk", he sings)

Wilbur has no one with whom to play, the Goose being too busy hatching her eggs, and Templeton (Paul Lynde), the self-centred rat, too preoccupied with gorging himself.

The haughty old sheep (Dave Madden) tells Wilbur that all pigs are slaughtered for food in the winter. Lonely and frightened, Wilbur hears a mysterious voice singing "Chin Up" to him. It is a large grey spider named Charlotte A. Cavatica (Debbie Reynolds), who tells Wilbur she wants to be his friend and will somehow try to save his life. Fern visits the barn and becomes friends with all the animals and Mrs. Arable (Martha Scott) worries that her daughter believes she can hear the animals talk.

The goose gives birth to seven goslings. One is a runt named Geoffrey (Don Messick) who becomes Wilbur's pal, joining him and the other animals in singing "We've Got Lots In Common". Wilbur, however, is still nervous about his fate, and is comforted to sleep by Charlotte singing him "Deep In The Dark". She spins through the night to the song ,"Charlotte's Web", weaving the words "Some Pig" into her web. The Zuckermans and their farm hand Lurvy (Herb Vigran) believe the words are part of some miracle.

To keep the scheme going, Charlotte designs new words into her web such as "terrific" and "radiant". Wilbur's dance makes him a local celebrity, and Mr. Zuckerman decides to enter him in the country fair, where he will be safe from slaughter forever if he wins a prize. Charlotte decides she must accompany Wilbur to the fair, but she is preparing her egg sac and nearing the end of her life cycle ("Mother Earth and Father Time"). Charlotte asks the reluctant Templeton to join them, and he agrees after the goose describes the fair as a scavenger's paradise for food ("A Veritable Smorgasbord").

Charlotte and Templeton hide in Wilbur's crate on the way to the fair. On a rafter in the pen, Charlotte works on her egg sac, weaving the word "humble" in her web. The Arables and Zuckermans enjoy all the exhibits at the fair.

A gigantic, obnoxious pig named Uncle (Herb Vigran) wins the top prize, but Wilbur is awarded a special medal for being "terrific", "radiant", and "humble", and for drawing so many tourists to the community. A barbershop quartet leads the crowd in singing "Zuckerman's Famous Pig".

As they prepare to leave, the languishing Charlotte tells Wilbur he has enriched her life, but she will not be going back to the farm. Wilbur sad but understanding, convinces Templeton to save Charlotte's egg sac in the crate. As the Zuckermans and Arables return home, Charlotte's last silk strand sways in the air.

Wilbur is lonely back at the farm. All winter long, he protects Charlotte's egg sac, and in the spring life renews itself. Even Templeton becomes a father. Wilbur watches proudly as Charlotte's egg sac hatches forth 514 baby spiders—all but three (who are too small) take to the air on silky parachutes.

The three small spiders stay on to be Wilbur's new friends, bearing children of their own. Wilbur will never be lonely again, but Charlotte will always be in his heart.

In author E. B. White's words, "It is not often that someone comes along who is a true friend and a good writer. Charlotte was both."

Title:	HEAVY TRAFFIC
Year:	1973
Country:	U.S.A.
Running time:	75 mins.
Medium:	Animated cartoon/colour
Director/Screenplay:	Ralph Bakshi
Production:	Steve Krantz
Voices:	Joe Kaufmann, Beverly Hope Atkinson, Franke de Kova, Mary Dean Lauria, Terri Haven
Photography:	Ted C. Bemiller
Editor:	Donald W. Ernst
Music:	Ray Shanklin, Ed. Bogas

Subject:

The adventures of a young cartoonist (Michael) whose Italian father (Angiel) is a member of the Mafia and has violent quarrels with Michael's Jewish mother Ida. Eventually Michael takes a black girl, Rosa, as his mistress. This angers Angiel who appeals to The Godfather without success.

The legless bouncer at the bar where Rosa worked kills the cartoon figure of Michael. The real Michael, who has been operating a pin table throughout, wanders the streets and meets the real Rosa.

Title:	THE NINE LIVES OF FRITZ THE CAT
Year:	1974
Country:	U.S.A.
Running time:	76 mins.
Medium:	Animated cartoon/colour
Director:	Robert Taylor
Producer:	Steve Krantz
Screenplay:	Fred Halliday, Eric Monte, Robert Taylor
Photography:	Ted C. Bemiller, Gregg Heschong
Editor:	Marshall M. Borden
Music:	Tom Scott
Voice of Fritz:	Skip Hinant

Subject:

Stoned on grass, Fritz escapes from his wife's nagging into the better times of his other lives: the time when he seduced his kid sister; the time when he was appointed Hitler's orderly; the time when he was blasted off to Mars in a rocket while copulating with black chick Thelma; the time in the future when he was sent by President Kissinger to carry a message to the President of the Black State of New Jersey and became involved in a war between two States.

Title:	JOURNEY BACK TO OZ
Year:	1974
Country:	U.S.A.
Medium:	Animated cartoon/colour
Director:	Hal Sutherland
Screenplay:	Fred Land, Norm Prescott
Producer:	Norm Prescott, Lou Scheimer
Lyrics and music:	Sammy Cahn, James Van Heusen
Songs:	Walter Scharf
Voices:	Milton Berle, Herschel Bernardi, Paul Ford, Margaret Hamilton, Jack E. Leonard, Paul Lynde, Ethel Merman, Liza Minnelli, Mickey Rooney, Rise Stevens, Danny Thomas, Mel Blanc, Dallas McKennon, Larry Storch

Subject:

Both the storyline as well as the characters are based on the successful live action film which was produced with Judy Garland in the nineteen-forties. New music and songs are introduced which carry the story and the animation.

FURTHER ANIMATED FEATURES COMPLETED AND EXPECTED TO BE FINISHED IN THE NEAR FUTURE.

1. Title: *A Thousand Intentions and One Invention*
    Country: Argentina

    An animated cartoon of 95 minutes by Manuel Garcia Ferre. Finished during 1972.

2. Title: *Wien*
    Country: Austria

    A film drawn directly onto film stock. Direction and production by Ernst Schmidt Jr.

3. Title: *Tintin et le Lac Aux Requins*
    Country: Belgium

    The second *Tintin* full length animated cartoon. 80 minutes long directed by Belvision Raymond Leblance-Hergé. Finished in 1972.

4. Title: *Kitan of the Amazon*
    Country: Brazil
    By de Anelio Latini-Filho.

5. Title: *Man the Polluter*
   Country: Yugoslavia/Canada
   35mm. and 16 mm., colour, 53 mins. 20 secs.
   Production, script and design: (Yugoslavia) Milan Blazekovic, Zlato Bourek, Nedeljko Dragic, Boris Kolar, Aleksandar Marks, Vladimir Jutrisa, Dusan Vokotic, Ante Zaninovic. (Canada) Don Arioli, Hugh Foulds, Chuck Jones, Wolf Koening, Kaj Pindal, Frank Nissem (Cinera Productions) Pino van Lamsweerde.

6. Title: *Robinson Colombus*
   Country: Denmark

   This film, based on the story of Robinson Crusoe, is by I. B. Steinna. Completed.

7. Title: *Maravillosos Cuentos Espanoles*
   Country: Spain

   This long film (approx. 82 minutes) is by Francisco Macian in Barcelona who made The Wizard Of The Dreams some years ago.

8. Title: *The Divine Comedy*
   Country: Spain

   The American producer Al Brodax who produced Yellow Submarine is co-operating with Salvator Dali in this project.

9. Title: *Gulliver's Travels*
   Country: Spain

   Another version of Swift's classic subject. Production by Delfont and direction by Cruz Delgado in Madrid and Barcelona.

10. Title: *Don Quixote*
    Country: Spain

    Cruz Delgado's original Servantez version of the popular Spanish hero. May not be commenced for a while.

11. Title: *The War Between Men and Women*
    Country: U.S.A.

    Based on the successful book, this feature is only partially animated under the direction of Melville Shavelson.

12. Title: *HEIDI*
    Country: U.S.A.

    In production with Hanna and Barbera studio in Hollywood.

13. Title: *Noah's Ark*
    Country: U.S.A.

    Another feature project from Hanna and Barbera organisation. This project is also being produced by Kinney's Unit Filmation.

14. Title: *Peanuts* (*No. 3*) *Race for your Life, Charlie Brown*
    Country: U.S.A.

    The third Charlie Brown animated feature by Bill Melendez and Co.

15. Title: *Timmy Me Grout Inside Out*
    Country: U.S.A.

    The production commenced at the beginning of 1972 by Dominic Orsatti. The film is directed by Alexander Cohen.

16. Title: *Misadventures of Don Juan*
    Country: U.S.A.

    Started October 1972 by director Emil Carle. Production by Dominic Orsatti.

17. Title: *Coonskin*
    Country: U.S.A.

    Director Ralph Bakshi made his name through "Fritz The Cat" and "Heavy Traffic" This feature is for Paramount Production and has been completed at the start of 1975.

18. Title: *The American Chronicles/The War Lords.*
    Country: U.S.A.

    Another of Ralph Bakshi's features for Paramount Pictures.

19. Title: *Hey Good Looking*
    Country: U.S.A.

    This picture by Ralph Bakshi is to be released by Warner Bros. Hollywood.

20. Title: *Je, Tu, Elles*
    Country: France

    This animated cartoon and live action feature by Peter Foldes has never been exposed in the cinemas so far. It is expected that it will be shown during 1975.

21. Title: *Le Sourire Vertical*
    Country: France

    Another live action and animated combined feature from France. Directed by Robert Laupoujade.

22. Title: *La Genese*
    Country: France

    Fully animated feature film by Pierre Alibert. Production by Films du Cypres. Completed in 1975.

23. Title: *A Season in Hell for Adam and Eve*
    Country: France/Czechoslovakia

    Based on the successful series of books by Jean Effel following his previous animated feature "The Creation of The World".

24. Title: *Daphnis and Chloe*
    Country: France

    Computer generated feature by Peter Foldes and Paul and Gaetan Brizzi (sponsored by the Arts Graphiques de la Societé Francaise de Production).

25. Title: *The Adventures of Baron Munchhausen*
    Country: France

    Yet another version of the famous German classic, by Jean Image.

26. Title: *The Twelve Works of Asterix*
Country: France, Completed 1976.

Production by the newly established studio in Paris, IDEFIX. Direction by Goscinny/ Uderzo. Artistic Director Gruel & Watrin.

The third full length animated cartoon based on the famous character Asterix drawn, designed, and written by Goscinny/Uderzo team. Animation superviser Pierre Watrin in Paris, and John Halas in London. Now finished.

27. Title: *The Cobbler and the Thief (Nashrudin)*
Country: Great Britain

This 78 minutes feature film directed by the Richard Williams Organisation has been in production for some time.

28. Title: *Tin Drums*
Country: Great Britain

Director Charlie Jenkins. The subject is based on the well-known novel of Gunter Grass.

29. Title: *The Tempest*
Country: Great Britain

George Dunning's version of Shakespeare's classic.

30. Title: *Alice Through the Looking Glass*
Country: Great Britain

Yet another version of Lewis Carroll's subject by Ray Jackson.

31. Title: *Watership Down*
Country: Great Britain/U.S.A.

One of the great contemporary classics by Richard Adams. Producer Martin Rosen. Direction: John Hubley.

32. Title: *Max & Moritz*
Country: Great Britain/Germany

A one hour special by John Halas in association with POLYMEDIA in Germany. The film is based on Wilhelm Busch's early strip cartoons with major emphasis on the characters of Max & Moritz.

33. Title: *Discovery of America*
Country: Great Britain

An hour long television film of the 40,000 years history of the American continent revealing new discoveries about it. Direction by John Halas for Educational Film Centre, London. A coproduction with other nations.

34. Title: *Lucky Luke*
Country: France

The second feature by the Idefix Studio in Paris featuring the character of Lucky Luke.

35. Title: *Ludas Matyi*
Country: Hungary

Based on the traditional character of Ludas Matyi, a small beanstalk type of figure. Directed by Atilla Dargay. Production by Pannonia Studio, Budapest.

36. Title: *The Divine Comedy*
Country: Italy

Production started some time ago under the direction of Nello Risi.

37. Title: *Hundred Thousand Leagues in Space*
Country: Italy

Mainly produced for television by Corona Films, Rome and directed by Marcello Baldi. Length 55 minutes. Finished 1962.

38. Title: *The Wizard of Oz*
Country: Italy

A remake of the successful fairy tale already made in live action in fully animated cartoon. Production by Studio Gibba. Direction by Gibba.

39. Title: *Kim*
Country: Italy

Based on Kipling's novel, another feature under the direction of Gibba. Production by Internat Film Enterprise.

40. Title: *Drywhat & Mighty Midget the Dwarf*
Country: Italy

The original title of the film is Il Nano e La Strega. It has been in production for some time, by Claudio Monti. Direction by Giorgio Librati.

41. Title: *Allegro Non Troppo*
Country: Italy.

A combined live action animation feature by Bruno Bozzetto in his comic style. Completed.

42. Title: *Robinson Crusoe*
Country: Rumania/Italy

The adventures of Robinson Crusoe is the first co-production between Corona Cinematog-Raphica Italy and Anima Films, Bucharest. Direction by Victor Antonesca and Gibba. Length, 80 minutes. Completed.

43. Title: *Homo Sapiens*
Country: Rumania

Ion Popesco—Gopo, the well known creator of the many films from Rumania, utilising the popularity of his main cartoon character.

44. Title: *Odyssey of the Zodiac*
Country: Switzerland

Direction is by Santiago Arolas.

45. Title: *The Boys of Captain Nemo*
Country: Czechoslovakia/Italy

Several short adventures of Captain Nemo are joined to make up the feature. A co-production between Czechoslovakia and Italy. The film is released in Italy under the title of I Regazzi del Capitano Nemo. The joint credit for direction is Karel Zeman and Paolo Hensch.

46. Title: *The Adventures of Buratino*
Country: USSR

The director of the film Babichenko is now working in the new animation studios of Moscow Television where he is making this 90 minutes feature. Finished 1970.

47. Title: *The Rescuers*
Country: U.S.A.

This new animated feature in production at the animation department of Walt Disney Studio is animation directed by the veteran Frank Thomas who has been with the organisation ever since 1934.

SOME NOTABLE ANIMATED FEATURE FILMS STARTED BUT NOT COMPLETED

1. Title: *Anatol at the Tower of Nesle*/France/1935
An attempt by Dubout the brilliant French cartoonist.

2. Title: *The Rainbow Road to Oz*/Canada
De Crawley Film.

3. Title: *The Pig and the Fly*/France/1935
Directors—Minima Indelli and Paul de Rounaix. Production by D.A.E.

4. Title: *Christopher Colombus*/France/1935
Directors—Minima Indelli and Paul de Roubaix. Production by D.A.E.

5. Title: *Around the World in 80 Days*/Great Britain/France/1939
This feature had been started during 1936 with the backing of Alexander Korda's London Film by Anthony Gross and Hector Hoppin. Sponsored by the British Film Institute, a seventeen minute section of it was completed in 1955 by Anthony Gross and Halas and Batchelor.

6. Title: *Tom Thumb*/France/1948
Direction by Rene Risacher. Production by Ecran Des Jeunes.

7. Title: *The Hobbit*/Great Britain/1972
A newly formed organisation by James Nurse, Euroanimation's attempt to film Tolkien's well-known novel for Rankin and Bass, New York. The project may be revived.

8. *Pinocchio*/Italy/1911.
The earliest attempt in Europe to produce a full length animated film by Cesore Antamaro.

9. Title: *The Life of Mussolini*/Italy/1923
The project appeared a good idea at that time, but never succeeded. By Guido Pregepi.

10. Title: *The Adventures of Pinocchio*/Italy/1940–42
There is sixty minutes of black and white section of the project still in existence. Directors—Raoul Verdini, Barbara Attalo and R. Bacchini. Production by C.A.I.P.

11. Title: *Tramy the Baby Trotter*/Italy/approx. 1966
Direction by Roberto Fabietti.

12. Title: *Rompicollo*/Italy/1953–54
Approximately two-thirds of the film was completed before the project ran into financial difficulties. Director—Giuseppe Ruccaglia.

13. Title: *L'Isola del Gabbiano Gregorio*/Italy/1967
Director—Antonio Attanassi.

14. Title: *Mister Touffe*/Switzerland/1929
The first attempt at cartoon feature in Switzerland by Vare.

15. Title: *Puss In Boots*/Switzerland/1965
Directors—Benny Meyer and F. G. Rindlisbacher.

16. Title: *Orpheus*/Czechoslovakia/——
Director and Producer—Richard Dillenz.

17. Title: *The Movies Take A Holiday*/U.S.A./1944
An anthology of avant-guard films based on the work of Renoir, Duchamps, Leger, Man Ray and Richter. Directors—Hans Richter and Herman Winberg. Length would have been 65 minutes.

FEATURE FILMS WITH INSUFFICIENT INFORMATION

It is regrettable that little knowledge is available regarding the Spanish feature "Oh Mi Karay Kiki" which was completed during 1950 by the same team who were involved with Suenos de Tay Pi, and the German productions "Reveil de Rubezahal" and "Die Sieben Raben" (Studio Dean).

Other features came and disappeared rather rapidly due to the fact that they were produced for television where they have only been seen once or twice. Into this category fall two Hanna and Barbera features, "Hey There It's Yogi Bear" in 1964, "A Man Called Flintstone" in 1967, and Rankin and Bass Japanese film made in 1971, "Santa Claus is Going to Town".

Little has been heard of the Harry Smith's (USA) film "Heaven and Earth Magic" a 75 minute film finished during the year 1965. Peter Foldes (France) combined film "The Ou Cafe" for French television also disappeared. So have the Japanese TOEI produced "The Fantastic World of Ukiyoe" made in 1969, length 70 minutes.

Not much information is available about the great Russian cartoonist's Ivanov-Vano's version of "Snow White" which was completed during 1952 in the studios of Soyuzmultfilm, length 55 minutes.

It would certainly be interesting to compare this film with the Walt Disney version.

The Chinese animation studio in Shanghai was an extremely active one before the war, but few have seen their long film in the west "The Princess with The Iron Fan" by Wan Lai Ming and Wan Kou Tchan produced in 1940.

The same applies to five long films produced in Seoul the capital of South Korea, serving the far eastern children's market.

The studio contains a staff of 150 artists some highly experienced. The list of films completed so far are:—

	Treasure Island
Duration:	74 mins.
Director:	Youngil Park
Production:	The Century Co. Ltd.
Subject:	Kangyoon Kim.

	Golden Ironman
Duration:	74 mins.
Direction and subject:	Youngil Park
Production:	The Century Co. Ltd.

	General Hong-Gil-Dong
Original title:	Hong -Gil-Dong Jang Koon
Duration:	58 mins.
Direction:	Yusoo Yong
Production:	The Century Co. Ltd.

	Hodond and Princess
Original title:	Hodong Wangja Wa Nang-nang Kongju
Duration:	56 mins.
Direction:	Yusoo Yong
Production:	The Century Co. Ltd.

	The War of Great Monsters
Duration:	80 mins.
Direction:	Yusoo Yong
Production:	The Century Co. Ltd.
Subject:	Hyunjae SUH

FEATURES ANNOUNCED AS FUTURE PROJECTS BY PRODUCERS AND DIRECTORS

Australia

The Astrasian Studio in Sydney, Australia, have announced the production of four feature films (no titles) in association with CBS-TV.

Argentina

Manuel Garcia Ferre who has already made some feature films has announced a new project. (No title).

Belgium

Valisa Films Productions in Brussels are making an 80 minute cartoon based on Picha's characters. It is called *Tarzoon, Shame of the Jungle*. As well as a further project entitled *The Flute of Six Schtroumpfs*. Both completed.

Brazil

Four announcements made. *The History of America* by Hamilton de Souza. *The Adventures of Picon-ze* by the Japanese born Ype Nakashima. *Viagem Ao Ceu* by Jorge Bastos, and *The Adventures of Curumin* by the experienced Alvaro Henrique Goncalves, and a project from Geraldo Sarno.

U.S.A.

A great many announcements have been made. *Space Survey* by Lester Novros, production by Graphic Films. *The Day I Met Zett* by the New York director Fred Moubgub. Another version of *Don Quixote* by Fred Calvert in Hollywood.

Another version of *Treasure Island, Oliver Twist, Cyrano de Bergerac, Swiss Family Robinson, Don Quixote, From The Earth To The Moon, Robin Hood, Noah's Ark, Knights of the Round Table, The Arabian Nights, Call of the Wild,* yet once again, *King Arthur* and *Huckleberry Finn.* The studio involved is the Kenney's Unit of Filmation, production by Hal Sutherland.

Nanny and the Professor is another of Fred Calvert's announcements.

Although started in South America *Winn Abojo* is prepared by director Emil Carle and producer Dominic Orsatti. The talented painter and abstract film maker Carmen D'Avino also announced that he is working on a long film with a combination of different techniques (no title yet).

Grease the rock musical is being transferred to film by Steve Krantz, and produced by Kenneth Waissman and Maxine Fox.

France

The director Jean Jabely intends to make the film *Minoie* based on the drawings of Phillipe Druillet. *Lon Sloane* has been announced as well as an animated feature of *Ben-Hur*.

Rene Laloux is adapting with Philip Caza the subject, *The Man, the Machine against Grandhar.*

Italy

Pulcinella Citrullo D'Acerra a combined live/animation project is being contemplated by Antonio Attanasi.

Sweden

A team film and AB started during 1973, *Agaton Sax*. An 80 minute subject based on the novel of Nils Olaf Franzen.

USSR

Sandor Reisnabuchler the Hungarian film director has been invited to Moscow to work in the studios of Soyuzmultfilm on *The Adventures of Babar the Wonderful Elephant* based on Jean de Brunhoff's orignial story.

Ivanov-Vano has also reworked and reanimated his feature film *The Hunch-Backed Horse* with new backgrounds, new music and better continuity. With quicker timing and up to date photography, this film can expect an entirely new lease of life.

COMBINED FEATURES, BUT SOME PREDOMINANTLY LIVE ACTION WITH ANIMATION INSERTS

1. Title: *Anchors Aweigh*/U.S.A./1946

   The famous musical, featuring Gene Kelly dancing with animated animals.

2. Title: *Mary Poppins*/U.S.A./1964

   Walt Disney's successful combined feature with some animated puffins dancing with humans with great precision. The director is Robert Stevenson, length 139 minutes.

3. Title: *Doctor Eliezer*/U.S.A./1969

   A totally abstract special effect film by Derek Lamb. Primarily shown in drive-in cinemas to stimulate the emotions of the audiences. Length 110 minutes.

4. Title: *German Dada*/Germany/1969

   Helmut Herbst's interesting experiment with live action, cutouts and animation.

5. Title: *Expo-71*/Japan/1971

   Juri Kuri's special effect film for the Kioto world exhibition. The film was just for the occasion. Length 60 mins.

INDEX AND APPENDIX TO CATALOGUE

Key to symbols:

(D)—Drawn on film
(C)—Animated cartoon
(P)—Animated puppets
(CO)—Animated cut-outs
(O)—Animated objects
(L)—Live action

(M)—Mixture of some or all of above media
(S)—Animated shadows or silhouettes
(TV)—Special production for television
(U)—Left unfinished
: : :—In preparation
*—In production
——Not included in catalogue
Number references refer to the catalogue

153	*The Little Snow Maiden*	(C)	1952	Ivan Ivanov-Vano
154	*The Twelve Months*	(C)	1956	Ivan Ivanov-Vano
154	*The Snow Queen*	(C)	1957	Lev Atamanov
154	*The Adventures of Buratino*	(C)	1959	Ivan Ivanov-Vano, Dimitri Babichenko
154	*I Drew the Man*	(C)	1960	V. and Z. Brumberg
155	*The Key*	(C)	1961	Lev Atamanov
155	*The Bath*	(P & L)	1962	Sergei Yutkievitch, Anatoli Karanovitch
155	*The Wild Swans*	(C)	1962	M. & V. Tsekhanovsky
155	*The Mechanical Flea*	(C-O)	1964	Ivan Ivanov-Vano
156	*The Blue Bird*	(C)	1972	V. Livanov
	SPAIN			
156	*The Knight Garbancito*	(C)	1947	Arturo Moreno
156	*Happy Holidays*	(C)	1948	Arturo Moreno
156	*Dream of Tai Py (Oh Mi Karay Kiki)*	(C)	1950 approx.	Jose Maria Blay, P. Winterstein
157	*Once Upon A Time*	(C)	1950	Alexandre Cirici-Pellicer
156	*The Magi of Dreams*	(C)	1966	Francisco Macian
157	*Scope, Colour, Muda 75 (Ere Erera Baleibu Icik Subua Arvaren)*	(D)	1970	Jose Antonia Sistiaga
157	*Cinderella*	(C)	—	Francisco Macian
157	*Magic Adventure*	(C)	1975	Cruz Delgado
	SWEDEN			
158	*Out of an Old Man's Head*	(C & L)	1968	Per Ahlin & Tage Danielsson
158	*Thundering Fatty*	(C & L)	1974	Per Ahlin
	UNITED STATES OF AMERICA			
158	*Snow White and the Seven Dwarfs*	(C)	1938	Disney
159	*Fantasia*	(C & L)	1939	Disney
161	*Gulliver's Travels*	(C)	1939	Dave Fleischer
161	*Mister Bug Goes to Town*	(C)	1940	Dave Fleischer
161	*Pinocchio*	(C)	1940	Disney
162	*Dumbo*	(C)	1941	Disney
163	*The Reluctant Dragon*	(C & L)	1941	Disney
163	*Bambi*	(C)	1942	Disney
163	*Victory Through Airpower*	(C)	1943	Disney
163	*The Three Caballeros*	(C & L)	1945	Disney
164	*Make Mine Music*	(C)	1946	Disney
164	*Song of the South*	(C & L)	1946	Disney
164	*Sinbad the Sailor*	(C)	1946	Disney
165	*Fun and Fancy Free*	(C & L)	1947	Disney
165	*So Dear to My Heart*	(C & L)	1948	Disney
165	*Melody Time*	(C & L)	1948	Disney
165	*Alice in Wonderland*	(P)	1948	Lou Bunin
165	*The Adventures of Ichabod and Mr Toad*	(C)	1949	Disney
166	*Cinderella*	(C)	1950	Disney
167	*Alice in Wonderland*	(C)	1951	Disney
167	*Peter Pan*	(C)	1953	Disney
167	*The Lady and The Tramp*	(C)	1955	Disney
168	*Sleeping Beauty*	(C)	1959	Disney
169	*A Thousand and One Arabian Nights*	(C)	1959	Jack Kinney (UPA)
169	*One Hundred and One Dalmatians*	(C)	1960	Disney
170	*Of Stars and Men*	(C)	1961	John Hubley
170	*Mister Magoo's Christmas Carol*	(C) (TV)	1962	Abe Levitow (UPA)
171	*Gay Purr-ee*	(C)	1962	Abe Levitow (UPA)
172	*The Sword in the Stone*	(C)	1963	Wolfgang Reitherman (Disney)
172	*Hey There, It's Yogi Bear*	(C)	1964	Hanna-Barbera
172	*The Man From Button Willow*	(C)	1965	David Detiege
173	*The Jungle Book*	(C)	1967	Wolfgang Reitherman (Disney)

BIBLIOGRAPHY   *BOOKS AND PAMPHLETS*

Asenin, Sergei V.   The Animated Film. Russian Edition, Moscow, 1974.

Bardeche, Maurice and Brasillach, Robert.   Histoire Du Cinema. Denoel, Paris, 1943.

Bassoto, Camillo.   Il Film Per Ragazzi E Il Documentario A Venezia 1949–1968. Mostra Cinema, 1968.

Benayoun, Robert.   Le Dessin Aminé Après Walt Disney. J. J. Pauvert, Paris, 1961.

Benesova, Dr. Marie.   Czechoslovak Animated Film. Czekoslovensky Film-export, Prague, 1967.

Buchmann, Dr. Mark   Jiri Trnka 20 Jahre Puppenfilm. Kunstgewerbemuseum, Zurich, 1966.

Chevalier, Denys.   J'aime Le Dessin Anime, Rencontres, Lausanne 1962.

Cuenca, Carlos Ferdandez.   Elmundo Del Dibujo Animado. San Sebastian, 1962.

Duca, J. M. L.   Le Dessin Anime, Prisma, Paris, 1948.
Histoire Du Cinema. Coll. Que sais-je No. 81—Presses Universitaires de France, 1947.

Disney, Walt.   The Art of Animation. Simon & Shuster, New York, 1959–1966.

Field, Robert, D.   The Art of Walt Disney. Macmillan-Collins, New York—London—Glasgow, 1942–1947.

Gasca, Luis.   Los Comics En La Pentala. Festival International Del Cine, San Sebastian, 1965.
Imagen Y Ciencia Ficcion. Festival International del Cine, San Sebastian, 1966.

Halas, John and Bob Privett.   How to Cartoon. 1951. Focal Press, London, Amphoto, New York.

Halas, John, and Roger Manvell.   The Technique of Film Animation. 1960 (4th edn. 1976), Focal Press, London, Hastings House, New York.

Halas, John, and Roger Manvell.   Design in Motion, 1963.

Halas, John   T.V. Graphics. Graphics Press, Zurich, 1966.

Halas, John and Walter Herdeg   Film and TV Graphics, 1965.

Halas, John   Animation in Great Britain in 1967. Pamphlet, Expo 67, Montreal, 1967.

Halas, John and Roger Manvell   Art in Movement, 1970. Studio Vista, London, New York.

Halas, John and contributors.   Computer Animation 1974. Focal Press, London, Hastings House, New York.

Halas, John and contributors.   Visual Scripting. 1976. Focal Press, London, Hastings House, New York.

Halas, John and Roger Manvell.   Animation Round the World. Society of Film & Television Arts, 1975.

Image et Son.   No. 204, April 1967, Paul Grimault Special.
No. 207, June–July 1967, French animation film-makers.

Jeanne, René, and Charles Ford.   Histoire illustrée Du Cinema. Marabout University, 3 Vols.

Kuttna, Mari   Hungarian Animation, Pannonia Studio, 1970.

Lapierre, Marcel.   Les Cent Visages Du Cinema.

Madsen, Dr. Roy.   Animated Film, Interland Publ. N.Y., 1968.

Maelstaf, Raoul.   Le Film D'animation en Belgique. Textes et Documentes Nos. 261–262, July–August 1970. Ministry of International Commerce and Foreign Affairs, Brussels.

Manvell, Roger.   The Animated Film. Illustrations by John Halas and Joy Batchelor, 1954. The story of producing Animal Farm.

Martin, André.   L'age D'or du Dessin Anime American 1906–1941, Tableau Synchroptique Cinematheque du Canada. Vanier 1967.

Müller, Horst.   DEFA Studio Für Trickfilme 1955–1964, Berlin, 1967.

Philippe, Pierre.   Un Petit Dictionaire du Cinema Francais D'animation. Pamphlet 1967.

Poncet, Marie Thérese.   Dessin Anime, Art Mondial. Cercle du Livre, Paris, 1956 Le Dessin Anime ED. du Cap Coll: Diagrammes du monde, Monte-Carlo, 1968.

Positif.	No. 31, Nov, 1959, animation in 1959, No. 54–5, July–August 1963, animation in 1963.
Rondolino, Gianni.	Il Lungo Metraggio D'animazione. Oggi. Revue Citta di Busto Arsizo No. 3 June, 1970.
Rondolino, Gianni.	The Story of Animated Film. Einaudi, Italy, 1974.
Sadoul, Georges.	Histoire Du Cinema Coll: J'ai lu Connaissance 1–1962. Histoire Generale Du Cinema, 5 Volumes, Denoel 1946–47–51–52–54, Paris.
Stephenson, Ralph.	Animation in the Cinema. Peter Cowie, IFG Series, London, 1967. New edition 1974.
Togawa, Nacki.	Animation Film in Japan. Pamphlet, Tokyo, 1967.
Zanotto, Piere.	Disegni E Pupazzi Animati Di Ieri E Di Oggi Ed. Quaderni Della Rivista del Cinematografeo Roam. 1966. L'impero Di Walt Disney Ed. R.A.D.A.R. Padova, 1967. Il Disengi Animati.

ARTICLES, CATALOGUES, REVIEWS

Baxter, Grange Grove.	Snow White Meets the Blue Meanies, Film No. 54 Spring 69.
Baldini, Rafaelo.	La Matita Che Graffia, Panorama, 12th Dec. 1968. (Italy).
Cinema 57.	No. 14, Jan, 1957, The Animation Cinema.
Cinema 65.	No. 98, July 1965, Animation II.
Cinemas.	Quarterly review of Journees du Cinema, Association Francaise pour la diffusion du Cinema, No. 3, L'animation aujourd'hui, & No. 7, L'animation dans le monde en 1960.
Comuzio, Ermanno.	Piccola Storia Del Disecnio Animato Italiano, Cineform No. 53, March 1966.
Dictionnaire du Cinema.	J. J. Pauvert edition.
Dictionnaire du Cinema.	Larousse edition.
Edera, Bruno.	The Full Length Animated Film CTVD No. 24, Fall 1969. 50 Anos De Cinema De Animacao De Longa Metrage. Bastidores 14.5.69, 28.5.69, 4.6.69, 11.69 (Portugal), Mar Alto 27.8.69, 24.9.69, 22.10.69, 26.11.69, 31.12.69, 28.1.70, Jornal Da Vosta Del Sol Feb 1970, Dec 1970.
International Film Guide.	1964, 65, 66, 67, 68, 69, 70, 71, 72, 73, 74, 75. Tantivy Press, London.
Martin, Andre.	Pour Qui Sont Les Trnkas, Cahiers du Cinema, Paris, Nos. 103, 104, 105, 107, Jan., March & May 1960.
Novum Gebrauchs Graphic/John Halas.	February 1975, Graphics in Motion I, May 1975, Graphics in Motion II, August, 1975, Graphics in Motion, III, November 1975, Graphics in Motion, IV, January 1976, Graphics in Motion V, April 1976, Graphics in Motion VI.
La Revue du Cinema.	Paris, Feb. 1947, animation special
Film.	No. 4 Special issue: the Animated film
ASIFA Bulletins	London, Paris, Bucharest and Budapest.

Index de la Cinematographie Francaise, Cinema International, Publications of Festivals at Annecy, Mamaia, Cambridge, Cannes, Tours, Cracow, Locarno, Oxford, Venice, etc. Illustrierte Film Buhne-Munich, Top-cel (organ of the New York Screen Cartoonists Local), L'Ecran Chinois, Le Film Sovietique, Hungaro Film Bulletins, Contemporary Films Catalogue (London), Making Film in New York (Special issue on animation, July–August, 1967), Entertainment World (31st Oct. 1969), UniJapan-Film and Uni-Japan Film Quarterly Catalogues, Unitalialfim Catalogues, Uniespana Film Catalogues, Unifrance-Film Catalogues, Ceskoslovensky Film Catalogues, American Film Institute Animation Issue (1974), and more recent publications.

CREDITS

The authors would like to thank:

Mr. Cosme Alves Neto, Cinematheque, Museum of Modern Art, Rio de Janeiro
Voltchenko Atamanov, Soyuzmultfilm, Moscow
Aveo Embassy Pictures, New York
Studios Belvision, Brussels
Arne Bostrom, Geneva
Bruno Bozzetto, Milan
Lou Bunin, Punch-Film Studio, New York
Freddy Buache, Swiss Cinematheque
A. Carvalhaes, Sao-Paulo
Cinematheque Quebecoise, Montreal
Contemporary Films, London
Guy L. Coté, Montreal
Crawley Films, Ottawa
Serge Danot, Paris
Defa-Film, Dresden
Det Danske Film Museum, Copenhagen
Deutsche Institut fur filmkunde, Wiesbaden
Walt Disney Studios, Burbank
George Dunning, TVC Studios, London
Eagle Films Ltd. Alan Wheatley, London
Jean Effel, Paris
Peter Foldes, Paris
Gamma-Film, Milan
Louis Gasca, San Sebastian
Gibba, Francesco Guido, Rome
Les Goldman, Van Nyus, California
Vasco Granja, Damaia, Portugal
Paul Grimault, Paris
Yoram Gross, Tel Aviv
Hanna-Barbera Productions, Hollywood
Peter Hellstern, Atlantic Film, Zurich
Helmut Herbst, Cinegrafic, Hamburg
John Hubley, Storyboard Films, New York
Jean Image Films, Paris
Feodor Khitrouk, Moscow
Gunnar Karlsson, Stockholm
Robert Lapoujade, Rebais
Kurt Linda, Munich
Studio Macian, Barcelona
Raymond Maillet, JICA, Paris
George Matolcsy, Pannonia Studio, Budapest
Max Massimino-Garnier, Milan
National Cinematografica of Argentina
Nippon Herald Motion Pictures Co., Tokyo
Pagot-Film, Milan
Parkfilm, Geneva
V. Privato-Gosfilmofond, Moscow
Adolfo Ridruejo, National Film Institute, Buenos Aires
F. G. Rindisbachler, Berne
Gianni Rondolino, Turin
Hans Scheugl and Ernest Schmidt, Wien
J. A. Sistiaga, Fuenterrabla
David R. Smith, Burbank
Toei Film Studios, Tokyo
Unifrance Film, Paris
Unijapan Film, Tokyo
Ivan Ivanov-Vano, Moscow
Valoria Films, Paris
Piero Zanotto, Venice
and all the others . . .

Also Published by Focal Press

COMPUTER ANIMATION
Edited by John Halas
176 pages, 213 photographs, 221 diagrams, casebound.

VISUAL SCRIPTING
Edited by John Halas
144 pages, 604 cartoon-illustrations, casebound.

THE TECHNIQUE OF FILM ANIMATION
by John Halas and Roger Manvell
4th edition, 351 pages, 234 photographs, 148 diagrams, casebound.

THE ANIMATION STAND: Rostrum Camera Operations
by Zoran Perisic
168 pages, 242 two-colour illustrations, paperback.

GRAMMAR OF THE FILM LANGUAGE
by Daniel Arijon
640 pages, 1,547 illustrations, casebound.

HOW TO CARTOON
by John Halas and Bob Privett
3rd edition, 132 pages, 117 diagrams and cartoon drawings, paperback.

HOW TO ANIMATE CUT-OUTS
by C. H. Barton
116 pages, 348 diagrams, paperback.

Forthcoming

THE PHOTOGUIDE TO SHOOTING ANIMATION
by Zoran Perisic
Approx 200 pages, 24 pp colour and b/w illustrations, 50 pp diagrams, paperback.

NC
1765   410758
.E23

Edera

Full Length Animated Feature
Films.